American Inside Out Evolution

Student's Book

Intermediate

SUE KAY
VAUGHAN JONES

macmillan education

ents

READING

Contemporary reading texts have been adapted and graded to suit each level. They have been selected not only for their language content but also for their interest and appropriacy. The texts are supported by recordings.

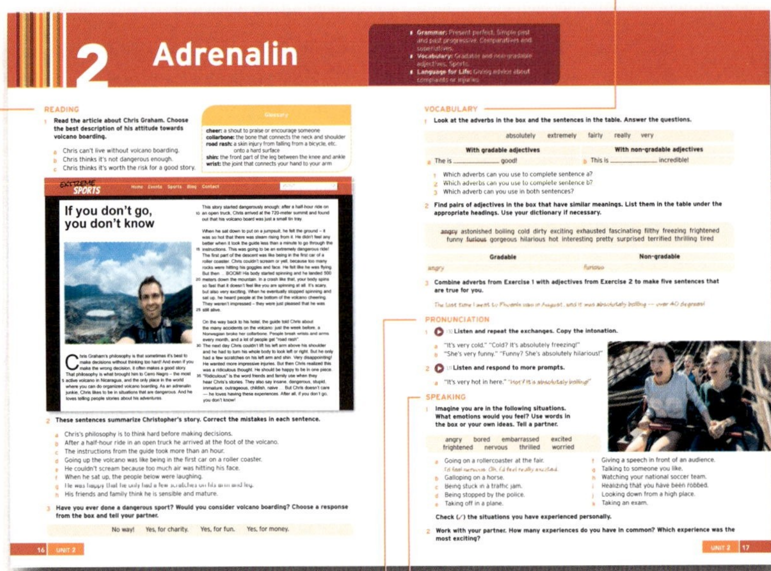

VOCABULARY

- Vocabulary is presented in a meaningful context and is related to the topics in the unit.
- Clear pictures help acquisition.
- There are practice activities to expand your knowledge of particular lexical sets and give you opportunities to use the new vocabulary in social exchanges.
- You will also listen to the words and repeat them before manipulating them in real social contexts.

PRONUNCIATION

Pronunciation work on particular areas of sound, stress, and intonation is integrated into every unit.

SPEAKING

You will have plenty of opportunities to speak throughout the unit using language learned.

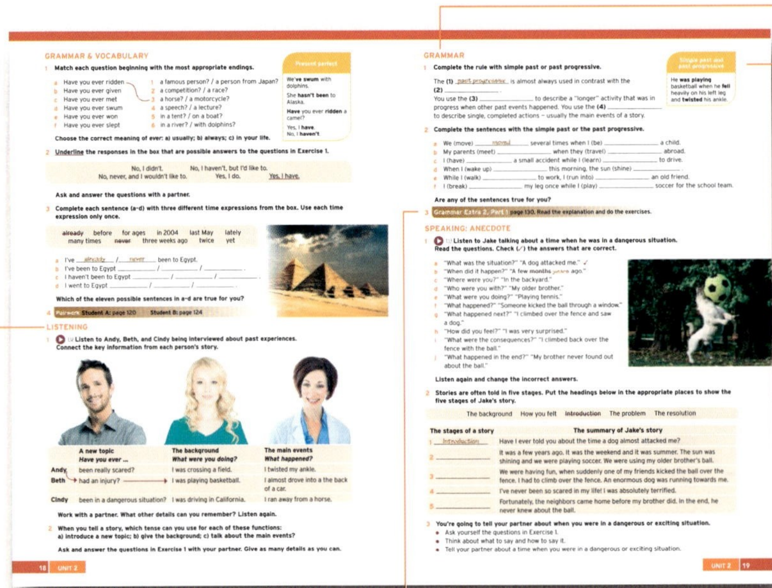

GRAMMAR

- Here you will explore new grammatical structures that have been contextualized in the reading / listening sections. You will focus on the way language works.
- A brief summary of the grammar point is provided in the box.
- Language is explored in realistic and meaningful practice exercises.
- You will use target language in controlled and personalized practice.

LISTENING

The listening activities include texts specially written for language learning – dialogues, conversations and monologues. They were carefully designed to develop real-life listening skills.

The Grammar Extra pages at the back of the Student's Book extend explanations and provide further practice.

LANGUAGE FOR LIFE

The Language for Life section gives you a portable toolkit of functional language. Here, you notice how language is more than just form. You will see language in fun, engaging social situations.

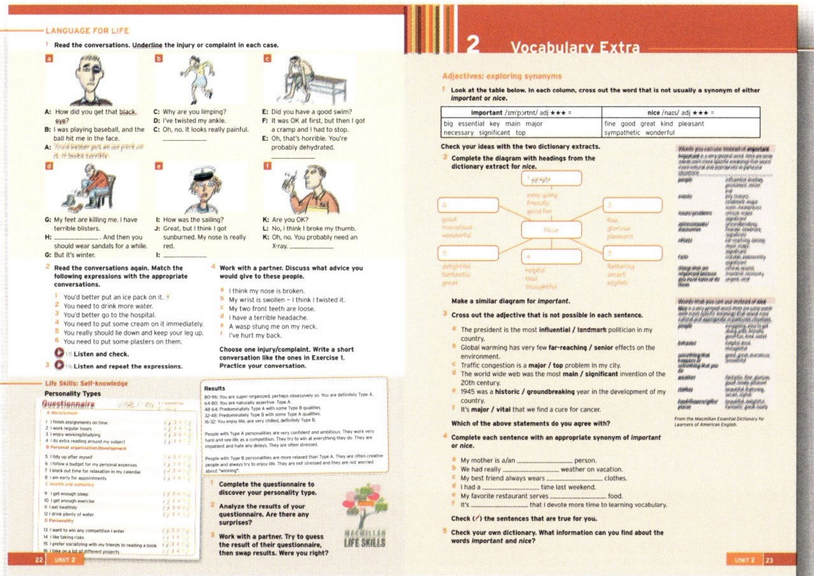

VOCABULARY EXTRA

The Vocabulary Extra pages at the end of every unit recycle the key vocabulary items taught in the unit. This provides an activated wordlist and a useful bank of vocabulary.

LIFE SKILLS

Developing life skills alongside language skills is an essential requirement to meet the demands of the contemporary world.

American Inside Out Evolution has a Life Skills section in every unit. Life Skills present activities in order for you to reflect on and discuss the skills you need for social and work situations in today's world.

REVIEW

There are Review units in the Student's Book. They review the new structures and vocabulary taught in the previous teaching units.

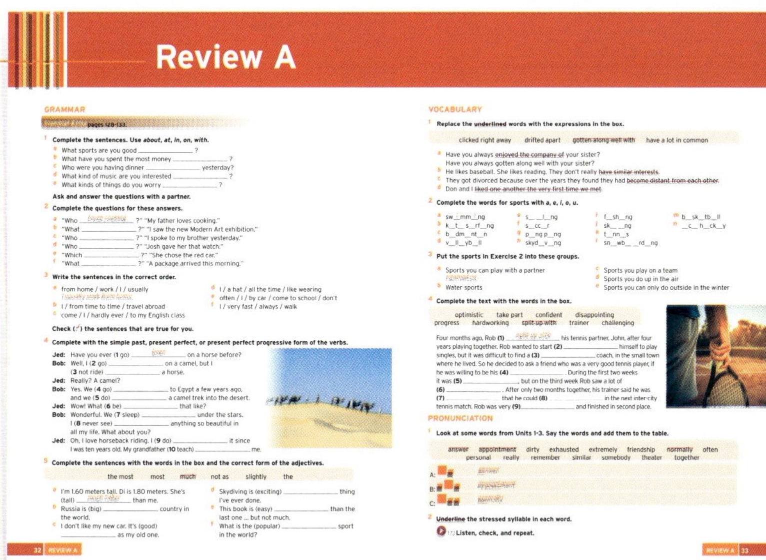

There is one Pairwork activity for every unit, which offers further speaking practice.

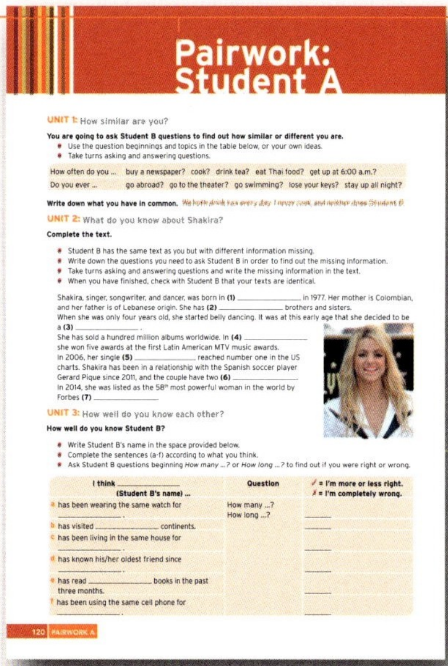

GRAMMAR EXTRA

The Grammar Extra pages at the back of the Student's Book provide a summary of the new grammatical structures, as well as extra practice.

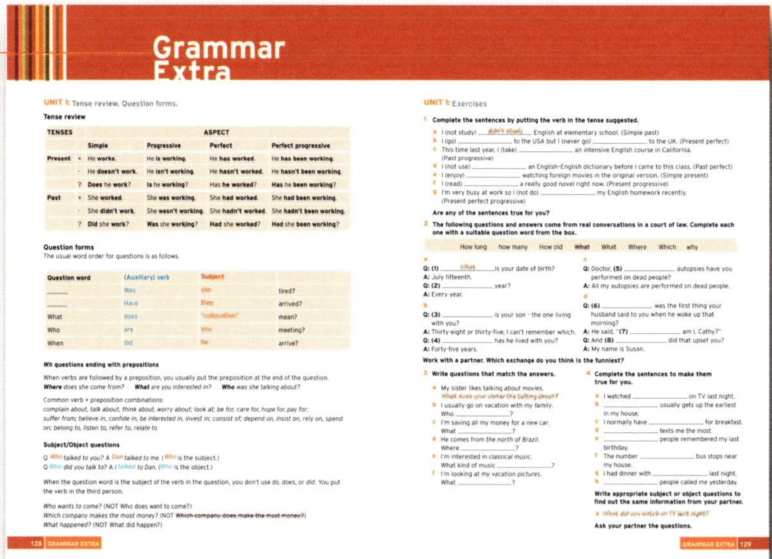

The Workbook provides a review of all the main points in the Student's Book, plus extra listening practice, pronunciation work, and a writing program.

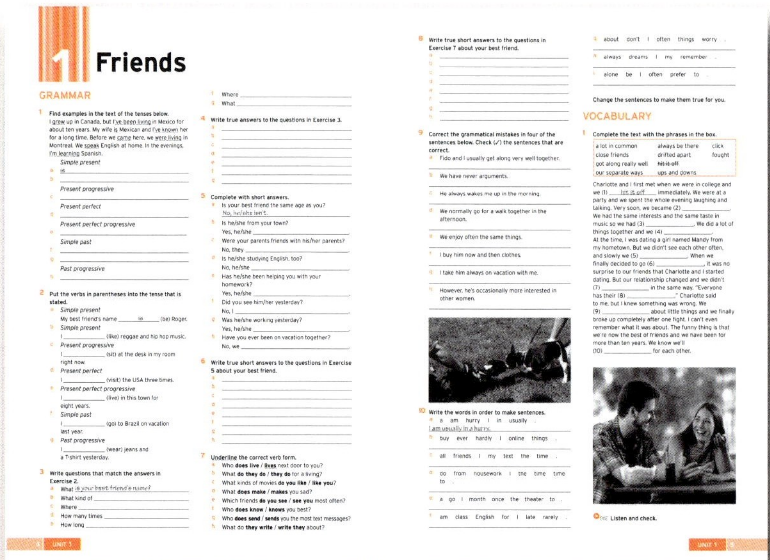

Student's Components

Student's Book with access code to Digital Student's Book

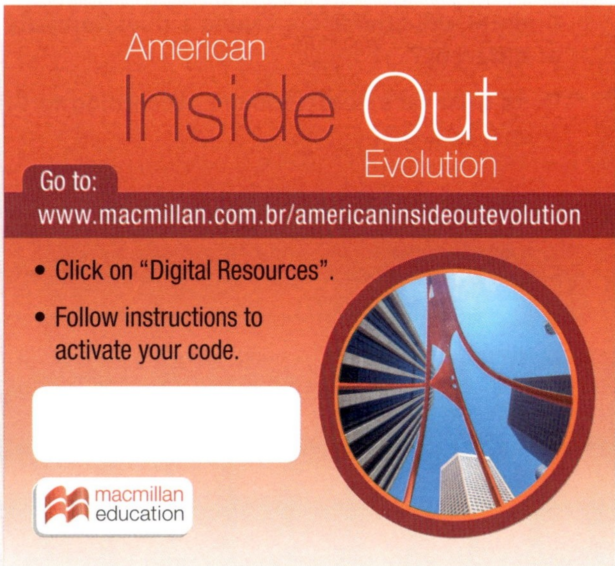

Workbook with access code to Digital Workbook

READING & SPEAKING

1 **Write down the names of three people who are important to you:**
a) a relative; b) a friend; c) a famous person.
Ask a partner about the people they have chosen. Find out as much as you can.

2 **Chantal and Louise are taking a questionnaire about their friendship. Will their answers be similar or different?**

3 **Read Chantal's questionnaire. According to Chantal's answers, which words best describe her friend, Louise?**

kind forgetful stylish disorganized thoughtful rich wise

magazine-y.com

magazine-y FASHION BEAUTY LIFESTYLE NEWS BLOG SUBSCRIBE search

Answer these questions about your best friend. Will your answers be the same?

1 When and where did you first meet your friend?
We met at work fifteen years ago. I got a job as a producer at a radio station in Boston and Louise was working in the publicity department.

2 What did you think of your friend when you first met?
I was a bit scared of her at first! She seemed very grown up — she's three years older than me — and quite serious. I also thought she dressed in a very fashionable way.

3 What did your friend think of you?
She probably thought I was a bit messy at work. But I made her laugh, so she obviously thought I was funny.

4 How did you get to know each other?
Louise was very nice to me when I arrived and helped whenever I had a problem. After a few weeks I invited her out to lunch to say thank you. We got on very well and started meeting up outside of work regularly.

5 How often do you see each other?
Louise lives in a different part of the country now, but we meet every three months or so. We speak on the phone at least once a week and keep in touch via social media all the time.

6 What makes your friend special to you?
She is very helpful and I can speak to her about anything. When I ask for her advice she is always smart and sensible. Also, we share a sense of humor, so we spend a lot of time laughing.

7 When did you last see your friend?
I saw her last week. She was visiting Boston for a conference. We met at our favorite restaurant and had lunch … and lots of laughs.

4 **Compare Louise's answers with Chantal's. Are they the same or different?**

1 We met about twelve years ago.
2 I thought she was disorganized.
3 I think she was a bit scared of me.
4 I invited her to lunch.
5 We meet every six months.
6 I like her sense of humor.
7 We met last week in Boston.

5 **Work with a partner. Choose five questions from the questionnaire and ask each other the questions about a close friend.**

SPEAKING & GRAMMAR

1 **Work with a partner. Match the beginnings (a-l) with the endings (1-12) of these questions.**

About you: Q & A

a) Where ...	1 you do for a living?
b) How many ...	2 music do you listen to?
c) What does ...	3 been to an English-speaking country?
d) Are ...	4 you doing at this time yesterday?
e) How often do you ...	5 are you from?
f) What do ...	6 you last go on vacation?
g) What kind of ...	7 you studying for any exams right now?
h) How long ...	8 brothers and sisters do you have?
i) Have you ever ...	9 do you admire most?
j) When did ...	10 your name mean?
k) What were ...	11 have you been learning English?
l) Who ...	12 see your parents?

Question forms

Where **is** he from?

Has he **been** here long?

What **was** he **doing**?

Who **saw** him first?

Ask each other the questions. How many of your answers are the same?

2 **Classify the questions (a-l) from the Q&A above in the following table of tenses.**

	Simple	Progressive	Perfect	Perfect progressive
Present	a, b, ...			
Past				

Which two tenses are not included in the Q&A?

3 **Questions sometimes end with a preposition; for example, questions *a* and *g* in the Q&A above. Rewrite these questions in the correct order.**

a learning / English / What / you / for / are / ?
What are you learning English for?
b are / at / you / kinds of things / What / good / ?
c kinds of things / What / in / are / interested / you / ?
d money / you / on / do / spend / the most / What / ?
e clubs or groups / What / to / belong / you / do / ?
f What / about / kinds of things / you / do / worry / ?
g lunch / you / usually / Who / have / do / with / ?
h in / you / do / confide / Who / ?

Ask your partner the questions.

4 **Look at these questions and answers. In which question is *Who* the subject?**

a "**Who** do you confide in?" "I confide in **John**."
b "**Who** confides in you?" "**John** confides in me."

Do you use the auxiliary *do* when *Who*, *What*, or *Which* is the subject?

5 **Grammar Extra 1** page 128. Read the explanation and do the exercises.

6 **Look at these sentences. Write questions with *Who*.**

a Jenny talks the most.
Who talks the most?
b Tom always remembers my birthday.
c Brad wears the best clothes.
d Becky texts me the most.
e David lives the closest to me.
f Rick has known me the longest.

Think about your close friends and answer the questions (a-f). Ask your partner.

PRONUNCIATION

1 1.02 **Listen and repeat the fractions in the box.**

$^1/_2$	$^1/_3$	$^1/_4$	$^3/_4$	$^4/_5$	$^1/_8$	$^3/_{10}$	$^1/_{20}$

2 **Match each percentage with the equivalent fraction.**

a 5% = $^1/_{20}$
b 12.5%
c 25%
d 30%
e 33.3%
f 50%
g 75%
h 80%

1.03 **Listen, check, and repeat.**

READING

1 **Write down the names of three friends. When was the last time you were in touch? How did you communicate? (e.g. face to face, text messages, by phone, Facebook etc.)**

2 **Work with your partner. Read the review of social media statistics. For each statement decide which alternative is most likely to be true.**

thereviewer.com

REVIEWER HOME ABOUT REVIEWS NEWS search

< previous next >

Social Media Trends

We conducted a review of the latest global statistics about how young people communicate with friends. Here are some of the most interesting results.

a **67% / 86%** of US adults aged 18-29 use at least one social media site.
b Most social media sites have more **female / male** users (in the USA).
c The average Facebook user has 155 Facebook friends, but how many friends would they turn to for help: **4 / 9**?
d The person with the highest number of followers on Twitter is **a pop singer / a footballer**.
e The key reason for using social media among young people aged 16-24 was **to keep in touch / to fill up spare time**.
f Facebook is currently available in **101 / 59** different languages.
g High levels of involvement with a smartphone can lead to **increased / decreased** levels of depression and stress.
h The percentage of people who check their phone within 5 minutes of waking up in the morning is **42% / 61%**.
i The most popular devices for accessing the internet are **smartphones / computers**.
j The percentage of US teenagers who feel they are addicted to their smartphone is **50% / 21%**.

1.04 **Listen and check your ideas. Which are the most/least surprising results?**

LISTENING

1 **Three people (Adam, Carole, and Sharon) were asked, "How do you usually contact people?" Guess their answers and complete their responses with the words in the box.**

spam instant chat voice email smartphone letters calls business online

Adam

Yes, I check my **(1)** ____________ email all the time at the office, but I hardly ever check my personal email. There's a lot of **(2)** ____________ today. I text from time to time, but I usually **(3)** ____________ message my friends. It's so much quicker, and I'm very bad at texting.

Carole

I regularly check my **(4)** ____________. Oh, and I use Skype for video calls now and then. One of my grandchildren lives in Australia and she **(5)** ____________ me on Skype every weekend. I never write **(6)** ____________ nowadays. It's a shame really, don't you think?

Sharon

I use my **(7)** ____________. I'm always **(8)** ____________ so I chat with several friends at the same time. I love to **(9)** ____________ but I like to make **(10)** ____________ videos too ... So I often use WhatsApp, Snapchat and Facebook.

2 1.05 **Listen and check your ideas for Exercise 1. How many of the sentences are true for you?**

GRAMMAR

1 **Add more adverbs of frequency from the sentences in the Listening section.**

Always	Often	Sometimes	Not often	Never
	normally	*occasionally*	*hardly ever*	
	regularly			

2 **Look at the sentence below. Decide which adverbs in the table normally go in position A and which ones normally go in position B.**

I **A** contact my friends by phone **B** .

Position A: always, ...

3 **Guess which adverbs from the table would make these statements true for your partner. Rewrite the sentences with the adverbs you have chosen.**

a He/She writes letters.
b He/She listens to classical music.
c He/She is late for appointments.
d He/She remembers friends' birthdays.
e He/She goes to the theater.
f He/She buys chocolate.

Ask your partner questions to check your ideas.

Do you ever write letters?

How often do you listen to classical music?

4 **Pairwork Student A:** page 120 **Student B:** page 124

Adverbs of frequency

Adverbs

be + adverb
I'm **always** online.

auxiliary + adverb + main verb
She doesn't **often** call me.

adverb + main verb
I **rarely** write letters.

Adverb phrases

I'm on the phone **all the time**.

They contact me **from time to time**.

He uses video chat **now and then**.

READING

1 **Look at the pictures of Max and Jen in college and Max and Jen now. Do you think the following statements are true or false?**

a Max and Jen had similar interests when they were in college.
b They chose similar careers when they graduated.
c They have similar jobs and lifestyles now.

Read their comments below and check your ideas.

Q&A

Catching up with

Max and Jen

Max and Jen met at college. Three years after they graduated we contacted them to ask them about their friendship. This is what they said:

How did you meet Max?
I first met Max when I was looking for someone to share the house I was renting. I put an ad online and he was the first person to answer it. When we met we clicked right away and I told him he could move in.

What kind of relationship did you have with Jen?
Jen and I got along very well together. When we first met we hit it off immediately and we ended up sharing a house for almost three years. We had our ups and downs, but we had the same attitude to the important things in life. The only thing we argued about was the housework. I like things to be clean and tidy, but Jen never seemed to notice when the house needed cleaning. I don't think she ever found out where we kept the vacuum cleaner!

What was it like living with Max?
It was fun living with Max. We soon found out that we had a lot in common and quickly became close friends. We had the same ideas about politics and other less important things, like cooking. We also liked the same music, and that's important when you're sharing a house. We fell out a couple of times about the housework. Max thinks I'm messy, but I think life's too short to worry about cleaning!

What did you do when you graduated?
When I finished college, I moved to New York City and got a job in a finance company. I have to work long hours and I don't really enjoy what I'm doing, but I earn a very good salary. I'm very ambitious and I enjoy spending money on travel, tech gadgets, and a nice car. Jen works very hard as well, but she's not earning much money.

What happened when you graduated from college?
When we graduated three years ago, we went our separate ways, and since then our lives have been very different. Max went off to the "big city" to make his fortune, and I went back to my hometown and got a job as a production assistant in an art gallery. I love my job, but I don't earn very much. I am living with my parents as I can't afford a place of my own. Max thinks I'm crazy. Money is very important to him now, but I get a lot of satisfaction from my job, and I can spend time with my family and friends. He's earning a lot of money, but he works very long hours and gets very stressed.

"We soon found out that we had a lot in common and quickly became close friends."

Are you still in touch with each other?
I still see Jen occasionally, but now that our lives are so different we have drifted apart a bit. We still have a good time when we meet and we know we'll always be there for each other.

10 11

2 **Underline the correct name**

a **Jen / Max** was looking for someone to share the house with.
b **Jen / Max** is a very neat person.
c **Jen / Max** lives with her/his parents now.
d **Jen / Max** has a well-paid job.
e **Jen / Max** loves her/his job.
f **Jen / Max** has a nice car.

VOCABULARY

1 **Complete these expressions about friendship from the article on page 12.**

- a we liked one another as soon as we first met = we clicked right away / we hit it off immediately
- b we had similar interests = *we had a lot* ______________
- c we got to know one another very well = *we became* ______________
- d we argued = *we* ______________
- e we became/have become more distant from each other = *we went our separate* ______________ / *we've drifted* ______________
- f we enjoyed each other's company = *we got along* ______________
- g we had good moments and bad moments = *we had our* ______________
- h I know I can count on her when I need a friend = *I know she'll always be* ______________

Look again at the text and check your answers.

2 **The following is a summary of Jen and Max's friendship. Put the lines of the summary in the correct order.**

met. They became close	☐
separate ways and they've drifted	☐
friends and got along	☐
Jen and Max hit it	1
in common. Now they have gone their	☐
off immediately when they first	2
fall out and they say that they are still	☐
there for each other.	☐
apart. They didn't	☐
well together. They had a lot	☐

3 **How many friends have you stayed in touch with from: a) elementary school; b) high school; c) college?**

Compare with a partner.

SPEAKING: ANECDOTE

1 1.06 **Listen to Antonia talking about a friend who is different from her and look at the questions. Which two questions does she not answer?**

- a What is your friend's name?
- b How long have you known each other?
- c Where did you meet?
- d Why did you become friends?
- e In what ways are you different?
- f What do you have in common?
- g Have you ever had a fight?
- h How often do you see each other?
- i What kinds of things do you do together?
- j When was the last time you saw your friend?

1. In Guatemala.
2. Backgrounds, tastes, personalities, looks.
3. We're both Red Sox fans.
4. Jackie.
5. Three or four times a year.
6. We go out for lunch; talk about baseball or Guatemala.
7. Ten years.
8. We were both in the same situation; both from the USA.

Match the questions with the answers (1-8). Listen again and check.

You're going to tell your partner about a friend who is different from you.

- Ask yourself the questions in Exercise 1.
- Think about *what* to say and *how* to say it.
- Tell your partner about a person who is important to you.

LANGUAGE FOR LIFE

1 1.07 **Listen to three conversations between friends. Are these statements true or false?**

a Cathy meets her friends by chance.
b The friends are all in a hurry.
c Cathy makes plans to meet her friends again.

2 **Work with a partner. Underline the most natural sounding alternatives (1-5).**

a

Cathy: Hey! How's it going?
Harry: Not bad.
Cathy: What have you been up to lately?
Harry: **(1) I haven't done a lot really. / Not a lot, really.** What about you?
Cathy: **(2) Oh, I've been doing this and that. / Oh, this and that.**
Harry: Hey, I have to run. I'll give you a call.

b

Cathy: Hello, stranger!
Jim: Cathy! How's life?
Cathy: Great! What are you up to these days?
Jim: **(3) Oh, keeping busy, you know. / Oh, I'm keeping busy, you know.**
Cathy: You should come over for dinner some time.
Jim: That would be great. Better get back to the office. See you.

c

Cathy: Hi. How are things going?
Ed: Fine. What about you?
Cathy: **(4) Oh, things are pretty good. / Oh, pretty good.** Are you doing anything special this weekend?
Ed: **(5) No, just taking it easy. / No, I'm just taking it easy.**
Cathy: Me, too.
Ed: Sorry, I can't stop. Take care.

3 **Complete the table with the highlighted useful phrases from the conversations.**

Greetings	How's it going?	a How's life?	b ________
Saying things are OK	Not bad.	c ________	d ________
Asking for news	What have you been up to lately?	e ________	
Saying you're in a hurry	Hey, I have to run.	f ________	g ________
Goodbyes	I'll give you a call.	h ________	i ________

1.08 **Listen and repeat all the expressions in the table.**

4 **Work with a partner. Practice the conversations.**

Life Skills: Communication

Non-verbal Communication

1 **Apart from words, what is involved in communication between two people? Discuss with a partner and tick the three most important features in this list.**

tone of voice	☐	volume of speech	☐
eyes	☐	hands	☐
posture	☐	intonation	☐
clothes	☐	feet	☐
speed of speech	☐		

2 **Match these emojis with the emotions.**

kind crazy impatient sad
embarrassed friendly angry

3 1.09 **Listen to four different people saying the same thing. Match each speaker with one of the emotions in Exercise 2. There are three extra descriptions. What did the people say to make you think they were embarrassed, impatient, etc.?**

4 **Role play this short dialogue with a partner three times. Each time choose a different emotion from Exercise 3 for Mom. Perform to the class. Can they identify the emotion correctly?**

Mom: Where are you going?
Teenager: I'm going to meet my friends. I always meet them on Fridays.
Mom: Will you be back for dinner? You're usually late.
Teenager: No. Please don't worry about me. I'll get something while I'm out.

MACMILLAN LIFE SKILLS

Vocabulary Extra

Using a dictionary

1 Work with a partner. What kinds of information about words can you find in a good dictionary? Look at this dictionary page and discuss the questions.

a How many different words are defined?
b Which words are more frequent: the red words (e.g. *friend*) or the black words (e.g. *frigate*)?
c Which words do you already know?
d Which words are completely new to you (you've never seen them before)?
e Which new words can you understand?
f In your opinion, which new words would be most useful to learn?

2 Match the following dictionary abbreviations/symbols with their meanings.

a abbrev	adverb
b adj	uncountable noun
c adv	synonym
d noun [C]	abbreviation
e noun [U]	transitive verb
f verb [I]	adjective
g verb [T]	opposite
h sth	countable noun
i =	intransitive verb
j ≠	something

Find an example of each abbreviation or symbol on the dictionary page.

a abbrev Fri. abbrev Friday

behavior: *She was in a frenzy of rage.* **2** a period when there is a lot of activity

fre•quen•cy /ˈfrikwənsi/ noun **1** [U] the number of times that something happens during a period of time: *We hope this treatment will reduce the frequency of heart disease.* **2** [C] the WAVELENGTH on which a radio program is broadcast

fre•quent¹ /ˈfrikwənt/ adj ★ happening often ≠ INFREQUENT: *Their arguments were becoming more and more frequent.* ♦ *He was a frequent visitor to our house.* ♦ *Inspections must be carried out* ***at frequent intervals*** (=regularly).

F

fre•quent² /friˈkwent/ verb [T] *formal* if you frequent a place, you go there regularly

fre•quent•ly /ˈfrikwəntli/ adv ★★ often ≠ RARELY, SELDOM: *He has frequently been compared to Michael Jackson.* ♦ *The ten most frequently asked questions are listed below.*

fresh /freʃ/ adj ★★★

1 new	6 with feeling of energy
2 food: not preserved	7 of flowers
3 food: still good to eat	8 water: with no salt
4 replacing sth	+ PHRASE
5 recently done/made	

1 clearly new and different: *We need a completely fresh approach to the problem.* ♦ *The program* ***takes a fresh look at*** *this difficult issue.* ♦ *She regarded the birth of her children as* ***a fresh start*** (=a chance to start living in a better way).
2 fresh food has not been preserved in any way: *You can use fresh or canned tomatoes for this recipe.*
3 food that is fresh is still good to eat because it was prepared or produced recently ≠ STALE: *Cooked meat will* ***stay fresh*** *for several days in the refrigerator.*
4 replacing or adding to a previous thing: *The police made a fresh appeal for witnesses.* ♦ *I've put fresh towels in your room.*
5 recently made or experienced: *fresh footprints in the snow* ♦ *The details are still fresh in my mind.*
6 if you feel fresh, you have a lot of energy
7 fresh flowers have been recently PICKED (=taken from the place that they were growing in)
8 fresh water is water in lakes and rivers that does not contain any salt
PHRASE **fresh from/out of sth** if someone is fresh from a particular place or situation, they have recently come from there: *He was just a kid, fresh out of law school.*
—**fresh•ness** noun [U]

ˌfresh ˈair noun [U] the air outside that is nice to breathe → BREATH

fresh•en /ˈfreʃ(ə)n/ verb [T] to make something fresher, cleaner, or more attractive
PHRASAL VERBS **ˌfreshen ˈup** to wash your hands and face and make yourself cleaner and neater
ˌfreshen sth ˈup *same as* **freshen**: *Freshen up your walls and ceilings with a coat of paint.*

fresh•ly /ˈfreʃli/ adv recently

fresh•man /ˈfreʃmən/ (plural **fresh•men** /ˈfreʃmən/) noun [C] *American* a student who is in their first year at a HIGH SCHOOL or university

fresh•wa•ter /ˈfreʃˌwɔtər/ adj living in water that does not contain salt

fret /fret/ verb [I] to worry about something continuously

fret•ful /ˈfretf(ə)l/ adj someone who is fretful is worried and unhappy

Fri. abbrev Friday

fri•ar /ˈfraɪər/ noun [C] a man who is a type of MONK (=a member of a Christian religious community)

fric•tion /ˈfrɪkʃ(ə)n/ noun [U] **1** disagreement: *There is some friction between the various departments.* **2** the fact that one surface rubs against another

Fri•day /ˈfraɪdeɪ/ noun [C/U] ★★★ the day after Thursday and before Saturday: *My birthday is on a Friday this year.* ♦ *The museum closes Fridays* (=every Friday). ♦ *She leaves next Friday.* ♦ *Let's go swimming* ***on Friday***.

fridge /frɪdʒ/ noun [C] *informal* ★ a REFRIGERATOR

fried /fraɪd/ adj cooked in hot oil

friend /frend/ noun [C] ★★★ someone who you know well and like who is not a member of your family: *She's visiting friends in Illinois.* ♦ *Helga is* ***a close friend*** *of mine.* ♦ *May I introduce Peter Flint, a very old* ***friend of the family***. ♦ *I'm having lunch with* ***an old friend*** (=someone who has been a friend for a long time). ♦ *She has a wide* ***circle of friends*** (=group of friends). ♦ *They used to* ***be friends*** (=with each other). ♦ *They* ***made friends with*** *the children next door* (=started to be their friends).

Words often used with **friend**
Adjectives often used with ***friend***
■ **best, close, dear, good, great, lifelong, old, trusted** + FRIEND: someone who you know very well

friend•ly /ˈfren(d)li/ adj ★★
1 someone who is friendly is always pleasant and helpful toward other people ≠ UNFRIENDLY: *He will be remembered as a kind, friendly person.* ♦ *The local people were very* ***friendly toward*** *us.*
→ SYMPATHETIC
2 if you are friendly with someone, you are their friend: *Janet and I used to* ***be*** *very* ***friendly***. ♦ *Doctors shouldn't get too* ***friendly with*** *their patients.*

-friendly /fren(d)li/ suffix **1** used for showing that something does not harm something else: *wildlife-friendly farming methods* ♦ *environmentally-friendly cleaning materials* **2** appropriate for a particular type of person: *child-friendly restaurants*

friend•ship /ˈfren(d)ʃɪp/ noun [C/U] ★ a relationship between people who are friends: *Whatever happened, I did not want to lose Sarah's friendship.* ♦ *his* ***friendship with*** *a local businessman* ♦ *She formed* ***a close friendship*** *with Vera Brittain.*

fries /fraɪz/ noun [plural] FRENCH FRIES

frig•ate /ˈfrɪgət/ noun [C] a small fast ship that is used by a navy

fright /fraɪt/ noun [singular/U] a sudden strong feeling of being afraid: *He was shaking with fright.* ♦ *Kelly cried out in fright.*

From the *Macmillan Essential Dictionary for Learners of American English.*

3 Refer to the dictionary page and discuss these questions with your partner.

a How many phrasal verbs are there?
b What are the eight most frequent adjective collocations for *friend*?
c Identify the five words with the letter combination *ie*. Which two of these vowel sounds – /aɪ/, /e/, /eɪ/, /ɪ/ – are possible ways of pronouncing *ie*?
Write an example word for each of the two sounds.
d What is the difference between *friendship* and *friendly*?

4 Check your own dictionary. How does it give the kinds of information discussed on this page?

READING

1 **Read the article about Chris Graham. Choose the best description of his attitude towards volcano boarding.**

a Chris can't live without volcano boarding.
b Chris thinks it's not dangerous enough.
c Chris thinks it's worth the risk for a good story.

Glossary

cheer: a shout to praise or encourage someone
collarbone: the bone that connects the neck and shoulder
road rash: a skin injury from falling from a bicycle, etc. onto a hard surface
shin: the front part of the leg between the knee and ankle
wrist: the joint that connects your hand to your arm

EXTREME SPORTS   Home   Events   Sports   Blog   Contact   search

If you don't go, you don't know

Chris Graham's philosophy is that sometimes it's best to make decisions without thinking too hard! And even if you make the wrong decision, it often makes a good story. That philosophy is what brought him to Cerro Negro – the most active volcano in Nicaragua, and the only place in the world where you can do organized volcano boarding. As an adrenalin junkie, Chris likes to be in situations that are dangerous. And he loves telling people stories about his adventures.

This story started dangerously enough: after a half-hour ride on an open truck, Chris arrived at the 720-meter summit and found out that his volcano board was just a small tin tray.

When he sat down to put on a jumpsuit, he felt the ground – it was so hot that there was steam rising from it. He didn't feel any better when it took the guide less than a minute to go through the instructions. This was going to be an extremely dangerous ride! The first part of the descent was like being in the first car of a roller coaster. Chris couldn't scream or yell, because too many rocks were hitting his goggles and face. He felt like he was flying. But then ... BOOM! His body started spinning and he landed 500 meters down the mountain. In a crash like that, your body spins so fast that it doesn't feel like you are spinning at all. It's scary, but also very exciting. When he eventually stopped spinning and sat up, he heard people at the bottom of the volcano cheering. They weren't impressed – they were just pleased that he was still alive.

On the way back to his hotel, the guide told Chris about the many accidents on the volcano: just the week before, a Norwegian broke her collarbone. People break wrists and arms every month, and a lot of people get "road rash". The next day Chris couldn't lift his left arm above his shoulder and he had to turn his whole body to look left or right. But he only had a few scratches on his left arm and shin. Very disappointing! He wanted more impressive injuries. But then Chris realized this was a ridiculous thought. He should be happy to be in one piece. "Ridiculous" is the word friends and family use when they hear Chris's stories. They also say insane, dangerous, stupid, immature, outrageous, childish, naive ... But Chris doesn't care — he loves having these experiences. After all, if you don't go, you don't know!

2 **These sentences summarize Chris's story. Correct the mistakes in each sentence.**

a Chris's philosophy is to think hard before making decisions.
b After a half-hour ride in an open truck he arrived at the foot of the volcano.
c The instructions from the guide took more than an hour.
d Going up the volcano was like being in the first car on a roller coaster.
e He couldn't scream because too much air was hitting his face.
f When he sat up, the people below were laughing.
g He was happy that he only had a few scratches on his arm and leg.
h His friends and family think he is sensible and mature.

3 **Have you ever done a dangerous sport? Would you consider volcano boarding? Choose a response from the box and tell your partner.**

No way!   Yes, for charity.   Yes, for fun.   Yes, for money.

VOCABULARY

1 Look at the adverbs in the box and the sentences in the table. Answer the questions.

absolutely extremely fairly really very

With gradable adjectives	With non-gradable adjectives
a This is ____________ good!	b This is ____________ incredible!

1 Which adverbs can you use to complete sentence a?
2 Which adverbs can you use to complete sentence b?
3 Which adverb can you use in both sentences?

2 Find pairs of adjectives in the box that have similar meanings. List them in the table under the appropriate headings. Use your dictionary if necessary.

~~angry~~ astonished boiling cold dirty exciting exhausted fascinating filthy freezing frightened funny ~~furious~~ gorgeous hilarious hot interesting pretty surprised terrified thrilling tired

Gradable	Non-gradable
angry	*furious*

3 Combine adverbs from Exercise 1 with adjectives from Exercise 2 to make five sentences that are true for you.

The last time I went to Phoenix was in August, and it was absolutely boiling — over 40 degrees!

PRONUNCIATION

1 1.10 **Listen and repeat the exchanges. Copy the intonation.**

a "It's very cold." "Cold? It's absolutely freezing!"
b "She's very funny." "Funny? She's absolutely hilarious!"

2 1.11 **Listen and respond to more prompts.**

a "It's very hot in here." *"Hot? It's absolutely boiling!"*

SPEAKING

1 Imagine you are in the following situations. What emotions would you feel? Use words in the box or your own ideas. Tell a partner.

angry bored embarrassed excited frightened nervous thrilled worried

a Going on a rollercoaster at the fair.
I'd feel nervous. Oh, I'd feel really excited.
b Galloping on a horse.
c Being stuck in a traffic jam.
d Being stopped by the police.
e Taking off in a plane.
f Giving a speech in front of an audience.
g Talking to someone you like.
h Watching your national soccer team.
i Realizing that you have been robbed.
j Looking down from a high place.
k Taking an exam.

Check (✓) the situations you have experienced personally.

2 Work with your partner. How many experiences do you have in common? Which experience was the most exciting?

GRAMMAR & VOCABULARY

1 Match each question beginning with the most appropriate endings.

a	Have you ever ridden	1	a famous person? / a person from Japan?
b	Have you ever given	2	a competition? / a race?
c	Have you ever met	3	a horse? / a motorcycle?
d	Have you ever swum	4	a speech? / a lecture?
e	Have you ever won	5	in a tent? / on a boat?
f	Have you ever slept	6	in a river? / with dolphins?

Choose the correct meaning of *ever*: a) usually; b) always; c) in your life.

Present perfect

We'**ve swum** with dolphins.

She **hasn't been** to Alaska.

Have you ever **ridden** a camel?

Yes, I **have**.
No, I **haven't**.

2 Underline the responses in the box that are possible answers to the questions in Exercise 1.

No, I didn't. No, I haven't, but I'd like to.
No, never, and I wouldn't like to. Yes, I do. Yes, I have.

Ask and answer the questions with a partner.

3 Complete each sentence (a–d) with three different time expressions from the box. Use each time expression only once.

already before for ages in 2004 last May lately
many times never three weeks ago twice yet

a I've ___already___ / ___never___ been to Egypt.
b I've been to Egypt ________ / ________ / ________ .
c I haven't been to Egypt ________ / ________ / ________ .
d I went to Egypt ________ / ________ / ________ .

Which of the eleven possible sentences in a–d are true for you?

4 Pairwork Student A: page 120 **Student B:** page 124

LISTENING

1 1.12 **Listen to Andy, Beth, and Cindy being interviewed about past experiences. Connect the key information from each person's story.**

	A new topic *Have you ever ...*	The background *What were you doing?*	The main events *What happened?*
Andy	been really scared?	I was crossing a field.	I twisted my ankle.
Beth	had an injury?	I was playing basketball.	I almost drove into the back of a car.
Cindy	been in a dangerous situation?	I was driving in California.	I ran away from a horse.

Work with a partner. What other details can you remember? Listen again.

**2 When you tell a story, which tense can you use for each of these functions:
a) introduce a new topic; b) give the background; c) talk about the main events?**

Ask and answer the questions in Exercise 1 with your partner. Give as many details as you can.

GRAMMAR

1 Complete the rule with simple past or past progressive.

The **(1)** past progressive is almost always used in contrast with the
(2) ________________ .
You use the **(3)** ________________ to describe a "longer" activity that was in progress when other past events happened. You use the **(4)** ________________ to describe single, completed actions – usually the main events of a story.

Simple past and past progressive

He **was playing** basketball when he **fell** heavily on his left leg and **twisted** his ankle.

2 Complete the sentences with the simple past or the past progressive.

a We (move) moved several times when I (be) ________________ a child.
b My parents (meet) ________________ when they (travel) ________________ abroad.
c I (have) ________________ a small accident while I (learn) ________________ to drive.
d When I (wake up) ________________ this morning, the sun (shine) ________________ .
e While I (walk) ________________ to work, I (run into) ________________ an old friend.
f I (break) ________________ my leg once while I (play) ________________ soccer for the school team.

Are any of the sentences true for you?

3 **Grammar Extra 2, Part 1** page 130. Read the explanation and do the exercises.

SPEAKING: ANECDOTE

1 1.13 **Listen to Jake talking about a time when he was in a dangerous situation. Read the questions. Check (✓) the answers that are correct.**

a "What was the situation?" "A dog attacked me." ✓
b "When did it happen?" "A few ~~months~~ years ago."
c "Where were you?" "In the backyard."
d "Who were you with?" "My older brother."
e "What were you doing?" "Playing tennis."
f "What happened?" "Someone kicked the ball through a window."
g "What happened next?" "I climbed over the fence and saw a dog."
h "How did you feel?" "I was very surprised."
i "What were the consequences?" "I climbed back over the fence with the ball."
j "What happened in the end?" "My brother never found out about the ball."

Listen again and change the incorrect answers.

2 Stories are often told in five stages. Put the headings below in the appropriate places to show the five stages of Jake's story.

The background   How you felt   ~~Introduction~~   The problem   The resolution

The stages of a story	The summary of Jake's story
1 Introduction	Have I ever told you about the time a dog almost attacked me?
2 ________________	It was a few years ago. It was the weekend and it was summer. The sun was shining and we were playing soccer. We were using my older brother's ball.
3 ________________	We were having fun, when suddenly one of my friends kicked the ball over the fence. I had to climb over the fence. An enormous dog was running towards me.
4 ________________	I've never been so scared in my life! I was absolutely terrified.
5 ________________	Fortunately, the neighbors came home before my brother did. In the end, he never knew about the ball.

3 You're going to tell your partner about when you were in a dangerous or exciting situation.

- Ask yourself the questions in Exercise 1.
- Think about what to say and how to say it.
- Tell your partner about a time when you were in a dangerous or exciting situation.

VOCABULARY & SPEAKING

1 **Work with a partner. List the sports in the box in different groups according to the criteria (a-f). A sport might belong to more than one group.**

badminton baseball basketball boxing bungee jumping cycling ~~fishing~~ golf horseback riding ice hockey judo karate kite surfing ping pong rock climbing running sailing scuba diving skating skiing skydiving snowboarding soccer surfing swimming tennis track volleyball windsurfing

a Water sports *fishing, ...*
b Team sports
c Indoor sports
d Sports that collocate with *play*
e Sports that are hardly ever shown on TV
f Sports that need special footwear

2 **Work with your partner. Tell each other about the following.**

a Sports you have tried
b Sports you do
c Sports you watch
d Sports you don't like

LISTENING & VOCABULARY

1 1.14 **Listen and guess which sports Toby and Kate are talking about.**

2 **Complete the table with words from the conversations.**

	Sport	Place	Equipment
Toby		*the ocean*	*a board*
Kate			

the ocean

a wetsuit

a harness

a kite

a board

mountains

waterproof clothes

climbing shoes

cliffs

ropes

Listen again and check your answers.

3 **Work with your partner. Choose five more sports to add to the table and complete the *Place* and *Equipment* columns for each one. Use your dictionary if necessary.**

GRAMMAR

1 Put the words in the box into four groups of three adjectives, according to how their comparative and superlative forms are made.

~~cold~~ fat happy ~~high~~ hot interesting lucky
popular pretty ~~quiet~~ relaxed sad

Group 1: cold – colder – coldest; high – higher – highest; quiet – quieter – quietest

Complete these rules for forming comparative and superlative adjectives.

1 For most one-syllable adjectives and some two-syllable adjectives, you add *er / est*.
2 For one-syllable adjectives which end in one vowel + one consonant, you double the consonant and add ______ .
3 For two-syllable adjectives which end in *y*, you replace *y* with ______ .
4 For most other two-syllable adjectives and for all three-syllable adjectives, you use ______ .

Comparatives and superlatives

He's **slightly taller than** me.
She's **much more mature than** he is.
They're just **as good as** we are.
It's **by far the biggest** one I've ever seen.

2 Look at the table and complete the sentences (a-f) to make true statements.

Sport	Estimated number of participants worldwide
Basketball	450 million
Soccer	265 million
Badminton	220 million
Baseball	65 million
Dragon boat racing	65 million
Tennis	60 million
Judo	28 million

a *Soccer* is much more popular than *judo* .
b ______ is slightly more popular than ______ .
c ______ is just as popular as ______ .
d ______ is a little less popular than ______ .
e ______ is a lot less popular than ______ .
f ______ is by far the most popular sport in the world.

3 Complete the following sentences with your own opinions about different sports.

a ______ is much ______ than ______ .
b ______ isn't nearly as ______ as ______ .
c ______ is just as ______ as ______ .
d ______ is the ______ I've ever ______ .
e ______ is much ______ than ______ .
f ______ is by far the ______ in the world.

Now find other people in the class who share your opinions.

4 **Grammar Extra 2, Part 2** page 130. Read the explanation and do the exercises.

SPEAKING

1 How well do you know the town/city where you are studying English? Discuss these questions with your partner.

Where is ...

- the nearest ski resort?
- the nicest swimming pool?
- the biggest soccer stadium?
- the best-equipped sports store?
- the most difficult street to park on?
- the most fashionable clothing store?
- the tallest/oldest/most famous building?
- the best store to find books in English?

2 Note your answers down. Now discuss in groups and decide how well you know the place where you are studying English.

LANGUAGE FOR LIFE

1 Read the conversations. Underline the injury or complaint in each case.

a

A: How did you get that black eye?
B: I was playing baseball, and the ball hit me in the face.
A: *You'd better put an ice pack on it. It looks terrible.*

b

C: Why are you limping?
D: I've twisted my ankle.
C: Oh, no. It looks really painful. ___________

c

E: Did you have a good swim?
F: It was OK at first, but then I got a cramp and I had to stop.
E: Oh, that's horrible. You're probably dehydrated. ___________

d

G: My feet are killing me. I have terrible blisters.
H: ___________. And then you should wear sandals for a while.
G: But it's winter.

e

I: How was the sailing?
J: Great, but I think I got sunburned. My nose is really red.
I: ___________

f

K: Are you OK?
L: No, I think I broke my thumb.
K: Oh, no. You probably need an X-ray. ___________

2 Read the conversations again. Match the following expressions with the appropriate conversations.

1 You'd better put an ice pack on it. *a*
2 You need to drink more water.
3 You'd better go to the hospital.
4 You need to put some cream on it immediately.
5 You really should lie down and keep your leg up.
6 You need to put some plasters on them.

1.15 **Listen and check.**

3 1.16 **Listen and repeat the expressions.**

4 Work with a partner. Discuss what advice you would give to these people.

a I think my nose is broken.
b My wrist is swollen – I think I twisted it.
c My two front teeth are loose.
d I have a terrible headache.
e A wasp stung me on my neck.
f I've hurt my back.

Choose one injury/complaint. Write a short conversation like the ones in Exercise 1. Practice your conversation.

Life Skills: Self-knowledge
Personality Types

Questionnaire

1 = never 2 = rarely 3 = sometimes 4 = often 5 = usually 6 = always

A Work/school	
1 I finish assignments on time	1 2 3 4 5 6
2 I work regular hours	1 2 3 4 5 6
3 I enjoy working/studying	1 2 3 4 5 6
4 I do extra reading around my subject	1 2 3 4 5 6
B Personal organization/development	
5 I tidy up after myself	1 2 3 4 5 6
6 I follow a budget for my personal expenses	1 2 3 4 5 6
7 I block out time for relaxation in my calendar	1 2 3 4 5 6
8 I am early for appointments	1 2 3 4 5 6
C Health and wellbeing	
9 I get enough sleep	1 2 3 4 5 6
10 I get enough exercise	1 2 3 4 5 6
11 I eat healthily	1 2 3 4 5 6
12 I drink plenty of water	1 2 3 4 5 6
D Personality	
13 I want to win any competition I enter	1 2 3 4 5 6
14 I like taking risks	1 2 3 4 5 6
15 I prefer socializing with my friends to reading a book	1 2 3 4 5 6
16 I take on a lot of different projects	1 2 3 4 5 6

Results

80-96: You are super-organized, perhaps obsessively so. You are definitely Type A.
64-80: You are naturally assertive. Type A.
48-64: Predominately Type A with some Type B qualities.
32-48: Predominately Type B with some Type A qualities.
16-32: You enjoy life, are very chilled, definitely Type B.

People with Type A personalities are very confident and ambitious. They work very hard and see life as a competition. They try to win at everything they do. They are impatient and hate any delays. They are often stressed.

People with Type B personalities are more relaxed than Type A. They are often creative people and always try to enjoy life. They are not stressed and they are not worried about "winning".

1 Complete the questionnaire to discover your personality type.

2 Analyze the results of your questionnaire. Are there any surprises?

3 Work with a partner. Try to guess the result of their questionnaire, then swap results. Were you right?

Adjectives: exploring synonyms

1 Look at the table below. In each column, cross out the word that is not usually a synonym of either *important* or *nice*.

important /ɪm'pɔrtnt/ adj ★★★ =	**nice** /naɪs/ adj ★★★ =
big essential key main major necessary significant top	fine good great kind pleasant sympathetic wonderful

Check your ideas with the two dictionary extracts.

2 Complete the diagram with headings from the dictionary extract for *nice*.

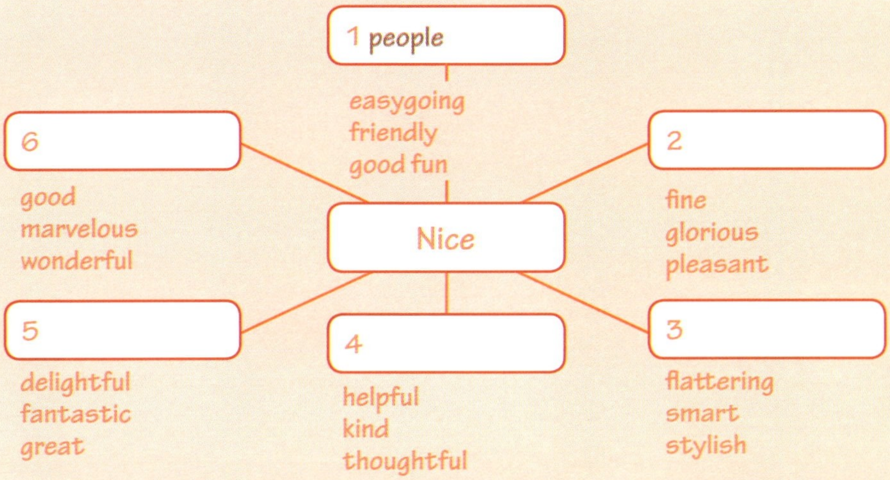

Make a similar diagram for *important*.

3 Cross out the adjective that is not possible in each sentence.

a The president is the most **influential / ~~landmark~~** politician in my country.
b Global warming has very few **far-reaching / senior** effects on the environment.
c Traffic congestion is a **major / top** problem in my city.
d The world wide web was the most **main / significant** invention of the 20th century.
e 1945 was a **historic / groundbreaking** year in the development of my country.
f It's **major / vital** that we find a cure for cancer.

Which of the above statements do you agree with?

4 Complete each sentence with an appropriate synonym of *important* or *nice*.

a My mother is a/an ________________ person.
b We had really ________________ weather on vacation.
c My best friend always wears ________________ clothes.
d I had a ________________ time last weekend.
e My favorite restaurant serves ________________ food.
f It's ________________ that I devote more time to learning vocabulary.

Check (✓) the sentences that are true for you.

5 Check your own dictionary. What information can you find about the words *important* and *nice*?

Words you can use instead of **important**

Important is a very general word. Here are some words with more specific meanings that sound more natural and appropriate in particular situations.

people	influential, leading, prominent, senior, top
events	key, historic, landmark, major, main, momentous
issues/problems	critical, major, significant
achievements/ discoveries	groundbreaking, historic, landmark, significant
effects	far-reaching, lasting, main, major, significant
facts	notable, noteworthy, significant
things that are important because you must have or do them	critical, crucial, essential, necessary, urgent, vital

Words that you can use instead of **nice**

Nice is a very general word. Here are some words with more specific meanings that sound more natural and appropriate in particular situations.

people	easygoing, easy to get along with, friendly, good fun, kind, sweet
behavior	helpful, kind, thoughtful
something that happens or something that you do	good, great, marvelous, wonderful
weather	fantastic, fine, glorious, good, lovely, pleasant
clothes	beautiful, flattering, smart, stylish
food/flowers/gifts/ places	beautiful, delightful, fantastic, great, lovely

From the *Macmillan Essential Dictionary for Learners of American English.*

READING

1 **Look at the pictures. What do you think the relationship is between Brad, Ann, Grace and Greg and the pictures on their phones? Discuss with a partner.**

2 **Read the descriptions and check your ideas.**

Who's on your screen?

Brad

This is my wife, Gina. She's taking a selfie with our two daughters. On the left is Phoebe, and on the right is Mia. Everyone is looking at the camera and they look pretty happy. I love this picture because they are all smiling, and for once the girls aren't fighting! I miss them all so much when I'm away. This picture cheers me up every time I look at it.

Ann

This is my first grandchild, Dexter. He's my son's child. He is 4 months old in this picture and he's looking straight at me! I visit him as often as I can, but my son lives three hours away, so it's not as often as I'd like. I adore him! His gorgeous little face brightens my day.

Grace

This is me with my two best friends, Amy and Beth. It's a picture from college a few years ago. I think we all look really nice, especially Beth. I remember it was just before the college ball, and we were getting ready for the party. It reminds me of some of the amazing times we had at college. I think they are the best friends I've ever had.

Greg

The picture I have on my phone at the moment is of my dog, Cookie. She's 5 years old and here she's chewing on a plastic toy. She's a lovely companion, but she's always running around and barking. Cookie's been my best friend for the last five years.

3 **Read the descriptions again and match each person with their reason for carrying the picture.**

a It reminds me of the amazing times we had. *Grace*

b I adore him!

c I love my dog.

d I miss them when I'm away.

What picture do you have on your phone, and why? Tell your partner.

GRAMMAR

1 Look at this sentence from the descriptions on page 24. Match each example of *look* (1 and 2) with the correct meaning. Then answer the questions.

Everyone ***(1) is looking*** *at the camera and they* ***(2) look*** *pretty happy.*

- *look* = to direct your eyes towards something
- *look* = to have a particular appearance

a Which example of *look* (1 or 2) describes an action – something "happens"?
b Which example of *look* (1 or 2) describes a state – nothing "happens"?
c Can you use progressive tenses with verbs when they describe a state?

2 Complete the descriptions using the simple present or the present progressive.

a She (look) ___looks___ like a nice woman. She (be) ________ related to the child in the picture. The child (be) ________ her son's first child.
b She (pose) ________ with her college friends. They (seem) ________ very happy together.
c He (smile) ________ and (show) ________ us a picture of his family.
d He (hold) ________ a picture of his dog. She (look) ________ like a nice pet.

Match the descriptions (a-d) with the people on page 24.

3 Do these verbs describe actions or states? Underline the correct verb forms.

a I **think / 'm thinking** pictures of friends and family **are / are being** important.
b I **have / 'm having** lots of pictures on my cell phone.
c Pictures **remind / are reminding** me of special occasions.
d I **hate / 'm hating** pictures of me.
e People **think / are thinking** that I **look / 'm looking** like my mother.

Are any of the sentences true for you?

Dynamic and stative meanings

Dynamic meaning

(Use simple or progressive forms)

He usually **smiles** all the time, but he **isn't smiling** now.

Stative meaning

(Use only simple forms)

She **likes** taking pictures.

(NOT ~~She's liking~~ ...)

Did you understand?

(NOT ~~Were you understanding?~~)

Note: Some verbs (e.g. *have, look, think*) can have both meanings:

I **think** my camera is useless. (stative: *think* = *have an opinion*)

I'**m thinking** of getting a new one. (dynamic: *think* = *plan*)

VOCABULARY

1 Combine these words and part-words to form at least ten more family words.

aunt boyfriend brother child cousin daughter ex- father girlfriend grand great- half- husband -in-law mother nephew niece only parent partner second single sister son step uncle wife

great-aunt, ex-boyfriend, brother-in-law, stepchild ...

2 Which family words in Exercise 1 can you use to describe yourself? Draw a diagram.

3 Refer to the people in your diagram in Exercise 2 and complete the following task.

- Underline the people who live closest to you.
- ~~Cross out~~ the people who you see least.
- Circle the person who you saw most recently.
- Put an asterisk * by the oldest person and two asterisks ** by the youngest.
- Put a check ✓ next to the person who you get along best with.

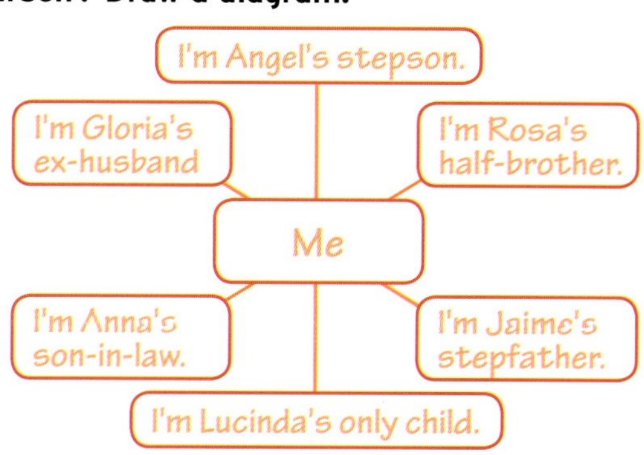

4 Tell your partner about some of the people in your diagram.

SPEAKING

1 Which of these "firsts" do you remember best?

your first broken heart | your first crush | your first dance | your first date | your first English class | your first friend | your first hero | your first home | your first kiss | your first love | your first vacation

2 Choose three "firsts" and tell your partner about them.

I remember my first hero – Roger Federer. He won the men's singles final at Wimbledon for the first time in 2003 and for the eighth time in 2017 ...

READING & LISTENING

1 Read about this first date. How do you usually meet people? Discuss with your partner.

firstdates.com

firstdates

HOME PROFILES QUESTIONNAIRE BLOG CONTACT search

21st Century Dating

Kim

How did you first meet?
During my friend's birthday party.

What were you hoping for?
I just wanted to meet nice people and enjoy the evening in good company.

What was your first impression of Dan?
Wow! He's quite handsome!

What did you talk about?
We mainly talked about our jobs and our families. It seems we both love cycling, so we talked about that too.

Were there any awkward moments?
Only at the beginning; we had just been introduced and I couldn't remember his name.

Would you like to see Dan again?
Yes, I think so. We talked about going for a cycle ride together …

Dan

How did you first meet?
Kim was at a birthday party. Actually, I was not directly invited but a friend of mine, who was invited, insisted I should go with him.

What were you hoping for?
I didn't know what to expect. I didn't know anybody except for my friend. I just hoped that the people there would be easy-going and nice to talk to.

What was your first impression of Kim?
I thought she looked very pretty. She was wearing a beautiful dress – I felt a bit scruffy next to her!

What did you talk about?
All sorts of things. Kim talked a lot about her family. It is quite big and she spends a lot of time with them.

Were there any awkward moments?
No, none at all. It turned out to be a great evening with good company.

Would you like to see Kim again?
Yes, definitely. I gave her my number so it is up to her. I hope she gets in touch. Fingers crossed!

2 Complete the sentences with *Kim* or *Dan*.

a ________________ was not familiar with people at the party.
b ________________ felt not well-dressed close to ________________ .
c ________________ felt bad because he/she could not remember ________________'s name.
d ________________ likes to spend time with the family.
e ________________ is expecting a phone call.

3 1.17 **Listen to Kim and Dan talking about their relationship one year later. Why do you think it didn't work out?**

VOCABULARY

1 Complete the statements with words from the box.

dating dreams ~~love~~ propose relationship sight split up

- **a** I don't believe in ___love___ at first _______________ .
- **b** _______________ is the best way to find a new boyfriend or girlfriend.
- **c** He plans to invite her to dinner in a restaurant by the sea and _______________ to her. It will be very romantic.
- **d** They had a long _______________ before they got married.
- **e** People don't usually marry the man or woman of their _______________ .
- **f** Couples soon _______________ and go their separate ways if they don't have anything in common.

2 Work with a partner. Which statements in Exercise 1 do you agree with?

GRAMMAR

Present perfect: simple & progressive

I've known her for a few weeks.
She's been dating my brother.
He's asked her to marry him twice already.

1 Complete the table with these example sentences (a-c) from Kim's story.

- **a** He's been on his own for a long time.
- **b** We've been trying to arrange another date.
- **c** I've relocated to San Francisco.

	What does the verb describe?	Verb form	Sentence a, b, or c?
1	A continued or repeated action that started in the past and is still happening now.	Present perfect progressive	
2	A state that started in the past and continues now.	Present perfect (simple form)	
3	A finished action that happened some time in the past. (You don't say when.)	Present perfect (simple form)	

2 Underline the correct verb form. What does the verb describe in each case? Refer to the table in Exercise 1 and discuss your ideas with your partner.

- **a** **I've learned / 've been learning** English for three years.
- **b** **I've had / 've been having** the same hairstyle since I was a teenager.
- **c** My sister **has gone out / has been going out** with the same person since college.
- **d** **I've been / 've been going** to the USA three times.
- **e** **I've known / 've been knowing** my best friend for over ten years.
- **f** **I've stopped / 've been stopping** using social media. It's a waste of time.

Are any of the sentences true for you?

3 Make questions using the simple or progressive form of the present perfect.

- **a** ever / cry / at the movies?
  Have you ever cried at the movies?
- **b** How many times / travel / by plane?
- **c** ever / read / the same book twice?
- **d** How long / have / your watch?
- **e** How many times / go / to the USA?
- **f** How long / go / to the same dentist?
- **g** ever / own / a pet?

Ask and answer the questions with a partner.

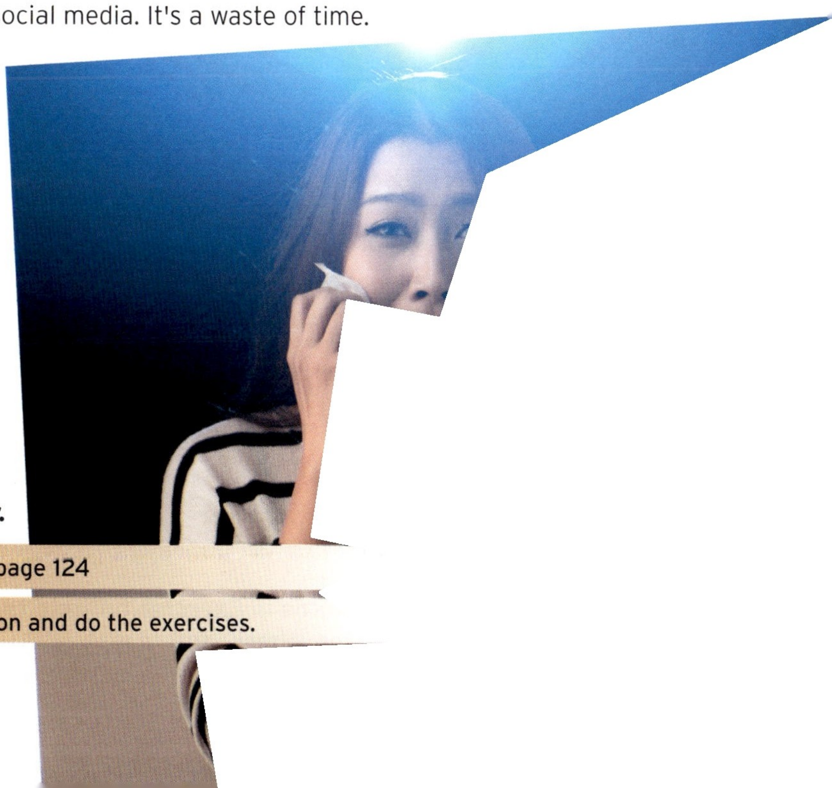

4 **Pairwork** **Student A:** page 120 **Student B:** page 124

5 **Grammar Extra 3** page 132. Read the explanation and do the exercises.

VOCABULARY

1 1.18 **Read and listen to six people talking about the important qualities they find in people they know. Which person is most/least like you?**

a I like a man who can take care of me. My ideal man has to be athletic, hard-working, down-to-earth, reliable, and romantic.

b Well, I'm pretty shy and sensitive. I feel good around my classmates who are outgoing and self-assured. They make me feel more confident.

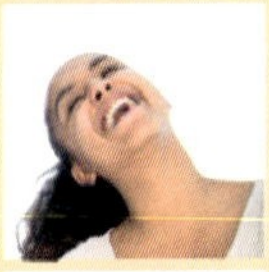

c I think the most important thing is a good sense of humor and a kind heart. My brother is witty, generous, and thoughtful.

d I couldn't live with a miserable, narrow-minded person. My roommates are cheerful, broad-minded, and optimistic.

e I'm looking for a good-looking, nice, faithful boyfriend who can cook really well.

f Big-headed, demanding, and self-centered people cannot be my friends. I like people who are modest, easygoing, and considerate.

2 **Complete the table with the highlighted words from Exercise 1. Use your dictionary if necessary.**

Words from the interviews		Words with similar meanings		Words with opposite meanings
a *faithful*	=	loyal	≠	unfaithful
b	=	considerate	≠	thoughtless
c	=	arrogant	≠	modest
d	=	realistic/practical	≠	unrealistic/impractical
e	=	confident	≠	insecure
f	=	sociable	≠	shy
g	=	optimistic	≠	miserable
h	=	selfish	≠	unselfish
i	=	trustworthy	≠	unreliable
j	=	amusing	≠	dull
k	=	tolerant	≠	narrow-minded
l	=	relaxed	≠	demanding

3 **What qualities do you look for in people? List the six most important qualities. Find someone else in the class who has chosen the same qualities.**

PRONUNCIATION

1 1.19 **Listen and repeat the words. Underline the stressed syllable for each word.**

a loyal cheerful faithful impractical
b interesting sociable miserable considerate
c ambitious demanding creative intelligent

2 1.20 **Look again at the words in Exercise 1. Circle the word in each group that has more syllables than the other words. Listen, check, and repeat.**

READING & SPEAKING

1 Complete the questionnaire. Choose only one answer (a-e) for each question.

gettingtoknow.com

gettingtoknow.com HOME PROFILES QUESTIONNAIRE BLOG CONTACT search

Describe yourself

1 The quality you admire most in other people is their ...
a) artistic talent.
b) ambition.
c) love of nature.
d) intellect.
e) sense of humor.

2 In a relationship, it's important to ...
a) give each other space.
b) respect each other's careers.
c) enjoy the same outdoor activities.
d) discuss things.
e) laugh together.

3 Your favorite place for dinner is ...
a) a cool new restaurant.
b) somewhere the rich and famous go.
c) a barbecue in the backyard.
d) a quiet place where you can talk.
e) a crowded place with loud music.

4 Your ideal weekend is ...
a) going to a jazz festival.
b) shopping in designer boutiques.
c) walking in the mountains.
d) going to the theater.
e) clubbing.

5 On a Saturday night, you're most likely to be ...
a) at the opening of a new art gallery.
b) making important new work contacts.
c) halfway up a mountain.
d) at home reading a novel.
e) in a crowded bar or nightclub.

6 You're most comfortable wearing ...
a) black clothes.
b) stylish clothes.
c) sports clothes.
d) jeans and a T-shirt.
e) colorful clothes.

7 On television you most like watching ...
a) foreign movies.
b) business news.
c) nature documentaries.
d) political debates.
e) comedies.

8 Which phrase best describes you?
a) I don't like following the crowd.
b) I live to work.
c) My idea of heaven is sleeping in a tent in the middle of nowhere.
d) I love a good argument.
e) Life's too short to stay at home – let's party!

Results

Mostly a: You are the artistic type. The artistic type is sensitive, creative, confident, and independent, but can be unreliable.

Mostly b: You are the career type. The career type is ambitious, sociable, serious, and hard-working, but sometimes dull.

Mostly c: You are the outdoor type. The outdoor type is down-to-earth, reliable, easygoing, and optimistic, but can be demanding.

Mostly d: You are the brainy type. The brainy type is intelligent, witty, interesting, and broadminded, but can be big-headed.

Mostly e: You are the party type. The party type is cheerful, funny, sociable, and outgoing, but sometimes selfish.

2 What does your score mean? Do you agree? Compare with a partner.

LANGUAGE FOR LIFE

1 1.21 **Listen to the conversation. Are these statements true or false?**

- **a** Mia and Rita know John very well.
- **b** Mia and Rita know Liz very well.
- **c** Mia is more critical than Rita.

2 Read the conversation. Match the highlighted phrases (1-8) with their more direct meanings (a-h) below.

Mia: So what do you think of Liz's new boyfriend?
Rita: John? He seems nice. I don't really know. **(1)** He wasn't very talkative.
Mia: Well, he's a little shy. And **(2)** Liz tends to dominate the conversation, doesn't she?
Rita: Yes, I guess so. But when John did say something, **(3)** it wasn't particularly interesting.
Mia: Oh, no. **(4)** You can be so mean.
Rita: I'm not mean – just honest.
Mia: But **(5)** he's not bad-looking, is he?
Rita: He's OK. Isn't he a little young for her?
Mia: Young? **(6)** Liz isn't exactly old.
Rita: That's true. But she looks older than she is.
Mia: Yes, I know what you mean. But she's so nice – she deserves someone really special.
Rita: Actually, **(7)** she can be really difficult.
Mia: Really?
Rita: Yes, **(8)** she can be a little bossy.
Mia: Oh, no. Why can't everybody be perfect, like us?
Rita: And so modest. Ha-ha!

- **a** it was boring 3
- **b** You're awful
- **c** Liz is young
- **d** He was very quiet
- **e** she's controlling
- **f** she's impossible
- **g** Liz talks too much
- **h** he's good-looking

3 1.22 **Listen and repeat the expressions (1-8) from the conversation.**

4 Match the comments (a-j) with their less direct versions (1-10).

- **a** She never stops talking.
- **b** The restaurant was awful.
- **c** He prefers older women.
- **d** She's rude.
- **e** He's big-headed.
- **f** They're unfriendly.
- **g** He never gets up before noon.
- **h** Sometimes she looks exhausted.
- **i** They're well-off.
- **j** She didn't help me at all.

1. She isn't particularly/exactly polite.
2. He tends to get up pretty late.
3. They're not particularly/exactly friendly.
4. She can be a little bit talkative.
5. The restaurant wasn't very/particularly good.
6. She can look a little tired.
7. They're not particularly/exactly poor.
8. He tends to go out with older women.
9. She wasn't particularly/exactly helpful.
10. He's not particularly/exactly modest.

Life Skills: Problem Solving
Problem Page

1 Look at the problem that was sent into an online Problem Page. Complete using the words in the box.

kind sociable rude older ~~lazy~~

AskAngie.com

Dear Angie,
I'm 16 and my mother is always saying that I am **(1)** ___lazy___ because I am always sitting around, looking at my phone and on social media. She says it is **(2)** __________ to be looking at your phone when somebody is talking to you. Mom says I should be more **(3)** __________ and talk to people. I just think **(4)** __________ people don't understand me! I will try to be **(5)** __________ to them because I love my family.
What should I do?
Yours,
Ellie

2 What answer would you give Ellie if you were Angie? Make notes and then compare with your partner.

3 Work in pairs to solve these problems.

- **a** My son spends a lot of time on social media.
- **b** I am allergic to cats. My new housemate has two cats which she loves. I feel bad telling her that I am allergic.
- **c** I don't want to go to university, but my parents are insisting that I should study something that will help me for my future.

MACMILLAN LIFE SKILLS

Sounds and spelling

1 **Say the words below. Look at the phonetic symbols and find the symbols for the vowel sounds and diphthongs in red.**

beige /beɪʒ/ boy /bɔɪ/ check /tʃek/ jump /dʒʌmp/
mother /ˈmʌðər/ mouth /maʊθ/ ring /rɪŋ/ shop /ʃɑp/

2 **Say the five words beginning with *hea* in the dictionary extracts. What do you notice about the pronunciation of the letters *ea*? Complete the table with the words in the box according to the pronunciation of the letters *ea*. Check your answers in a dictionary.**

~~bear~~ break breath dear dream great
health learn meat near search wear

/e/	/ɜː/	/i/	/ɪr/	/eɪ/
bear				

3 **Say the four words (bought – talk) in the dictionary extracts. Which vowel sound do all the words have in common? What do you notice about the spellings? Connect the words according to their vowel sounds. Check your answers in a dictionary.**

a /ə/ —— arrive —— color —— husband —— people
b /i/ —— bean pretty niece police
c /u/ —— blew fruit shoe through
d /ɪ/ —— busy key gym women

4 **Read the six words (economical – politician) in the dictionary extracts. How is the main stress indicated? Underline the stressed syllables in the noun phrases below and practice saying the phrases.**

a an economical economist
b a philosophical philosopher
c a political politician

5 **Look at the phonetic transcriptions for six words from Units 1-3. Say the words and complete the spellings. Check in a dictionary.**

a /ɔlˈðoʊ/ although
b /ˈdɔtər/ d_ _ gh_ _ _
c /ɪˈnʌf/ e_ _ _ gh
d /læf/ _ _ _ gh
e /ˈneɪbər/ _ _ _ gh_ _ _
f /ˈθɔtləs/ _ _ _ _ gh_ _ _ _ _

6 **Check your own dictionary. Find six more words from Units 1-3 that are difficult to spell or pronounce. Practice saying them.**

Phonetic symbols

Vowel sounds	Diphthongs	Consonants	
i	ɜr	p	ʒ
ɪ	eɪ	b	h
e	aɪ	t	hw
æ	ɔɪ	d	x
ɑ	oʊ	k	tʃ
ɔ	aʊ	g	dʒ
ʌ	ɪr	f	m
ʊ		v	n
u		θ	ŋ
ə		ð	w
		s	r
		z	l
		ʃ	j

head /hed/ noun ★★★

hear /hɪr/ verb ★★★

heard /hɜrd/ verb ★★★

heart /hɑrt/ noun ★★★

heat /hit/ noun ★★★

bought /bɔt/ verb ★★★

caught /kɔt/ verb ★★★

draw /drɔ/ noun ★★★

talk /tɔk/ verb ★★★

economical /ikəˈnɑmɪk(ə)l/ adj

economist /ɪˈkɑnəmɪst/ noun

philosopher /fɪˈlɑsəfər/ noun

philosophical /ˌfɪləˈsɑfɪk(ə)l/ adj

political /pəˈlɪtɪk(ə)l/ adj ★★★

politician /ˌpɑləˈtɪʃ(ə)n/ noun ★★

From the *Macmillan Essential Dictionary for Learners of American English.*

GRAMMAR

Grammar Extra pages 128–133.

1 Complete the sentences. Use *about, at, in, on, with.*

a What sports are you good ________ ?
b What have you spent the most money ________ ?
c Who were you having dinner ________ yesterday?
d What kind of music are you interested ________ ?
e What kinds of things do you worry ________ ?

Ask and answer the questions with a partner.

2 Complete the questions for these answers.

a "Who __loves cooking__ ?" "My father loves cooking."
b "What ________ ?" "I saw the new Modern Art exhibition."
c "Who ________ ?" "I spoke to my brother yesterday."
d "Who ________ ?" "Josh gave her that watch."
e "Which ________ ?" "She chose the red car."
f "What ________ ?" "A package arrived this morning."

3 Write the sentences in the correct order.

a from home / work / I / usually
I usually work from home.
b I / from time to time / travel abroad
c come / I / hardly ever / to my English class
d I / a hat / all the time / like wearing
e often / I / by car / come to school / don't
f I / very fast / always / walk

Check (✓) the sentences that are true for you.

4 Complete with the simple past, present perfect, or present perfect progressive form of the verbs.

Jed: Have you ever (**1** go) __been__ on a horse before?
Bob: Well, I (**2** go) ________ on a camel, but I (**3** not ride) ________ a horse.
Jed: Really? A camel?
Bob: Yes. We (**4** go) ________ to Egypt a few years ago, and we (**5** do) ________ a camel trek into the desert.
Jed: Wow! What (**6** be) ________ that like?
Bob: Wonderful. We (**7** sleep) ________ under the stars. I (**8** never see) ________ anything so beautiful in all my life. What about you?
Jed: Oh, I love horseback riding. I (**9** do) ________ it since I was ten years old. My grandfather (**10** teach) ________ me.

5 Complete the sentences with the words in the box and the correct form of the adjectives.

the most	most	~~much~~	not as	slightly	the

a I'm 1.60 meters tall. Di is 1.80 meters. She's (tall) __much taller__ than me.
b Russia is (big) ________ country in the world.
c I don't like my new car. It's (good) ________ as my old one.
d Skydiving is (exciting) ________ thing I've ever done.
e This book is (easy) ________ than the last one ... but not much.
f What is the (popular) ________ sport in the world?

VOCABULARY

1 **Replace the underlined words with the expressions in the box.**

clicked right away | drifted apart | ~~gotten along well with~~ | have a lot in common

a Have you always enjoyed the company of your sister?
Have you always __gotten along well with__ your sister?
b He likes baseball. She likes reading. They don't really have similar interests.
c They got divorced because over the years they found they had become distant from each other.
d Don and I liked one another the very first time we met.

2 **Complete the words for sports with *a, e, i, o, u*.**

a sw_i_mm_i_ng
b k__t__ s__rf__ng
c b__dm__nt__n
d v__ll__yb__ll
e s__ __l__ng
f s__cc__r
g p__ng p__ng
h skyd__v__ng
i f__sh__ng
j sk__ __ng
k t__nn__s
l sn__wb__ __rd__ng
m b__sk__tb__ll
n __c__ h__ck__y

3 **Put the sports in Exercise 2 into these groups.**

a Sports you can play with a partner
badminton, ...
b Water sports
c Sports you play on a team
d Sports you do up in the air
e Sports you can only do outside in the winter

4 **Complete the text with the words in the box.**

optimistic | take part | confident | disappointing
progress | hardworking | ~~split up with~~ | trainer | challenging

Four months ago, Rob **(1)** __split up with__ his tennis partner, John, after four years playing together. Rob wanted to start **(2)** ________ himself to play singles, but it was difficult to find a **(3)** ________ coach, in the small town where he lived. So he decided to ask a friend who was a very good tennis player, if he was willing to be his **(4)** ________. During the first two weeks it was **(5)** ________, but in the third week Rob saw a lot of **(6)** ________. After only two months together, his trainer said he was **(7)** ________ that he could **(8)** ________ in the next inter-city tennis match. Rob was very **(9)** ________ and finished in second place.

PRONUNCIATION

1 **Look at some words from Units 1-3. Say the words and add them to the table.**

~~answer~~ ~~appointment~~ dirty exhausted extremely friendship ~~normally~~ often
personal really remember similar somebody theater together

A: ■ ▪	answer
B: ▪ ■ ▪	appointment
C: ■ ▪ ▪	normally

2 **Underline the stressed syllable in each word.**

1.23 **Listen, check, and repeat.**

READING & LISTENING

1 Read about five young people who share a house talking about each other. Who has been in the house the longest?

facebook.com

Peter Home

Peter
News Feed
Messenger

EXPLORE
Pages
Groups
Events
Friend List
Games
On This Day
Live Video
Pokes
Pages Feed
Suggested Edits
See More

Peter
March 9 at 2:07pm

House Share

Like Comment Share

24

Peter I've lived in the house for three years. I get on very well with everyone, but I suppose I'm closest to Nathan. He's a very chilled guy. We have quite a lot in common: we share the same taste in music and we have a similar sense of humor. We often go out in the evenings together to see bands and have some pizzas.

Alice I really enjoy living here. I've been here for four years. Gretchen and I are the best of friends. I like all the boys too, but Peter and Nathan can be a bit annoying sometimes. They are not very tidy and they sometimes forget to do their chores. Luke isn't here very much so I probably don't know him as well as I know the others.

Nathan This is a great house. I've been here for just over two years. I've shared lots of houses before, but this is by far the nicest group of people I have ever lived with. Peter is my mate. We have a real laugh together. The girls are great, but they do nag a bit! I think they have higher standards when it comes to housework, etc. I think life's too short to worry about being tidy ...

Gretchen I'm the newest person in the house. I arrived about a year ago. I am very happy here, as the atmosphere is very relaxed. Alice and I get on very well and often cook together. Nathan and Peter are very funny – they make me laugh. I don't see so much of Luke, but I enjoy his company when he is around.

Luke I've lived here for nearly two years. All my housemates are very nice. I haven't had any problems with any of them. I have to travel abroad a lot for my job, so I am often away for several weeks at a time. I always get a nice welcome when I get back. It definitely feels like home.

2 Read the housemates' comments above and underline the correct words below.

a Peter and Nathan have **similar / different** interests.
b Peter thinks Nathan is **anxious / chilled**.
c Alice and Gretchen enjoy **dancing / cooking** together.
d Alice thinks Peter and Nathan are **too tidy / not tidy enough**.
e Nathan **hasn't / has** shared a house before.
f Luke spends a lot of time **at the house / away**.
g Nathan **enjoys / doesn't enjoy** housework.

3 1.24 **Listen to a conversation between Alice and Gretchen. What is Alice's news?**

4 Listen again. Are these statements true or false?

a Gretchen already knew Alice's news.
b Peter is moving to Spain.
c Valeria works at the university in Seville.
d Gretchen won't miss Luke.
e Alice wants to give Luke a surprise farewell party.
f Luke usually goes to the pub in the evenings.

WRITING & SPEAKING

1 Read the email and match the descriptions (a-f) with the paragraphs (1-6).

- **a** Opening phrase
- **b** Signing off (+ your name)
- **c** Main message
- **d** Greeting (+ name) *Paragraph 1*
- **e** Extra information (often attachments)
- **f** Closing phrase

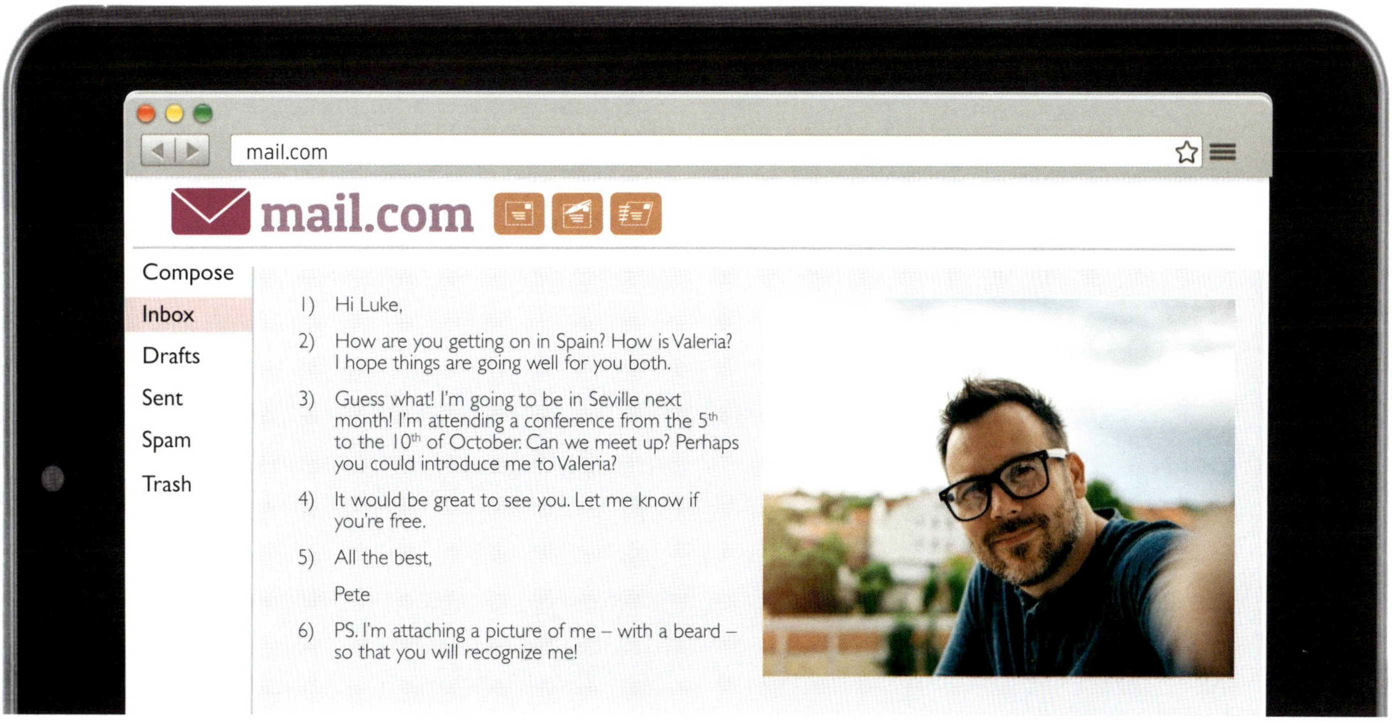

1) Hi Luke,

2) How are you getting on in Spain? How is Valeria? I hope things are going well for you both.

3) Guess what! I'm going to be in Seville next month! I'm attending a conference from the 5th to the 10th of October. Can we meet up? Perhaps you could introduce me to Valeria?

4) It would be great to see you. Let me know if you're free.

5) All the best,

Pete

6) PS. I'm attaching a picture of me – with a beard – so that you will recognize me!

2 In which paragraph (1-6) in the email in Exercise 1 could you use the following words and phrases?

- **a** Best wishes *5*
- **b** Dear Luke
- **c** Hello there!
- **d** How are things going?
- **e** I'm really looking forward to seeing you
- **f** I'm sending you a video clip
- **g** Lots of love
- **h** Regards
- **i** Thank you for your email

3 Imagine you are Luke. Write an email reply to Peter.

Hi Peter,
Thanks for your email ...

4 Work in pairs or small groups. Discuss the questions.

- **a** How often do you send email?
- **b** How many emails do you send and receive in a day/week?
- **c** Are your emails mainly work-related or personal?
- **d** Do you text more than you email?

5 Choose one of the emails below and write it.

a Write an email to a friend.
- You are replying to an email from your friend.
- Thank them for their email.
- You have some exciting news about another friend. Give details.
- Send a picture with your email.

b Write an email to a friend.
- You went to dinner at your friend's house.
- Thank your friend for the meal.
- Make positive comments about the food.
- Send some pictures with the email.

READING

1 **Think of a festival you know or have heard about. How much do you know about it? Discuss with a partner.**

a What is the name of the festival?
b When does it take place?
c What do you know about its history?
d How do the people celebrate?
e How does the festival end?

2 **Now read this travel blog about an unusual Filipino festival and find answers to the questions above.**

thecurioustraveler.com

thecurioustraveler.com HOME BLOG GALLERY CONTACT

THE MASSKARA FESTIVAL, BACOLOD

I recently traveled to the Philippines and headed to Bacolod in the Visayas region to experience the festival there. I heard that Filipinos know how to throw a party, but this was something special. I don't think I'll ever get over how warm and welcoming the people were.

Amazing "fiestas" occur in every city and town in the Philippines throughout the year. Many originated from Spanish colonial times when people held big religious festivals to attract people to Christianity. The MassKara festival in Bacolod, which takes place on the third weekend of October, started as recently as 1980. Bacolod is famous for its sugarcane, but in the 80s there was a crisis in the province. Two disasters struck at once: the sugar industry collapsed, and over 700 people died in a ferry disaster.

People know Bacolod as the "City of Smiles", but it wasn't a happy place. The residents decided to create something to smile about, so they came up with a "smiling festival". The name "MassKara" comes from "mas", Spanish for *many*, and "cara", the word for *face*. The festival is a noisy, busy, joyful, colorful mix of street dancers and musicians, who all dress up in bright clothes and smiling face masks — the *many faces*. MassKara is a declaration that, no matter how bad things looked, the people of Bacolod knew that things would get better and they would pull through to brighter times.

The festival starts with a dance contest where participants show off their skills, a beauty pageant, street food banquets, as well as lots of live music. MassKara feels like a mixture of Mardi Gras, the Carnival in Rio, and the Venice Carnevale, but at the same time it is distinctly Filipino, which makes it feel completely authentic.

On the first morning, after performing in the main arena, dancers progress through the streets in a giant parade all the way back to the main plaza. Here the top performers from each group compete for the prize.

In the evening, people parade around town on colorful electric floats, called the Electric MassKara, and the performers get down to some serious dancing. The final event is the Electric MassKara Elimination. Once again, the top dance groups compete until it's finally over and the winners are announced. I have no idea how the dancers keep it up all day. Just an hour of dancing wears me out.

The evening I was there, the Bacolodons carried on celebrating through the night at the street food stalls and bars. And the noise! Fireworks go off every few minutes – I'm surprised the town didn't burn down with all the sparks. This curious traveler joined in the festivities and ended up partying until the small hours before heading for his hotel, tired but smiling.

I set off the next day for my one-hour flight to Manila. I'm already looking forward to coming back next year!

VOCABULARY

1 Complete this description of the MassKara festival with the words in the box.

~~festival~~ pageant music street food masks
parade statues fireworks procession

MassKara takes place on the third weekend in October every year. The main feature of the **(1)** *festival* is the range of smiling face **(2)** ________ worn by the dancers. The festival includes a beauty **(3)** ________ and live **(4)** ________. There is a big **(5)** ________ through the streets. People enjoy **(6)** ________ at the banquets. Unlike other festivals in the Philippines which have religious origins, there are no costumes in the **(7)** ________, or any **(8)** ________ of religious figures. Lots of color and drama is provided by the stunning **(9)** ________ and masks of the dancers!

2 Write a short summary of a festival you know. Read your summary to your partner.

VOCABULARY & GRAMMAR

1 The nine phrasal verbs in the table are from the article on page 36. Find them in the text and match each one to a word or phrase in the box with the same meaning.

Intransitive	Transitive	
	Separable	**Inseparable**
~~go off~~		get down to something
set off	show something off	look forward to something
end up	wear something out	get over something
		carry on something

anticipate recover display proudly depart finish
~~explode~~ start destroy by overuse continue

Go off = explode

Phrasal verbs

Intransitive
(no object)
go off set off end up

Transitive
(takes an object)

a) separable
show sth **off**
wear sth **out**

b) inseparable
come up with sth
get over sth
get down to sth
carry on sth

2 Which of these sentences is grammatically incorrect? Cross it out.

a You can **look** the word **up** in a dictionary.
b You can **look** it **up** in a dictionary.
c You can **look up** the word in a dictionary.
d You can **look up** it in a dictionary.

Complete the rule with *always*, *sometimes*, or *never*.

When the object of a separable phrasal verb is a pronoun (*me*, *you*, *it*, etc.), it ________ comes between the verb (*look*) and the particle (*up*).

3 Put the words in parentheses in the correct order to make phrasal verb sentences with pronouns.

a I hate cleaning up the mess after I've had a party. (I hate / it / cleaning / up)
I hate cleaning it up.
b When my boss has a party, I take care of her children. (I / of / take care / them)
c I usually try on several outfits before I go to a party. (I / try / on / them)
d I always want to turn the music down at parties. (I / want to / down / turn / it)
e It's difficult to come up with ideas for gifts. (It's difficult to / them / with /come up)
f I'm looking forward to my next birthday party. (I'm / to / looking forward / it)

4 Pairwork Student A: page 121 **Student B:** page 125

LISTENING

1 **Think about last New Year's Eve. Work with a partner and ask and answer these questions.**

a Where were you?
b Who were you with?
c What did you do?

2 **What do you know about the Chinese New Year? Decide whether you think the statements below are true or false.**

a The Chinese New Year takes place *in early January*.
b Just before the New Year, people *clean their houses to sweep away bad luck*.
c Some people also *put up red decorations to scare away bad luck*.
d The traditional New Year's Eve dinner is *Peking duck*.
e People usually spend New Year's Eve with *their friends*.
f On New Year's Eve, people *stay in and watch TV*.
g At midnight on New Year's Eve, people *set off fireworks and firecrackers*.

1.25 **Listen to Hua and check your ideas. Correct the statements that are false.**

3 **Work with a partner. Rewrite the statements in Exercise 2 with information about New Year's Eve celebrations in your country.**

VOCABULARY

1 **Underline the correct verbs in the following extract from the interview about the Chinese New Year.**

I'm going to help my mother **(1) do / make** the housework. We're going to sweep away all the bad luck and **(2) do / make** room for good luck to come in.

2 **Complete the questions with the correct form of *do* or *make*.**

a Do you always ________________ New Year's resolutions?
b Who usually ________________ the cooking in your house?
c Have you ever ________________ a promise that you didn't keep?
d Are you ________________ any sports right now?
e When was the last time you ________________ a wish? Did it come true?
f When you ________________ the shopping, do you usually ________________ a list first?

Ask your partner the questions.

3 **Work with a partner. Decide whether the words in the box collocate with *do* or *make*. Use your dictionary if necessary.**

a comment | a decision | a job | a mistake | a noise | a profit | a suggestion | an excuse | arrangements | money | progress | some decorating | some exercise | some research | some skiing | something clear | sure | the ironing | your homework

Choose six collocations and use each one to write an example sentence that is true for you.

I haven't made any arrangements for New Year's Eve yet.

GRAMMAR

1 1.26 **Read and listen to Part 1 of a conversation between two roommates. Why is Sandy unhappy?**

Zoë: Hi!
Sandy: Oh, hello.
Zoë: You don't look very happy. Did something happen at work?
Sandy: No, work's fine. David hasn't called, and we're supposed to be going to a party tonight. What are you doing tonight? Do you want to come to the party with me?
Zoë: I'd love to, but **(1)** Steve's coming over, and **(2)** we're going to plan our summer vacation.
Sandy: Oh, well, what am I going to do? ... I know – **(3)** I'll call James.

2 Three different ways of talking about the future are highlighted in the conversation. Which form is used to talk about ...

a a spontaneous decision (you speak at the moment you decide to do something)?
b an intention (you speak after you have already decided to do something)?
c an arrangement (you speak after you have already arranged to do something)?

Future forms

Do you have any plans for the weekend?

A spontaneous decision: *will*

No, I don't. I think **I'll call** Jan and see if she's free.

An intention: *(be) going to*

Not yet. **I'm going to call** Jan and see if she's free.

An arrangement: present progressive

Yes, I do. I**'m having** lunch with Jan on Saturday.

3 Read Part 2. Underline the most appropriate future form.

James: Hello.
Sandy: Hi, James, it's Sandy. What **(1) will you do / are you doing** tonight?
James: Nothing! Well actually, **(2) I'll meet / I'm meeting** Alex and Suzy downtown, but ...
Sandy: Do you want to come to a party? Alex and Suzy can come, too.
James: Yes, that sounds great. **(3) I'm meeting / I'll meet** them at the Star Shopping Center at 8:30.
Sandy: OK, **(4) I'll see / I'm going to see** you there. ... (*Hangs up the phone.*) Hey, Zoe. **(5) I'll go / I'm going** to the party with James.
Zoë: Good idea.
Sandy: And next time I see David, **(6) I'm telling / I'm going to tell** him the relationship is definitely over.
Zoë: Hmm. **(7) I'll believe / I'm believing** that when I see it.

1.27 **Listen and check.**

4 Complete Part 3 by putting the verb in the most appropriate future form.

Zoë: Hello.
David: Is Sandy there, please?
Zoë: Yes, just a minute – I (**1** get) ________________ her for you. ... It's David.
Sandy: Oh, hello, David.
David: Look, I'm really sorry I didn't call earlier, but I'm still at the office and ...
Sandy: Oh, that's all right. I forgot you were going to call anyway.
David: Listen, I'm afraid I can't come to the party. I (**2** have) ________________ dinner with some important clients tonight.
Sandy: It doesn't matter – I (**3** go) ________________ to the party with someone else.
David: Oh, OK, well I (**4** call) ________________ you.
Sandy: When? I mean, all right. Goodbye.
David: Bye.
Zoë: So?
Sandy: Well, he apologized – and he (**5** have) _____ dinner with an important client. Anyway, I have to go. See you later.

1.28 **Listen and check.**

5 1.29 **Listen to Part 4. Is there a future for Sandy and David?**

6 **Grammar Extra 4** page 134. Read the explanation and do the exercises.

SPEAKING & READING

1 **Work with a partner. Discuss when and why people have these types of parties.**

- a housewarming party
- an 18th birthday party
- an office party
- a farewell/leaving party
- a surprise party
- a costume party

What other parties can you think of?

2 **Discuss what makes a good party. Write a list and agree on the three most important "ingredients". Read the blog post and find out how many of your ingredients are mentioned.**

The worst party ever

I have to tell you about the party I went to last night! Everyone agrees — it was the worst party ever!

My friend Gregg, the host, is great but he's not the most organized person in the world. Planning and delegation are not his strong points. He made a few key mistakes:

Firstly, he only decided at the last minute to throw the party, so he sent a general invitation via social media. Not just his friends saw it but also the friends of his friends — and their friends too. Everybody in the town came! He couldn't greet his guests let alone mingle with them. By about 11 p.m. you couldn't move and basically the house was a mess.

Then, after he had already invited some of the guests, he decided to have a costume party. So some people wore costumes and some didn't, and everyone ended up feeling embarrassed. Awkward!

As for the food — because he had only decided to throw a party at the last minute, he didn't have enough time to get the food and drink sorted out. No one had anything to eat. Someone really should have gone to the store and gotten some party food.

That wouldn't have mattered if the atmosphere and the music had been cool. Sadly the atmosphere was more like *ice cold*. The sound system wasn't powerful enough, so you couldn't hear it, and nobody was dancing. And anyway, if you could hear it, the music was terrible. By midnight there was no drink, food, or music, so everyone just drifted away.

Poor Gregg. He didn't delegate key tasks to anyone else, so there was no one to greet guests, no one to take care of the bar or the food, and no one to do the music. He ended up running around with a dustpan and brush desperately trying to clean up the mess – his parents would be back in the morning. And he certainly didn't enjoy the party. I guess he won't hold another one any time soon. And anyway, I'm not sure anyone would come …

VOCABULARY

1 **Use the words from the box to complete the three golden rules for giving a party.**

mess ~~delegate~~ greet enjoy dustpan

Three golden rules

1 Always **(1)** ___*delegate*___ ! You can't do everything yourself. You need four helpers: someone to meet and **(2)** ______ the guests; someone to take care of the bar; someone to take care of the food; and someone to do the music.

2 Don't worry about the **(3)** ______! It's no fun for party guests to see the host running around holding a **(4)** ______ and brush.

3 **(5)** ______ yourself! If your guests see you are happy and relaxed, they will be too.

2 **Find words or phrases from the blog post above to complete the descriptions.**

a You can ask people to wear a ___*costume*___ for your party.

b You are a g______ when you go to a party.

c You receive an i______ from someone who wants you to go to their party.

d You try to create a good a______ to get people in the mood for your party.

e You m______ so that you can talk to as many people as possible at a party.

f You are the h______ when you throw a party.

3 **Have you ever thrown a party? What was it like? Tell your partner.**

GRAMMAR

1 **Complete the table.**

People	everybody	**(1)** somebody	**(4)** ________	**(7)** ________
	everyone	**(2)** ________	**(5)** ________	no one
Things	everything	something	**(6)** ________	**(8)** ________
Places	everywhere	**(3)** ________	anywhere	**(9)** ________

2 Underline the correct pronoun to complete the conversation.

Mom: Is that you, Dylan? You're late. Where have you been?
Dylan: **(1) Nowhere. / Anywhere.**
Mom: But you're an hour late!
Dylan: OK, I went to the park.
Mom: Who with?
Dylan: **(2) Anyone. / No one.** I went on my own.
Mom: Where's Sophie?
Dylan: I don't know. **(3) Out somewhere / Nowhere.**
Mom: What happened?
Dylan: **(4) Nothing! / Anything!** Stop asking questions.
Mom: What do you want for dinner tonight?
Dylan: **(5) Anything. / Everything.** I don't care.
Mom: We could try that new Chinese restaurant – **(6) everyone / someone** says it's great.
Dylan: OK.
Mom: Good. Now, what did you do at school today?

anybody, somebody, etc.

Somebody is coming.

I can't hear **anything**.

I've looked **everywhere**.

No one cares.

1.30 **Listen and check. Do you know anybody like Dylan?**

PRONUNCIATION

1 1.31 **Listen and repeat the sentences.**

a I wanna be famous.
b It's gonna be good.
c He's gonna have a party.
d D'ya wanna come over for dinner?

Rewrite the sentences in Exercise 1 in full.

SPEAKING: ANECDOTE

1 1.32 **Listen to Paul talking about a costume party he went to and look at the questions. Which question does he not answer?**

a Whose party was it?
b Why did she have a party?
c What kind of party was it?
d Was there a theme?
e Where was the party?
f How many people were there?
g How many people did you know?
h What did you eat and drink?
i What was the music like?
j Did you dance?
k Did you stay until the end?

1 It was a costume party.
2 At least seventy.
3 At Maggie's house.
4 Everybody dressed up as something beginning with *M*.
5 It was fantastic.
6 My friend Maggie's.
7 Not everybody.
8 Because she was moving abroad.
9 Thai food and some kind of tea.
10 Yes, a lot.

Match the questions with the answers (1-10). Listen again and check.

2 **You are going to tell your partner about a party you've been to.**

- Ask yourself the questions in Exercise 1.
- Think about what to say and how to say it.
- Tell your partner about the party.

LANGUAGE FOR LIFE

1 1.33 **Read and listen to Rose speaking to four friends. Which friend doesn't she know very well?**

a
Rose: Do you want to go to the movies tonight?
Ian: Yes, good idea. What are you going to see?
Rose: The new James Bond movie.
Ian: Oh, no. I've already seen it.
Rose: Oh, what a shame. Is it any good?
Ian: No, it's terrible.

b
Rose: Would you like to come to the movies tonight?
Lucy: I'd love to, but I'm working tonight.
Rose: Oh, too bad.
Lucy: I know. What are you going to see?
Rose: The new Bond movie.
Lucy: Oh, I've heard it's really good – the best one so far.

c
Rose: Are you doing anything tonight?
Megan: No, why?
Rose: I'm going to see the new Bond movie. Do you want to come?
Megan: No, I'm afraid I can't. I have to get up really early tomorrow. Why don't you ask Alan?
Rose: Alan? I don't know him well enough.
Megan: Don't be silly. He'd be really happy.

d
Rose: Hi, Alan. It's Rose.
Alan: Hi, Rose. How are you?
Rose: Good, thanks. I was wondering if you'd like to go to the movies tonight.
Alan: Yes, that sounds great. What's playing?
Rose: Well, I was thinking of seeing the new James Bond movie.
Alan: Great. What time do you want to meet?

2 Read the conversations again. Look at the highlighted expressions. Find:

- **a** three ways of inviting somebody to do something
- **b** two ways of accepting an invitation
- **c** two ways of refusing an invitation
- **d** one way of asking somebody if they are free to go out
- **e** two ways of sounding disappointed

1.34 **Listen, check, and repeat the expressions.**

3 Work with a partner. Practice the conversations in Exercise 1.

4 Work with a partner. Write a conversation based on the situation below.

- **Student A:** You want to meet up with Student B and go somewhere. Make at least three suggestions.
- **Student B:** You don't want to go anywhere with Student A. Make excuses.

Practice your conversation. Take turns being Student A and Student B.

Life Skills: Social Skills

A Shopping Trip

1 1.35 **Listen to the conversation in a store. How many times do you hear the words *thanks* or *thank you*, *please* and *sorry*?**

2 Select the appropriate polite response for these situations. (There may be more than one.)

1

- **a** I'll get a kilo of apples.
- **b** A kilo of apples please.
- **c** Apples, a kilo, quickly! Thanks!

2

- **a** Sorry, but you were in my way!
- **b** Watch where you're going!
- **c** I'm so sorry, I didn't see you.

3

- **a** Get a move on!
- **b** I can do it myself, thank you.
- **c** Thank you very much.

4

- **a** Thank you but I can manage myself. After you.
- **b** Don't patronize me!
- **c** That's kind, thank you.

3 Discuss with a partner. When and how often do you use the words *please*, *thank you* and *sorry* in your culture? Are there other ways to express yourself without using those words?

MACMILLAN LIFE SKILLS

Phrasal verbs

1 Work with a partner. Decide which particle in each list does not go with *take* to form a phrasal verb. Cross it out.

a	about	after	in	on	up
b	apart	at	down	off	out
c	back	over	through	to	without

Check in the dictionary entry. Check (✓) the phrasal verbs you know.

2 Complete the table with the dictionary entry for each phrasal verb.

~~I don't take after my mom.~~ Sorry, I take it back.
The plane is taking off. Why did you take him on?
He took to them immediately. We've taken it up.

Intransitive	Transitive (separable)	Transitive (not separable)
		take after sb

Where does the dictionary put the object (*sb/sth*) when the phrasal verb is: a separable; b not separable?

3 Many phrasal verbs have both literal and idiomatic meanings. Underline the idiomatic meanings of these phrasal verbs.

a take back: **return sth you bought / admit that you said sth wrong**
b take down: **write sth / dismantle a structure**
c take in: **understand and remember sth / allow sb to stay in your home**
d take off: **remove clothing, etc. / aircraft: start flying**
e take out: **get sth official from a bank, etc. / remove sth from a pocket, etc.**
f take up: **fill space or time / start doing sth new**

Check your ideas in the dictionary extract.

4 Complete the sentences with phrasal verbs from Exercise 3.

a I'm a nervous flyer: I don't mind __taking off__ but I hate landing.
b I usually ________ a travel insurance policy when I travel abroad.
c I'm going to ________ jogging one of these days.
d When I realize that I'm wrong about something, I always ________ it ________ .
e I find that explanations in English are sometimes difficult to ________ .
f If I don't ________ some notes in class, I can never remember what the class is about.

Are any of the sentences true for you?

PHRASAL VERBS **'take ,after sb** to look or behave like an older relative
,take sth a'part to separate an object into its pieces: *Ben was taking apart an old bicycle.*
,take sth 'back 1 to take something that you have bought back to a store because it is broken or not appropriate **2** to admit that something that you said was wrong: *I'm sorry – I take it back.*
,take sth 'down 1 to separate a large structure into its pieces **2** to write information on a piece of paper: *The police took down our addresses and phone numbers.*
,take sb 'in 1 to allow someone to stay in your house or your country **2 be taken in** to be tricked so that you believe something that is not true
,take sth 'in 1 to understand and remember something that you hear or read: *I'm not sure how much of his explanation she took in.* **2** to make a piece of clothing more narrow or more tight, so that it fits you
,take 'off 1 if an aircraft takes off, it leaves the ground and starts to fly ≠ LAND **2** to become successful or popular very fast: *Her business has really taken off.* **3** *informal* to leave a place suddenly
,take sth 'off 1 to remove a piece of clothing from your body ≠ PUT STH ON **2** to spend a particular amount of time away from work: *I'm taking Monday off to go to the game.*
,take 'on sth to develop a particular character or appearance: *Our website is taking on a new look.*
,take sb 'on 1 to start to employ someone **2** to fight or compete against someone
,take sth 'on to accept some work or responsibility
,take sb 'out to take someone to a place such as a theater or a restaurant and pay for them: *She's taking her parents out for dinner.*
,take sth 'out 1 to remove something from a place: *Henry took out his wallet.* **2** to get something officially: *When you take out an insurance policy, read the small print.*
,take sth 'out on sb to treat someone badly because you are angry, upset, or tired, although it is not their fault
,take (sth) 'over to begin to do something that someone else was doing: *Jane **took over as** director after Richard retired.*
,take sth 'over to take control of something, especially another company
,take sb 'through sth to explain something to someone in detail
'take to sth to start doing something as a habit: *Recently he's taken to wearing a hat.*
'take to sb/sth to begin to like someone or something: *I took to John immediately.*
,take 'up sth to fill a particular amount of space or time: *These files take up a lot of disk space.*
,take sth 'up to start doing something regularly as a habit, job, or interest: *Chris has taken up jogging.* ♦ *The new teacher will **take up** her **position** in May.*
,take sb 'up on sth to accept an offer or invitation that someone has made: *I've decided to take you up on that job offer.*
,take sth 'up with sb to complain to someone about a problem

From the *Macmillan Essential Dictionary for Learners of American English.*

5 Look at the sentences. Decide which alternative is not possible in each case. Cross it out.

a People say I take after my **mother / father / ~~dog~~**.
b My **career / business / car** never really took off.
c I've never taken out a **rent / mortgage / bank loan**.
d Recently, I've taken to **wearing a suit / walking to work / having a baby**.
e I'd like to take up **swimming / sleeping / yoga**.

Check your own dictionary. What example sentences does it give for the phrasal verbs in Exercise 5?

READING

1 **Read through the questions below and guess how your partner would answer.**

quiz.com

Are you crazy about cheese?

1 Do you think about cheese several times a day?
2 Do you have cheese with everything?
3 Have you tried more than 10 different kinds of cheese?
4 Do you ever order a cheese board in a restaurant rather than ice cream?
5 Is a cheese sandwich your favorite kind of sandwich?
6 Do you spend several minutes at the cheese counter in your local store?
7 Do you have a favorite kind of cheese?
8 Do you ever dream about cheese?

If you answered yes to at least three of the questions, you're probably crazy about cheese!

Compare your answers. Who likes cheese the most? Could you live without cheese for a week?

2 **Decide whether the following statements about cheese are true or false.**

Cheese Trivia

a Cheese is made from the milk of cows, sheep and goats. True.
b France is the biggest producer of cheese.
c There are 87 different types of cheese.
d Parmesan is a soft French cheese.
e The moon is made of cheese.
f Cheese is a good source of protein and calcium.
g Eating a lot of cheese can lower your cholesterol.

1.36 **Listen and check your answers.**

3 **Look at the following statements and choose a word from the box to fill the blank. Use plural forms if the words are countable.**

apple ~~fish~~ fruit milk vegetable meat chocolate vitamin potato

a The best British dish is ____fish____ and chips.
b You should eat plenty of fresh ________ and ________ every day.
c Vegetarians believe no one should eat ________.
d The best way to eat ________ is as French fries.
e I like to put lots of ________ in my coffee.
f ________ are sweet and juicy and good for you.
g Eating a balanced diet should give you all the ________ you need.
h The Swiss eat more ________ per person than any other nation.

Work with a partner. Which statements do you agree/disagree with.

Nouns and quantity expressions

Countable nouns

Use: *none, not any, a few, several, some, many, a lot, lots, plenty*

Uncountable nouns

Use: *none, not any, a little, a bit, some, much, a lot, lots, plenty*

not enough = less than you need

too much/many = more than you need

GRAMMAR

1 **Complete the statements with either *Countable* or *Uncountable*.**

(1) ________________ nouns have a singular and a plural form. You can use *a/an* and numbers with them. You use the plural form when you are talking in general.

an apple / apples → *Apples are good for you.*

(2) ________________ nouns have only one form. You can't use *a/an* or numbers with them. Most (but not all) have a singular form.
knowledge (NOT ~~a knowledge~~) → *Knowledge is power.*

2 **The uncountable noun *chocolate* can also be countable (*a chocolate*). Which other nouns in the box can sometimes be countable, depending on the context?**

bread cake cheese coffee meat money nature pasta rice salad yogurt

3 **Complete the questions with *many* or *much*. Four answers are given for each question. Cross out the answer that is not possible.**

So far today, ...

a how ____many____ friends have you texted?
None / A couple / ~~A little~~ / Lots.

b how ______________ time have you spent online?
None / Very little / Not enough / A lot of.

c how ______________ phone calls have you made?
Very few / Two or three / Lots / So much.

d how ______________ chocolates have you had?
None / Several / Not enough / Too much.

e how ______________ money have you spent?
Not many / A bit / A lot / Way too much.

f how ______________ work have you done?
None / Enough / Plenty / Lots of.

Underline the answers that are true for you or write true answers of your own. Ask your partner the questions.

4 **Grammar Extra 5** page 136. Read the explanation and do the exercises.

VOCABULARY

1 **Match words from column A with words from column B to make common collocations.**

A	B
a a bar of	1 bananas / flowers
b a bowl of	2 chocolate / soap
c a box of	3 donuts / gum
d a bunch of	4 honey / instant coffee
e a jar of	5 chocolates / matches
f a pack of	6 fruit / sugar

2 **Work with a partner. Add the words in the box to column B to make more collocations.**

cereal grapes keys mustard raspberry jelly rice seeds rice seeds soup spaghetti tea tissues tools

Tell your partner how often you buy, consume, or use these items.

SPEAKING

1 **Add the names of different people in the class. Try to make true sentences.**

a ____________ is a vegetarian.
b ____________ is a good cook.
c ____________ always has a big breakfast.
d ____________ drinks a lot of coffee.
e ____________ doesn't like fish.
f ____________ always has lunch in the same place.
g ____________ often eats fast food.
h ____________ usually has water with dinner.

2 **Ask questions to check your ideas.**

Veronica, are you a vegetarian?

VOCABULARY & PRONUNCIATION

1 **Look at the picture. How many items of food can you name?**

2 **Look at the lists. What types of food do the colors represent?**

a veal cod limes trout beans tuna
b leeks plums clams figs shrimp peaches
c turkey olives mussels melons mushrooms sardines
d garlic cherries lobster onions grapefruits zucchinis
e peppers bacon salmon spinach mangoes cauliflower
f sausages lettuces cabbages oranges radishes potatoes
g eggplants strawberries cucumbers celery raspberries tomatoes

1.37 **Listen, repeat, and mark the stressed syllable. What is different about the last word in each row?**

3 **Complete the questions with the most appropriate contrasting word from the box.**

~~cooked~~	tap	frozen	heavy	mild	sweet	weak	white

a Raw or ___cooked___ vegetables?
b Light meals or ____________ meals?
c Red meat or ____________ meat?
d Fresh fish or ____________ fish?
e Strong coffee or ____________ coffee?
f Strong cheese or ____________ cheese?
g Bottled water or ____________ water?
h Bitter chocolate or ____________ chocolate?

Ask the questions and find out your partner's preferences.

LISTENING

1 **Work with a partner. Look at the pictures of different things that people eat around the world. What do you imagine they taste like?**

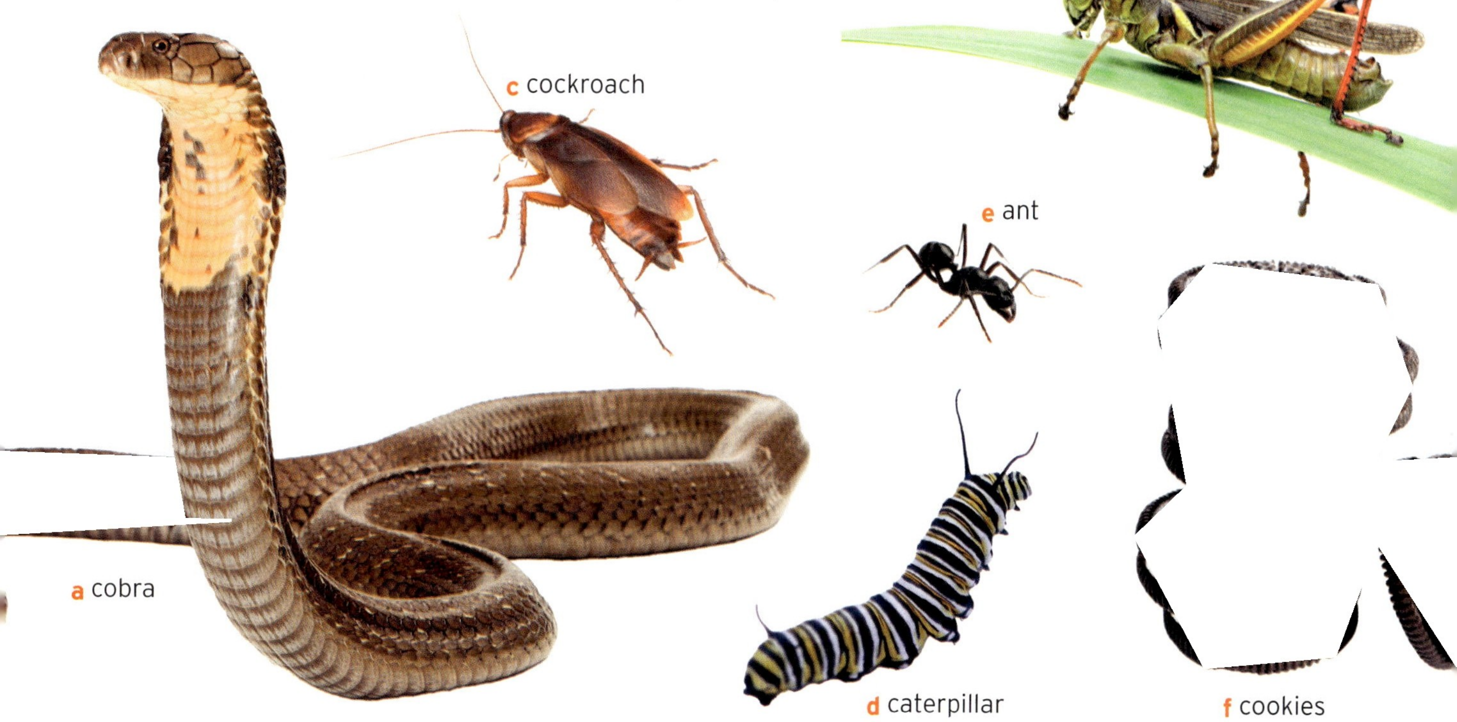

2 1.38 **Listen to an interview with somebody who has tried all these things. Match each dish (a-f) with the adjectives (1-6) he uses to describe them.**

a baked cobra in China	1 dry, bland
b fried grasshoppers in Thailand	2 crunchy, sweet, fruity
c roasted cockroaches in Indonesia	3 sweet, delicious
d boiled and sundried caterpillars in Africa	4 crispy, tasty, greasy
e roasted chocolate ants in Colombia	5 meaty, tough, chewy, delicious
f chocolate cookie pizza	6 sweet, crisp

VOCABULARY & SPEAKING

1 **Add words to the table from Listening Exercise 2.**

Ways of cooking food	Ways of describing taste	Ways of describing texture
boil	bitter	creamy
broil	salty	dry
bake	spicy	
	bland	

2 **Work with a partner. Take turns describing one of the items of food in the box for your partner to guess what it is.**

apples canned anchovies crème caramel curry dark chocolate cookies fresh bread fried eggs meat which is overcooked milk chocolate pizza plain white rice raw carrots salted peanuts seafood strong coffee your mother's cooking

It's crunchy on the outside and chewy on the inside.

Fresh bread?

Yes, that's right.

They're crunchy and salty.

Apples?

No, apples aren't salty.

Peanuts?

That's right.

3 **What are the best and worst meals you've ever had? Describe them to your partner.**

READING

1 **Bella is training to be a chef. She writes a blog called *For the Love of Food*. Why is she so interested in food?**

fortheloveoffood.com

HOME ABOUT RECIPES BLOG CONTACT

FOR THE
LOVE
OF
FOOD

Becoming A World-Class Chef

by Bella

Hi everyone, here's an update on my progress towards becoming a world-class chef! I have finished my college course (yay!) and I have been lucky enough to get a job at the Three Sisters restaurant in central London. I will be a VERY junior assistant in the kitchen, but I'm so excited to be joining such a famous place. It has a fantastic reputation for exciting and original food.

People often ask me why I'm so interested in food. Well, I have always loved food and my earliest memories are of eating! When I was growing up we didn't have much money, so my dad would grow lots of vegetables each year. I used to pick peas in the garden and eat them straight from the pod – they were so sweet and delicious. My mom used to keep chickens so that we would always have fresh eggs. I would collect the eggs when they were still warm and have them for breakfast with toast "soldiers".

So we always had fresh food, but it was also very simple. The first time I went to a restaurant – I was 12 years old – I was amazed by all the different flavors. My mom started to let me cook at home. I used to experiment with all sorts of different ingredients – sometimes it worked and sometimes it really didn't! But I always learned from my mistakes and that's really important in cooking. Whenever I got home from school, I would go straight into the kitchen rather than doing my homework. My parents used to get very frustrated with me, but they also enjoyed the meals I made them!

I feel at my happiest when I am in a kitchen and I love to make other people happy through my food. I am lucky to have found my passion. Wish me luck in my next challenge!

2 **Look at the following statements about Bella. Are they true or false?**

a Bella's mom grew vegetables. False
b Bella collected peas and boiled them for breakfast.
c Bella's family didn't have a lot of money when she was growing up.
d She first went to a kitchen when she was twelve years old.
e Bella experimented with different ingredients.
f Bella's mom let her cook at home.
g Bella went straight to the kitchen when she got home from school.
h Bella's parents enjoyed her cooking.
i Bella loves to make people happy with her food.

Rewrite the sentences in Exercise 2 in the first person. Change the information so that the sentences are true for you.

a My mom grew vegetables.

GRAMMAR

1 Work with a partner. Look again at the statements (a-i) in Exercise 2 on page 48. Number each statement *1*, *2*, *3*, or *4* according to the descriptions in this table.

Description	Alternative verb structures
1 Describes a repeated action in the past	*used to* + verb or *would* ('d) + verb
2 Describes a state in the past	*used to* + verb
3 Describes a single action in the past	None
4 Describes an action or state in the present	None

used to/would

used to: for repeated actions or states in the past

He **used to be** very thin.

He **didn't use to eat** much.

Did he **use to go** running?

Yes, he **did**.

No, he **didn't**.

would ('d): for repeated actions in the past

I'**d** walk to school every morning.

2 Look at the sentences (a-j) below about childhood and answer the questions.

1 In which sentences can you replace the underlined verb with *used to* + verb?
2 In which sentences can you replace the underlined verb with *would* ('d) + verb?

When I was a child ...

a I cycled to school every morning.
b I played soccer after school every day.
c I went on a school trip to the USA.
d I was afraid of the dark.
e I didn't believe in ghosts.
f My mother did all the cooking.
g I didn't like vegetables.
h I broke my leg skiing.
i I started learning the piano.
j I went swimming every Sunday.

Are the sentences true for you? Rewrite all the sentences so they are true for you. Use *used to* + verb or *would* ('d) + verb where possible.

3 **Pairwork Student A:** page 121 **Student B:** page 125

SPEAKING: ANECDOTE

1 1.39 **Listen to Julio from Brazil talking about his life when he was a child between the ages of five and ten. Which two questions does he not answer?**

a How many people were in your family?
b Who used to do most of the cooking?
c Did you use to help in the kitchen?
d Were there some things you didn't use to like eating?
e What time did you use to have lunch?
f Where did you use to have lunch?
g What time did you use to have dinner?
h Which room did you use to eat dinner in?
i Did your family use to eat in restaurants much?
j What did you use to eat on Sundays?
k What was your favorite dish when you were a child?

1 At seven o'clock.
2 Five.
3 In the kitchen.
4 My mother.
5 Pasta.
6 Rice and beans.
7 Yes, I used to chop the vegetables.
8 Yes, meat.
9 Yes, every Saturday.

Match the questions with the answers (1-9). Listen again and check.

2 You are going to tell your partner about your life when you were a child between the ages of five and ten.

- Ask yourself the questions in Exercise 1.
- Think about *what* to say and *how* to say it.
- Tell your partner about your life when you were a child.

LANGUAGE FOR LIFE

1 ▶ 1.40 **Listen to a conversation in a restaurant. Match the conversation to picture *a* or picture *b*.**

2 ▶ 1.41 **Listen to another version of the conversation. What differences do you notice?**

3 ▶ 1.42 **Listen and repeat the expressions from the conversation.**

a Excuse me. We're ready to order now.
b Can we have two cups of coffee and the check, please?
c Yes, a table for two in the name of Brown.
d Yes, two lemonades, please.
e I'll have the grilled salmon.
f Do you have anything near the window?
g No, I'm all right, thank you.
h I'll have the lamb, please.
i It was great, thank you.
j Not quite. Could you give us a few more minutes?

4 **Complete the restaurant conversation with the useful phrases from Exercise 3.**

Waiter: Good afternoon. Do you have a reservation?
Man: **(1)** Yes, a table for two in the name of Brown.
Waiter: Oh, yes. Is this table OK for you?
Man: **(2)** ______________________ ?
Waiter: Yes, of course. Follow me.
Waiter: Are you ready to order yet?
Woman: **(3)** ______________________ ?
Waiter: Of course. Would you like to order some drinks?
Woman: **(4)** ______________________ .
Woman: **(5)** ______________________ .
Waiter: Very good. What can I get you?
Woman: **(6)** ______________________ .
Waiter: OK. And sir?
Man: **(7)** ______________________ .
Waiter: Would you like to see the dessert menu?
Woman: **(8)** ______________________ .
Man: **(9)** ______________________ ?
Waiter: Certainly. How was your meal?
Woman: **(10)** ______________________ .

Listen again to the full conversation (▶ 1.43) and check your answers. Practice the conversation with a partner.

Life Skills: Critical Thinking
Advertising

1 **Are you influenced by advertising? Which of these products would you buy? Why?**

2 **What techniques do the advertisers use to encourage you to buy their products? Match the products with the selling concept.**

nostalgia 1b
lifestyle envy ______________
economy/value for money ______________
nature/purity ______________
good health ______________
science ______________

3 **Work in pairs. Choose a current advert you like. Identify the key selling concept in the advert. Present your analysis to the class, using either a poster or a digital slide.**

MACMILLAN LIFE SKILLS

Nouns and articles

1 **The table shows how articles combine with different types of nouns. Complete the first column with the correct noun type from the box.**

Countable nouns   Plural nouns   Uncountable nouns

Noun type	Singular			Plural	
	no article	with *a/an*	with *the*	no article	with *the*
a ______	*book*	*a book*	*the book*	*books*	*the books*
b ______	*advice*	x	*the advice*	x	x
c ______	x	x	x	*jeans*	*the jeans*

Copy the table and add the nine nouns on the right (behavior–sheep) in the dictionary extracts. There are three examples for each type of noun.

behavior /bɪˈheɪvjər/ noun [U] ★★★

child /tʃaɪld/ (plural **children**) noun [C] ★★★

clothes /kloʊðz/ noun [plural] ★★★

index /ˈɪnˌdeks/ (plural **indexes** or **indices**) noun [C] ★★

knowledge /ˈnɑlɪdʒ/ noun [U] ★★★

pants /pænts/ noun [plural] ★★

research /rɪˈsɜrtʃ/ noun [U] ★★

scissors /ˈsɪzərz/ noun [plural]

sheep /ʃip/ (plural **sheep**) noun [C] ★★

2 **Check your own dictionary. How does it show you whether a noun is countable, uncountable, or plural?**

Look up the nouns in the box. What do they all have in common?

equipment   happiness   health   luck   luggage   money   news   weather

3 **Read the dictionary entry for *the* and classify the five examples given under the following headings.**

The person or thing has already been mentioned	The person or thing is known about	The person or thing is "the only one"
	Have you locked the door?	

The is used as the **definite article** before a noun.

1 talking about sb/sth when you know who or which used before a noun when that person or thing has already been mentioned or is known about, or when there is only one: *Have you locked the door?* ♦ *I have to take care of the children.* ♦ *She brought me some cake and coffee, but the cake was stale.* ♦ *The sun was hidden behind a cloud.* ♦ *the best hotel in Paris*

DO NOT use **the** when you are referring to things or people in a general way: *Children need love and attention.*

From the *Macmillan Essential Dictionary for Learners of American English.*

4 **Complete this poem by asking yourself the questions about each noun. If you know the answer, put *the*. If you don't know the answer, put *a*.**

There was **(1)** ___*a*___ **young lady** from Niger
Who smiled as she rode on **(2)** ______ **tiger**.
They came back from **(3)** ______ **ride**
With **(4)** ______ **lady** inside
And **(5)** ______ **smile** on
(6) ______ **face** of
(7) ______ **tiger**.

- Which young lady?
- Which tiger?
- Which ride?
- Which lady?
- Which smile? Which face?
- Which tiger?!

5 **Read the dictionary note about the use of *the* to refer to things or people in a general way. Cross out *the* if it is incorrect in these generalizations.**

a ~~The~~ dogs have a better sense of smell than ~~the~~ cats.
b The life gets harder as you get older.
c The time is more important than the money.
d The salmon is richer in omega-3 oils than the cod.
e The children are getting fatter: they don't do enough exercise.
f It's impossible to live without the music.

Do you agree or disagree with the generalizations? Discuss with a partner.

SPEAKING & READING

1 **What do these expressions mean to you? Are there similar ones in your language?**

a The early bird catches the worm.
b There's no time like the present.
c Better late than never.

2 **Complete the questionnaire. Compare your results with a partner.**

Time Management Questionnaire

Scoring: 2 = Always 1 = Sometimes 0 = Never

- I do the most important things first. ________________
- I complete what needs to be done during the day. ________________
- I always get work done on time. ________________
- I feel I use my time effectively. ________________
- I try to complete difficult or unpleasant tasks without delay. ________________
- I force myself to make time for planning. ________________
- I get up early in the morning during my vacation. ________________
- I prepare a daily or weekly "to do" list. ________________
- I make a list of tasks with the most important tasks at the top. ________________
- I am able to meet deadlines without rushing at the last minute. ________________
- I keep up-to-date on all my tasks. ________________
- I avoid distractions. ________________
- I avoid spending too much time on trivial matters. ________________
- I spend enough time on my work or studies. ________________
- I have a weekly schedule. ________________
- I try to do the most important tasks during my most energetic periods of the day. ________________
- I make good use of my down time. ________________
- I often reassess my activities in relation to my goals. ________________
- I only look at social media and my emails after I've finished my tasks. ________________
- I am satisfied with the way I use my time. ________________

Results

35 to 40: You have outstanding time management skills.
29 to 34: You have strong time management skills.
20 to 28: You are managing your time fairly well, but sometimes feel you need some help.
15 to 19: You are stressed because you are not managing your time well.
Less than 15: You don't have any time management skills.

What does your score mean? Do you agree? Compare with a partner.

GRAMMAR

1 Underline the correct preposition in these sentences.

a I work best at / during night.
b We have a big family dinner **on / in** Sundays.
c I start work every morning **at / on** 9:00 a.m.
d I usually get home **in / on** time to read my children a bedtime story.
e I never take a nap **at / in** the afternoon.
f My birthday is **at / in** March. In fact, it's **in / on** March 6.
g I swim in the ocean as much as possible **during / at** vacations.
h My boss never starts meetings **in / on** time. She's always late.
i I did a lot of sightseeing **in / during** my last trip abroad.
j My mother was born **in / at** the fifties.

Are the sentences true for you? Are they true for your partner? Ask questions.

What time of day do you work best?

What do you do on Sundays?

Prepositions of time

at
night/five o'clock/2:45 p.m., etc.

on
Sunday/Monday, etc.
Friday night/Sunday morning, etc.
the weekend
May 1/June 22, etc.

in
the morning/ afternoon/evening
the spring/summer, etc.
January/February, etc.
the sixties

during
a whole period of time
an event or activity
(e.g. *the war/a visit/a flight*)

on time (at the right time)

in time (before it's too late)

2 **Grammar Extra 6, Part 1** page 138. Read the explanation and do the exercises.

VOCABULARY

1 **Look at the calendar. Imagine today is February 15 and follow the instructions.**

a ~~Cross out~~: St. Valentine's Day and the leap year day.
b Underline: the day before yesterday, the weekend before last, the day after tomorrow, the Monday after next.
c Circle: tomorrow, next Saturday, a week from today, a week from tomorrow.
d Put in parentheses ( ): in four days, two weeks ago, all of last week (Mon–Fri).

Apart from February 15, which other ten dates are still free?

February

Mon	Tue	Wed	Thu	Fri	Sat	Sun
		1	2	3	4	5
6	7	8	9	10	11	12
13	14	15	16	17	18	19
20	21	22	23	24	25	26
27	28	29				

2 **Use expressions from Exercise 1 to tell your partner about some of the things you've done recently or plan to do in the future.**

The day before yesterday I went out till 4:00 a.m. The weekend after next is my birthday.

PRONUNCIATION

1 1.44 **Listen and write the order in which you hear these groups of ordinal numbers.**

a 1st 2nd 3rd 4th 5th ☐ b 1st 4th 5th 3rd 2nd ☐ c 4th 5th 1st 2nd 3rd [1] d 5th 1st 4th 3rd 2nd ☐

Dictate the ordinal numbers 1st – 5th in any order to your partner. Check what they have written.

2 **Practice saying these important dates in the US calendar.**

a 02/14
b 04/01
c 07/04
d 10/31
e 12/31
f 12/25

1.45 **Listen, check, and repeat. Why are they important?**

READING

1 **Do you have any study tips for learning English? Tell a partner.**

2 **Read the article. Which tip do you think is the most useful?**

The Study Guru HOME ABOUT STUDY METHODS BLOG CONTACT

Time-saving tips for students

1 **DO NOT TRY TO MULTI-TASK**
Science has proven that people do not become more efficient by multi-tasking. People say that if you are texting while you're watching TV, you are multi-tasking. You aren't. You're just switching your attention from one thing to the other very quickly, losing focus and concentration. Do one thing at a time well rather than several things badly.

2 **DRAWERS WASTE TIME**
Drawers are a good place to put things so that they are neat and out of sight, right? Wrong! When you want to find something you have to root through drawer after drawer. If you want to find things quickly, put them on shelves. Your house may look like a store, but you will find things far quicker.

3 **JUST CLEAN UP!**
OK , so you're a student and students have better things to do than keep things spick and span, right? But if you find a place for everything and keep putting them back in those places, then it's impossible to lose anything (unless you have a roommate).

4 **THE TV AND YOUR MUSIC IS NOT HELPING YOU CONCENTRATE**
You're the internet generation, so you want audio-visual stimulation. Many people feel uncomfortable in silence. But it has been proven time and again that any noise or movement will put you off. Learn to love the silence.

5 **TIREDNESS IS A PRODUCTIVITY KILLER**
Sometimes you don't notice tiredness. You may want to do your work, but you find that you can't focus. This is because you are tired. You should take a nap – it really helps. If you sleep for 20 minutes you should feel so much better.

6 **SET A TIMER ON THE BORING THINGS YOU DO**
If you have a boring report to write, you can sit around and stare at the walls or you can push yourself to get it done. Put a timer on and time how long each chapter is taking you. Simply knowing how much time you are wasting is often enough of a motivation to get on with it

7 **SET A TIME LIMIT ON BORING TASKS**
If the previous tip didn't work for you, then set a time limit for the boring task. Start by allocating 30 minutes for that task and then stop and do something else. And then repeat this process.

8 **LEARN KEYBOARD SHORTCUTS**
You often have to work on a desktop computer when you're a student. If you don't know the keyboard shortcuts, you're wasting a lot of time.

9 **HEALTHY MEALS REALLY DO MAKE YOU MORE PRODUCTIVE**
It sounds like something your grandma would tell you, but the fact is that eating a fruit and vegetable diet for a week will improve your mood significantly. After a week, you'll feel physically better and you'll be far more productive. It's true and you should try it at least once to test it out.

10 **MAKE A LIST**
Print out this list and stick it on your wall where you can see it easily. Add a couple more tips from your own experience.

VOCABULARY

1 **Replace the underlined phrases with the correct form of the highlighted phrasal verbs and expressions from the article in the Reading section.**

a Every time I lose my keys I search the dresser. *root through*
b A strong cup of coffee helps me to continue with my work.
c I am the type that finds any tiny noise will distract me.
d My roommate keeps the room very clean and tidy.
e When buying a new pen, I always check if it works before buying it.
f I find it helpful to fix a deadline for a project.

2 **Are any of the sentences true for you? Compare with your partner.**

GRAMMAR

1 Look at the table and complete the explanation with must or should.

	Urgent	Not urgent
Important	I must do it today.	I must do it soon.
Not important	I should do it today.	I should do it soon.

(1) ___Must___ and **(2)** ______ are modal verbs. You can use them to give advice. **(3)** ______ is much stronger than **(4)** ______ . **(5)** ______ means it is important or necessary to do something. **(6)** ______ means it is a good idea to do something.

Copy the table and write things that you need to do in each square. Use *must* and *should* to tell your partner about your priorities for today/this week/this month.

> **Modal verb structures**
>
> I **must** arrive on time.
>
> I **mustn't** be late.
>
> You **should** go to bed earlier.
>
> You **shouldn't** stay up so late.
>
> He **has to** take a test, but she **doesn't have to** take it.
>
> They **can** wait in here, but they **can't** leave early.

2 Des O'Brien talks about the advantages and disadvantages of working from home. Read what he says and underline the appropriate verb structures.

"I love working from home. I **(1) don't have to / have to** drive to work, I **(2) mustn't / don't have to** sit in traffic, and parking is not my problem anymore. I **(3) can't / don't have to** get dressed in the morning – I **(4) can / have to** wear my sweatpants all day. In fact, I **(5) don't have to / mustn't** get up in the morning at all! If I want, I **(6) must / can** work all night. It's up to me. There's nobody to tell me, 'You **(7) can / must** be punctual. You **(8) mustn't / don't have to** make personal phone calls. You **(9) can't / don't have to** do your shopping online ...' There are only a couple of downsides. I **(10) can / have to** call somebody if I want to talk, and I can't blame anything on anybody else – I'm the only person here!"

1.46 **Listen and check. Talk to your partner about other advantages or disadvantages of working from home.**

3 Complete the table with an appropriate heading:
It's necessary; It's permitted; It's not permitted; It's not necessary.

A: It's necessary	B: ______	C: ______	D: ______
have to	don't have to	can	can't
must			mustn't

4 Complete the sentences with a modal from the table in Exercise 3. Use an appropriate tense.

a I ___don't have to___ work tomorrow. It's a national holiday.
b I ______ renew my passport. I've got a foreign business trip coming up.
c Yesterday I ______ put on a suit. We had an important meeting.
d I ______ forgot to buy a card for my boss. It's her birthday tomorrow.
e I ______ park near the office anymore. It's become a "residents only" zone.
f My parents weren't strict. I ______ watch TV whenever I wanted to.

Are any of these sentences true for you?

5 **Grammar Extra 6, Part 2** page 138. Read the explanation and do the exercises.

LISTENING

1 **Look at three people in their different work places. What jobs do you think they do and how do you think their working conditions compare?**

a

b

2 1.47 **Listen and check your ideas.**

3 **Read about the working conditions for each job. Are the sentences true or false? Listen again to check.**

Job 1	Job 2	Job 3
a You can get extra pay for working overtime.	a You are allowed to work at home whenever you want.	a You often have to work on weekends.
b Women aren't allowed to wear jeans.	b You aren't supposed to have any breaks.	b You can't work for more than twelve hours in a week.
c You aren't allowed to have relationships with other people in the company.	c You can wear whatever you want.	c You're supposed to wear a hat all the time.

4 **Replace each highlighted expression in Exercise 3 with *should*, *shouldn't*, *mustn't*, or *can* so that the sentences have the same meaning.**

Would you like to do one of these jobs?

VOCABULARY

1 **Replace the underlined expressions with expressions in the box.**

open-plan office qualifications shifts unsociable hours works flexible hours work to a deadline

- a Have you had a job where you had to work in the evenings and on weekends?
- b What are the advantages and disadvantages of an office with no dividing walls?
- c Are you the type of person who works well when they have to finish a job by a certain time?
- d Do you know anybody who can start and finish work when they want?
- e What is the job of your dreams, and what special diplomas or degrees do you need to do it?
- f If the salary was high, could you work twelve-hour periods of time, sometimes at night?

2 **Work with a partner. Ask and answer the questions in Exercise 1. What are your ideal working conditions?**

3 **Pairwork Student A:** page 121 **Student B:** page 125

WRITING

1 Here are some examples of phrases often used in business emails. Complete them using the words in the box.

able	apply	appreciate	complain	confirm	attaching
	hearing	May 16	response	~~Unfortunately~~	

a *Unfortunately*, I am not available on the date you suggest in your email.
b Thank you for your email of _______________ .
c I am _______________ my résumé for your attention.
d I would _______________ it if you could send me some information about your school.
e I would be _______________ to attend an interview at any time convenient to you.
f I am writing to _______________ about the damage caused by your company when they delivered a couch to my home last week.
g We look forward to _______________ from you as soon as possible.
h We would appreciate it if you could _______________ your reservation in writing.
i I am writing in _______________ to your advertisement in *The Washington Post*.
j I would like to _______________ for the position of IT assistant at your school.

2 Match each of the phrases (a-j) in Exercise 1 with one of the functions (1-10) below.

1 asking for information
2 applying for a job
3 thanking someone for their email
4 closing an email
5 giving bad news in an email
6 giving good news
7 complaining
8 responding to an advertisement
9 asking for confirmation
10 saying that you are sending something

3 Antonia Clifford is interested in applying for the position of flight attendant. Do you think her email is a suitable for a job application? Why? Why not?

Worldwide Airlines

HOME BOOK A FLIGHT JOBS CONTACT

Flight attendants

Worldwide Airlines is currently seeking friendly, service-oriented people who take pride in their performance and appearance.

- Applicants must be over twenty years of age and have at least two years' post high school education or work experience.
- Physical requirements: able to lift, push, and pull heavy articles as required.
- Minimum height 1m60. Maximum height 1m85.
- Languages: able to read, write, speak, and understand English. Other languages an advantage.
- Interested candidates can write to the following address for an application form and further information: jobs@worldwideairlines.com

mail.com

Compose
Inbox
Drafts
Sent
Spam
Trash

To: jobs@worldwideairlines.com
Cc:
Subject: Job Application
From: antoniaclifford@mail.com

Dear Mr. or Mrs.

I saw your advertisement in the Morning Post and I want to be a flight attendant. I am 21 years old and I just graduated from college. I have put my résumé with this email so that you can see what I've done and I'd love to come for an interview any time you like.

How about sending me an application form and some more information about the job?
I can't wait to hear from you!

Lots of love,
Toni

4 Improve Antonia's email by using some of the phrases in Exercise 1.

LANGUAGE FOR LIFE

1 Read and match the conversations (a-c) with the pictures (1-3).

1

2

3

a **A:** **(1)** We're ahead of schedule.
B: Yes, hopefully we'll be there **(2)** before dinner.
A: Oh, yes, I think so. In fact, we may even **(3)** be early.
B: Well, that's OK. If we have some time before dinner, we can go to the gym.
A: The gym? I'd rather **(4)** find something to do in the mall!

b The Global Earth Party will put the environment at the top of the agenda. We've asked the same question **(5)** repeatedly: when will the government do something about global warming? **(6)** We don't have much time left – we need to act now. Vote for the Global Earth Party today!

c **C:** Come on, guys. Stop running. OK, **(7)** one by one. Ruben, stop pushing. Let's go back to class.
D But we didn't have time to finish our game.
C: Yes, I know, **(8)** time goes very quickly when you're having fun. But we have work to do.

2 Replace the underlined phrases in Exercise 1 with the time expressions below (a-h).

- a We're running out of time
- b We're making good time
- c have time to spare
- d time and time again
- e one at a time
- f in time for
- g time flies
- h kill time

1.48 **Listen to the conversations and check your answers.**

3 1.49 **Listen and repeat the expressions from the conversations.**

4 Work with a partner. Choose three of the expressions from Exercise 2 and include them in a short conversation. Practice your conversation.

Life Skills: Organization
Preparing for a Trip

1 1.50 **Listen to Sandy talking to a friend about her upcoming trip. Is she well prepared? Put a check (✓) beside the things she has done and a cross (✖) beside the things she hasn't.**

- a renew passport
- b buy tickets
- c buy walking boots
- d buy a camping stove and cooking equipment
- e buy sunscreen
- f buy water purifying equipment
- g buy sleeping bag
- h plan the itinerary

2 Work in pairs to sort these actions in order of priority, from first (a) to last (h).

- a book flights ☐
- b plan itinerary ☐
- c check passport ☐
- d pack backpack for trip ☐
- e buy camping equipment ☐
- f test camping equipment ☐
- g buy hiking boots ☐
- h break in hiking boots ☐

3 Work with a partner. Add a time period against each action to show how much before the departure date it should be done, then add it to the calendar at the appropriate date.

check passport – 3 months – 31st December

4 You are going on a beach holiday in 2 months' time. Organize your calendar to show what you need to do, and when.

December

Mon	Tue	Wed	Thu	Fri	Sat	Sun
				1	2	3
4	5	6	7	8	9	10
11	12	13	14	15	16	17
18	19	20	21	22	23	24
25	26	27	28	29	30	31 check passport

MACMILLAN LIFE SKILLS

Words that are sometimes confused

1 **Read the information about the difference between *job* and *work*. What is the key grammatical difference between the words?**

2 **Complete the questions with *job/jobs* or *work*. In which sentences are both possible?**

a What kind of ________________ does your father do?
b Is it easy to find ________________ in your country?
c How many different part-time ________________ have you had?
d What time do most people start ________________ in your country?
e Have you ever been offered a ________________ in a foreign country?

Ask your partner the questions.

- You can refer to what someone does in order to get paid as their **work** or their **job**: *Do you find your work* OR *your job interesting?* ♦ *What kind of work* OR *job does he do?*
- **Work** is uncountable with this meaning, so it never has **a** in front of it and is never plural: *He's looking for work.* ♦ *It's fascinating work.* ♦ *Has he found a job?* ♦ *She has had many different jobs.*

3 **Look at more words that are sometimes confused. Complete the dictionary examples (a-g) with the correct alternative. Use the dictionary definitions to help you.**

a actually / currently
- *We've spoken on the phone, but we've never ________________ met.*
- *This is the best recording ________________ available on CD.*

b travel / trip
- *The whole family went on a ________________ to Florida.*
- Foreign ________________ never really appealed to him until he retired.

c career / course
- *He has just started out on a ________________ as a photographer.*
- She's on a management ________________ this week.

d fun / funny
- *Our day at the beach was a lot of ________________.*
- Don't laugh; it isn't ________________.

e borrow / lend
- *Could you ________________ me your umbrella?*
- Can I ________________ your umbrella?

f argue / discuss
- *Don't ________________ with me – you know I'm right.*
- We're meeting to ________________ the matter next week.

g lose (lost) / miss (missed)
- *I ________________ the last train home again.*
- I ________________ my bag. Have you seen it?

4 **Complete the questions with an appropriate word from Exercise 3. You may have to change the form of the word.**

When was the last time you ...
a ___argued___ with your parents?
b heard a really ____________ joke?
c went on a foreign ____________?
d ____________ books from a library?
e read a book about ____________?
f did a training ____________?
g ____________ a bus?
h ____________ some money to a friend?
i ____________ your house keys?
j thought about changing your ____________?

Ask your partner the questions.

5 **Check your own dictionary. What example sentences does it give for the words on this page?**

actually /ˈæktʃuəli/ adv ★★★ **1** used for emphasizing what is really true

argue /ˈɑrˌɡju/ verb ★★★ **1** [I] to discuss something that you disagree about, usually in an angry way = QUARREL

borrow /ˈbɑroʊ/ verb ★★ **1** [T] to receive and use something that belongs to someone else, and promise to give it back

career[1] /kəˈrɪr/ noun [C] ★★ **1** a job or profession that you work at for some time

course[1] /kɔrs/ noun [C] ★★★ **1** a series of classes in an academic subject or a practical skill

currently /ˈkʌrənt(ə)li/ adv ★★★ at the present time

discuss /dɪˈskʌs/ verb [T] ★★★ **1** to talk about something with someone

fun[2] /fʌn/ adj enjoyable

funny /ˈfʌni/ adj ★★★ **1** someone or something that is funny makes you laugh

lend /lend/ (past tense and past participle **lent** /lent/) verb ★★★ **1** [T] to give someone something for a short time, expecting that they will give it back to you later

lose /luz/ (past tense and past participle **lost**/lɔst/) verb ★★★ **2** [T] to be unable to find someone or something

miss[1] /mɪs/ verb ★★★ **3** [T] to be too late for something such as a train or bus

travel[2] /ˈtræv(ə)l/ noun [U] ★★★ the activity of traveling

trip /trɪp/ noun [C] ★★ an occasion when you go somewhere and come back again

From the *Macmillan Essential Dictionary for Learners of American English.*

GRAMMAR

Grammar Extra pages 134-139.

1 Correct the three sentences where the pronoun is in the incorrect position.

a He had a cold but he got over **it** quickly. ✓
b I've used these boots so much I've worn out **them**.
c I dropped the plant on the floor and had to clean up **it**.
d If you don't understand the word, look **it** up.
e Before you buy that shirt, you should try on **it**.

2 Complete the sentences. Use *will*, *going to*, or the present progressive.

a "It's too hot." "OK, I (open) ___'ll open___ a window."
b I (train) ________ to be an actor when I graduate.
c She (meet) ________ Jon and Sue at eight o'clock.
d I don't want to go out. I (stay in) ________ and read my book.
e I can't get through to Dave. Oh, I know, I (try) ________ calling him on his cell phone.
f He (arrive) ________ on the 11:15 train from New York.

3 Complete the sentences with the words in the box.

anyone anything ~~everywhere~~ no one nothing nowhere someone

Rod: Where have you been? I've been looking **(1)** ___everywhere___ for you.
Dana: Over there. I was talking to **(2)** ________ .
Rod: Who? Is it **(3)** ________ I know?
Dana: No, it's **(4)** ________ you know – a new person in my office. ... Hey, is there **(5)** ________ to eat?
Rod: No. There's **(6)** ________ to eat or drink – and **(7)** ________ to sit! ... I've had enough. Do you want to go?

4 Check (✓) the three correct sentences.
Change the incorrect sentences. Use *used to*, *didn't use to*, or *would*.

When I was young, ...
a I'd have blond hair. I used to have blond hair.
b I used to have a dog.
c I wouldn't believe in ghosts.
d I'd love everything my mother cooked.
e I'd go swimming on Saturdays.
f I didn't use to play a musical instrument.

Which sentences are true for you? Compare with a partner.

5 Underline the correct preposition.

We got married **(1) in** / **on** a warm Saturday **(2) at** / **in** the spring. We had a party **(3) in** / **on** the evening. **(4) During** / **On** the party, we danced and everyone had a great time. **(5) At** / **On** ten o'clock **(6) at** / **in** night, we drove to the airport to go on my surprise honeymoon. **(7) During** / **In** the flight, my husband told me we were going to Cuba. We landed **(8) at** / **on** four o'clock **(9) in** / **on** Sunday morning. **(10) At** / **In** eight o'clock **(11) during** / **on** Sunday evening, the island experienced a terrible hurricane. We flew out **(12) at** / **on** Monday morning after the shortest honeymoon in history!

VOCABULARY

1 **Rewrite the sentences. Replace the <u>underlined</u> words with the phrasal verbs in the box.**

are heading for | are putting on | go off | ~~go on~~ | got over | join in

a We can't <u>continue</u> like this, Ron.
We can't go on like this, Ron.
b Fortunately, the bomb didn't <u>explode</u>.
c Saskia and Freddie <u>are organizing</u> a big party.
d He never <u>recovered from</u> his wife's death.
e Hello? Yes, we <u>are moving towards</u> Boston now.
f This is fun! Why don't you come and <u>participate</u>?

2 **Complete the sentences with the words in the box.**

atmosphere | costume | guests | host | ~~invitation~~ | mingle

I once received an **(1)** *invitation* to a party. It was a **(2)** ________ party. The theme of the party was horror movies. I went as Frankenstein's Monster. When we arrived, the **(3)** ________ greeted us and showed us into the main room. He was dressed as Count Dracula. My wife, the Bride of Frankenstein, and I immediately started to **(4)** ________ , but it's not so easy introducing yourself to people dressed as monsters and mummies! Three other **(5)** ________ were dressed as Frankenstein's Monster. Even so, there was a really good **(6)** ________ , and the party was a great success.

3 **Complete the lists with the words in the box.**

~~bake~~ | bland | boil | crisp | crunchy | delicious | disgusting | dry | fry | roast | tasty | tough

Cook in oven: 1 *bake*, 2 ________
Cook in water: 3 ________
Cook in oil: 4 ________
Taste (positive): 5 ________ , 6 ________
Taste (negative): 7 ________ , 8 ________
Texture: 9 ________ , 10 ________ , 11 ________ , 12 ________

4 **Write the date for each of the following.**

a today
b the day before yesterday
c the day after tomorrow
d a week from today
e the Tuesday before last
f the Monday after next

PRONUNCIATION

1 **Look at some words from Units 4–6. Say the words and add them to the table.**

~~arrangement~~ | banana | career | cucumber | decision | excuse | happiness | organize | parade | permission | relax | résumé | sardines | sausages | suggestion

A: ■ ■	
B: ■ ■ ■	*arrangement*
C: ■ ■ ■	

2 **<u>Underline</u> the stressed syllable in each word.**

1.51 **Listen, check, and repeat.**

READING & LISTENING

1 Read the posts about two unusual festivals and answer the questions.

a Which is the older festival?
b What special food or drinks do people have at each festival?

WIKIPEDIA
The Free Encyclopedia

Main page
Contents
Featured content
Current events
Random article
Donate to Wikipedia
Wikipedia store

Interaction
Help
About Wikipedia
Community portal
Recent changes
Contact page

Main Page Talk   Read View Source View History   search wikipedia

The Palio di Siena

The Palio di Siena is a famous horse race held in Siena, Italy. The race circles the Piazza del Campo and involves ten horses and riders representing ten of the city wards in Siena.

The tradition started in the 16th century, when the Grand Duke of Tuscany banned bullfighting. City wards started holding races instead — first on buffalo, then on donkeys and eventually horses. The first modern Palio took place in 1633, and today the race is held twice a year: on July 2 and August 16.

The race itself usually lasts for no more than 90 seconds. Bareback riders circle the Piazza three times. Many riders fall off their horses in this dangerous race – but a horse that has thrown its rider can still win the prize.

Visitors come from all over the world to watch the race, as well as the famous two-hour pageant that precedes the race itself. The parade is called the "Corteo Storico" and includes colorful flags, traditional costumes and riders armed with swords. There are also food stalls and bars, where visitors can enjoy local delicacies such as cured meats.

Palio di Siena horse race

HOME VISIT EXHIBITS ANIMALS EVENTS LEARN RESEARCH SUPPORT ABOUT SEARCH

BugFest, North Carolina Museum of Natural Sciences

Every September since 2003 more than 35,000 visitors come to BugFest to experience over 100 exhibits, crafts, games, and activities. We provide the opportunity for you to interact with scientists so you can learn about the fascinating world of bugs. We also have our Café Insecta, where the brave can sample buggy dishes prepared by local chefs. The best part is it's all free!

- Enjoy the entertaining displays, exhibits and activities — both inside and outside the museum.
- Learn about arthropods, which make up three-quarters of all animals on Earth, during fascinating presentations.
- Taste delicious dishes featuring insects as a major ingredient and sample our toasted cockroach at Café Insecta.
- Learn how to keep your own hive at a Beekeeping Workshop.
- Bring an unusual bug to the Stump the Experts table.
- Enjoy the live bands and bug stations.
- Join the moths, fireflies and katydids for an exhilarating evening of nocturnal activities at the Evening Insectival.
- Enjoy the live bands and street carnival.

2 Read the texts again. Are these sentences true or false? Correct the false sentences.

a The Palio is held once a year in July. *False. It is held twice a year, in July and August.*
b The Palio di Siena is a competition between different groups in the town.
c The horses do not have saddles.
d The race cannot be won by riderless horses.
e At the BugFest festival you can have toasted spiders.
f The BugFest festival has a street carnival and live bands.
g Café Insecta serves dishes made with honey.

3 1.52 **Listen to the conversation and write what food and drinks Carol's family has at Christmas.**

a Christmas Eve *fish (usually salmon), fruit dessert*
b Christmas Day (breakfast)
c Christmas Day (lunch)
d The day after Christmas Day

4 Listen again and underline the correct information.

a Carol's **mom / dad** is having a party on Christmas Eve.
b Carol's **mom / dad** used to make dinner on Christmas Eve.
c Carol's family **gets up late / opens presents** on Christmas morning.
d Carol's dad **is single / has remarried**.
e On Christmas afternoon, Carol's family **stays at home / goes out for a walk**.

WRITING & SPEAKING

1 Work with a partner. Match the questions (a-e) with the answers in note form (1-5).

a What's the name of the festival and where does it take place? 3
b When is the festival and how long does it last?
c Who started the festival and when?
d What happens at the festival (traditions, entertainment, customs)?
e What do people eat?

< Notes Done

1 Parades, parties, dancing in the street; people wear costumes
2 Rich food, King Cake
3 Mardi Gras, New Orleans, USA
4 January and February; several weeks
5 French settlers, centuries ago

2 Match the parts of the text below with the questions (a-e) in Exercise 1.

festivals.com

MARDI GRAS

Mardi Gras has been celebrated for centuries – since French settlers first came to the USA and built the city of New Orleans. ☐

People eat all kinds of rich food. There's a special cake called a "King Cake," which is gold, green, and purple – the colors of Mardi Gras. Inside the cake is a gold bean, which will bring good luck to the person who finds it. ☐

Mardi Gras takes place in February in the city of New Orleans, in the USA. ☐

In the two weeks just before "Fat Tuesday" there are parades and all-night parties, with music and dancing in the streets. Everybody wears colorful clothes and costumes. In the parades, people throw beads and money. ☐

It's a big carnival that lasts several days.

Mardi Gras starts in January and lasts for several weeks. It ends at midnight of the day called "Fat Tuesday", or "Mardi Gras" in French. ☐

3 Think about a festival you have been to. You are going to tell your partner about it.

- Interview your partner using the questions in Exercise 1
- Write their answers in note form.

4 Write a paragraph describing your partner's festival.

7 News

LISTENING

1 **Look at the picture and discuss the questions with a partner.**

a Who are the most photographed celebrities in your country?
b Which celebrities are in the news right now and why?
c How do you think celebrities feel about being photographed by the paparazzi?

2 **You are going to listen to an interview with Jack, an experienced paparazzo. What do you think his views are about the following? Underline *OK* or *not OK*.**

a **It's OK / not OK** when paparazzi take pictures of celebrities' glamorous lifestyles.
b **It's OK / not OK** when paparazzi take unflattering pictures of celebrities.
c **It's OK / not OK** when paparazzi take pictures of celebrities doing ordinary things.
d **It's OK / not OK** when paparazzi take pictures of celebrities' children.
e **It's OK / not OK** when paparazzi follow celebrities everywhere.
f **It's OK / not OK** when celebrities refuse to cooperate with the paparazzi.
g **It's OK / not OK** when celebrities complain about the paparazzi.

2.02 **Listen and check your ideas.**

Do you agree with Jack? Discuss your own views with a partner.

GRAMMAR

1 Complete the following sentences about photographing celebrities. Use the verbs in the box.

agrees asked enjoy explained tell

a People ______________ seeing pictures of celebrities doing ordinary things.
b Kate Moss ______________ us not to take photos of her daughter.
c We've ______________ that we don't want to upset her.
d Nicole Kidman always ______________ to smile for the camera.
e Celebrities ______________ us that we're invading their privacy.

Verb patterns

I **can't stand waiting** around.
She **promised to come**.
We explained that it was difficult.
He **asked me to wait.**
They **told us that** they need time.

2 Use the verbs from Exercise 1 to complete the table of verb patterns.

Verb + *ing*-form	Verb + *to*-infinitive	Verb + *that*	Verb + sb + (*not*) *to*-infinitive	Verb sb + *that*
• can't stand doing sth	• need to do sth	• realize that ...	• tell sb to do sth	• warn sb that ...
• don't mind doing sth	• promise to do sth	• say that ...	• warn sb not to do sth	• **(5)** ________ sb that ...
• **(1)** ________ doing sth	• try to do sth	• suggest that ...	• **(4)** ________ sb to do sth	
	• want to do sth	• think that ...		
	• **(2)** ________ to do sth	• **(3)** ________ that ...		

3 In these statements two verbs are possible, and one is not. Cross out the verb that is not possible.

a I **asked / told / ~~said~~** him to stop, but he pushed the camera in my face and continued taking pictures.
b I just **try / want / enjoy** to lead a normal life, but these people are making it impossible.
c When a celebrity gets aggressive, I **tell / explain / say** that I'm just doing my job.
d I **told / warned / suggested** him to stop taking photos of my daughter or I'd sue him.
e If they don't enjoy the attention, I **think / suggest / tell** that they should change jobs.
f They're hypocritical. On the one hand they **need / agree / don't mind** to have their pictures in the press, and on the other hand they **warn / tell / explain** us that we're invading their privacy.

Who do you think made each statement: a paparazzo or a celebrity? Compare your ideas with a partner.

VOCABULARY

1 Complete the sentences with these adjectives from the interview in the Listening section.

desperate hypocritical insensitive ~~obsessed~~ photogenic unflattering

a There is a lot of gossip about celebrities. Some people are ___*obsessed*___ with them!
b Some magazines print ______________ pictures of celebrities.
c I think it's ______________ to take pictures of celebrities when they are upset or sick. It's just not right.
d Some people say they're not interested in celebrities, but then read about them in magazines. I think they're ______________ .
e I hate pictures of myself because I always look terrible. I'm not very ______________ .
f Many fans are ______________ to see celebrities when they are showing up at a gala or festival.

2 Are any of the views in Exercise 1 true for you? Discuss with a partner.

READING & VOCABULARY

1 Match the news stories (1-5) with the headlines (a-e). Compare with a partner.

News in brief HOME NEWS CONTACT

1
Pennsylvania police posted a mug shot of a burglar online yesterday, asking for information from the public. The man was a fugitive as he had escaped from prison last month. They were surprised when the criminal himself posted the photo on his own social media account. He added the comment, "Lol, I love it!" He was arrested 45 minutes later when he responded to a message inviting him for an interview. It was the police posing as journalists!

2
Twenty-eight-year-old James Allen was in court after the attempted robbery of a convenience store. He was foiled by the door! Holding a plastic gun and wearing a thick mask, he couldn't get the electric doors open. He then removed his mask in full view of the security camera before running away. A store employee recognized Allen when he came back to the store the next day. He will be sentenced next month.

3
Polish author Krystian Bala committed a murder and almost escaped punishment ... until he wrote a book that gave away clues! His novel *Amok* became a bestseller in Poland, but the police noticed that the details of a murder in the book were similar to a case they were investigating. The police discovered that the victim had been romantically involved with Bala's ex-wife. Bala was convicted and sentenced to 25 years in prison.

4
A San Francisco thief pedaled his bike up to a woman on the sidewalk, grabbed a phone out of her hands, and rode away. Unknown to him, the woman was in the middle of demonstrating the phone's new tracking device – which worked! The thief was captured just minutes later.

5
In El Paso, Texas, a man entered a church and got away with the safe. But safes are heavy, and he only got a few yards before dropping it on a neighbor's lawn. He tried to open it right there, and that's when he was met by the home's occupant – a police officer!

a **SAFE AND SECURE**
b **SOCIAL MEDIA STUPIDITY**
c **UNMASKED**
d **A NOVEL CRIME**
e **TRACK IT DOWN**

Which stories do you like best?

2 Complete the sentences using highlighted words from the stories in Exercise 1.

a A *police officer* is a person who fights crime and tries to catch criminals.
b A ______________ is someone who has been attacked or robbed.
c A ______________ is a crime involving the killing of a person.
d A ______________ is someone who has escaped from jail and is hiding from the police.
e A criminal is ______________ when they are prevented from carrying out a crime.
f When a criminal is ______________ they are taken prisoner.

3 Use these words from the stories in Exercise 1 to complete three more stories.

mug shot burglar arrested robbery convicted sentenced

NICE JUDGE

(1) ______________ Frank Gort broke down in court and cried when he was **(2)** ______________ to seven years in jail, claiming it was his unlucky number. An understanding judge in San Antonio, Texas gave him eight years instead.

LIKELY CRIMINAL

Jon Reardon, wanted for theft, loved his **(3)** ______________ on the Cascade Country Crimestoppers social media page so much, that he "liked" it. He was **(4)** ______________ a few weeks later.

SOCIAL MEDIA PROFILE

A couple, arrested this week for the **(5)** ______________ of an Ohio bank, posted photos on social media posing with the cash in the days after the crime. Known criminal John Morgan, a **(6)** ______________ robber, and his wife, Julie, also got tattoos celebrating their success.

PRONUNCIATION

1 2.03 **Listen and repeat the past participle endings for regular verbs commonly used in the passive.**

ed = /t/	ed = /d/	ed = /ɪd/
asked based	believed called	arrested decided

***ed* is pronounced as an extra syllable only after the sounds /t/ or /d/. True or false?**

2 **Practice saying the past participle for the verbs in the box. Add them to the correct column in the table in Exercise 1.**

check describe escape expect force involve name need report stop treat use

2.04 **Listen, check, and repeat.**

GRAMMAR

1 **Rewrite the following in the passive to recreate sentences from the news stories on page 66. Make the underlined words or phrases the subject of the passive verb.**

a Someone stole a safe. *A safe was stolen.*
b Someone captured the thief. *The thief …*
c Someone arrested the man. *The man …*
d Someone grabbed it. *It …*

How is the passive formed? Find other examples of passive structures in the same news stories on page 66.

Passive

be + past participle

It **had been done.**
It **was done.**
It **was being done.**
It **has been done.**
It **is done.**
It **is being done.**
It **is going to be done.**
It **will be done.**

2 **Look at your sentences (a–d) above. Check (✓) the following explanations if you think they are correct.**

a In sentences *a*, *b*, *c*, and *d* the object of the active verb has become the subject of the passive verb.
b In sentences *a*, *b*, and *c* the "doer" of the action (= the agent) is either unknown, unimportant, or obvious.
c In sentence *d* the "doer" of the action (= the agent) is mentioned after the verb using *by*.

3 **Rewrite these newspaper extracts in the passive to make them sound more natural. Don't mention the agent.**

a The Oscar committee has announced the Oscar nominations.
The Oscar nominations have been announced.
b Doctors are treating the troubled movie star for "exhaustion" at Meadows Rehabilitation Center in Arizona.
c The record company has released the singer's long-awaited album to rave reviews.
d Kidnappers released the hostages last night and they are on their way home to their relieved families.
e The central bank will reduce interest rates by 1% before the end of the year according to most financial observers.
f People have accused the fashion industry of encouraging young girls to go on starvation diets.

Would you want to read more about any of the stories above?
What kinds of topics do you like reading about in the newspaper?

4 **Pairwork Student A:** page 122 **Student B:** page 126

5 **Grammar Extra 7** page 140. Read the explanation and do the exercises.

READING & LISTENING

1 **Match each picture (a-f) with an appropriate newspaper headline (1-6).**

a

b

c

d

e

f

1 ULTIMATE COSMIC COINCIDENCE
2 HIT AND RUN JOGGER ARRESTED
3 WILDFIRES RAGE IN SOUTHERN FRANCE
4 DELEGATES WALKOUT
5 PRESIDENT QUITS AFTER CORRUPTION PROBE
6 TATTOO STUDENT BARRED

What do you think each news item is about? Which story would you read first?

2 **Find an underlined headline word in Exercise 1 that has the same meaning as the phrases below.**

a unplanned departure *walkout*
b leaves his job
c are spreading out of control
d left the scene of an accident
e things happened at the same time
f the biggest and best
g has been excluded
h investigation

Are there any similar stories in the news today?

3 2.05 **Listen and match the radio news items (a-f) with the headlines (1-6) in Exercise 1.**

4 **Work with a partner and complete the task.**

- Write a news story based on one of the following three headlines (a-c).
- Invent any extra information you need.
- Broadcast your news to the rest of the class.

a FANS BARRED FROM SOCCER WORLD CUP FINAL
b CHIEF FIRE OFFICER QUITS AFTER FIRES RAGE AT BEACH RESORT
c HIT AND RUN DRIVER CAUGHT AFTER POLICE PROBE

READING & WRITING

1 **Complete the email from Pia to her friend Ian. Use the words in the box.**

Actually Anyway Apart apparently doing forward
Good ~~great~~ happy heard let news sorry touch

mail.com

Compose
Inbox
Drafts
Sent
Spam
Trash

To: ian@mail.com
Cc:
Subject:
From: pia@mail.com

Hi Ian,
Thanks for your email. It was **(1)** ___great___ to hear from you. I'm **(2)** ________ I haven't replied sooner, but work's been really stressful. More about that in a minute. But first, I was really **(3)** ________ to hear about your promotion. You deserve it – you've worked so hard. **(4)** ________ job! I wish you were still living in Berlin, so we could go out and celebrate.
Anyway, back to my stressful job! **(5)** ________, it's much better now that there has been some restructuring within the company.
The good **(6)** ________ is that we've got a new boss, and he's quite dynamic. He's already made a few changes, and the best thing is that he wants me to travel more, so I'll be able to see all my friends back home more often.
Talking of friends, have you **(7)** ________ about Anna and Giorgio? They've split up! I have no idea why, but **(8)** ________, Giorgio's gone back to Italy and Anna's refusing to talk to anybody about it. Please **(9)** ________ me know if you hear any more about it.
(10) ________ from that, everything's fine here in Berlin. It's getting pretty hot, and I'm looking **(11)** ________ to going on vacation in August. What are your vacation plans?
(12) ________, I'd better get back to work now, but be in **(13)** ________ soon and tell me how you're **(14)** ________.

Lots of love,
Pia

2 **Read the email again and answer the questions.**

a Who lives in Berlin?
b Who used to live in Berlin?
c Who got promoted at work?
d Who's got a new boss?
e Who's split up?
f Who's gone back to Italy?

3 **Work with a partner. Use the sentence beginnings below to invent a reply from Ian to Pia's email.**

mail.com

Compose
Inbox
Drafts
Sent
Spam
Trash

To: pia@mail.com
Cc:
Subject:
From: ian@mail.com

Dear Pia,

It was great …
I'm sorry …
I was so happy …
By the way, Giorgio called me. Apparently …
Apart from that, I'm looking forward to my vacation. I'm going …
Anyway, …

Lots of love,

P.S. Guess what! …

Compare your email with other people in the class. Choose the email with the best ideas.

LANGUAGE FOR LIFE

1 Match the two pictures to two of the conversations (a-h).

1

2

a **A:** How's Leanne?
B: Actually, we've split up.
A: Oh, I'm sorry to hear that. / How exciting!
B: It's OK. Um, this is Cassandra.

b **C:** Hello. You're looking really happy with yourself.
D: I am! I just passed my driving test!
C: Oh, no. That's terrible! / Good job! Was it your first time?
D: No, my sixth.

c **E:** Guess what! I've won a vacation to Florida.
F: I'm sorry to hear that. / Lucky you! Is it a vacation for two?
E: Yes, I'm taking my mom.
F: Oh.

d **G:** You don't look very happy.
H: No, I just got my exam scores. I failed them all.
G: Good job! / Oh, no, that's terrible! What happened?
H: I didn't do any work.

e **I:** Do you like this bunch of flowers? They are for my wife.
J: They are lovely! What are you celebrating?
I: We've just had a baby.
J: Oh, congratulations! / How annoying!

f **K:** You don't usually take the bus!
L: No – my car's broken down again.
K: How annoying! / Good job!
L: I know. But it is twenty-five years old.

g **M:** What did you do last night?
N: I watched a documentary about snow leopards.
M: Oh, that sounds interesting. / Oh, I'm sorry to hear that.
N: Yes ... unfortunately, I fell asleep halfway through.

h **O:** What are you doing today?
P: I'm taking my first sailing class.
O: How exciting! / Oh, no, that's terrible! Are you nervous?
P: I am actually. I can't swim.

2 Work with a partner. Read the conversations (a-h) which show people responding to good and bad news. In each case, underline the appropriate response.

2.06 **Listen and check.**

3 Classify the useful phrases that you heard in Exercise 2 in the table below.

Positive responses	Negative responses
	Oh, I'm sorry to hear that.

2.07 **Listen, check, and repeat.**

4 2.08 **Listen to some more pieces of good and bad news and respond appropriately.**

Life Skills: Accessing and Analyzing Information

A Hurricane

1 Discuss with a partner where you go for the news.

a

9 a.m. August 24

b

10 a.m. August 24

c

At least 2 die in Hurricane Lucy

Hurricane Lucy hit the US early on Thursday morning. All the roads coming from the Texas coast were full of cars. The mayor of Rockport, Texas, told residents who decided to stay to write their social security number on their arm. This would help rescue services identify them.

Sunday August 27

d

2 a.m. August 24

Which of the above media published the story first? Which do you think is the most accurate? Why?

MACMILLAN LIFE SKILLS

Verb patterns

1 Complete the common verb patterns (a-j) with *ask*, *explain*, *say*, or *tell*.

a explain / **say** + (that)
b **explain** / ________ / **say** how/ what, etc.
c ________ / **say** sth to sb
d ________ sth on / about
e ________ sb + (that)
f ________ / **tell** sb why/ how, etc.
g ________ / **ask** sb sth
h ________ / **tell** sb about sth
i ________ sb for sth
j ________ / **tell** sb to do sth

Check your answers in the dictionary extracts. Which verbs almost always have a person (sb) as a direct object?

2 Say or tell? Underline the correct verbs in these sentences.

a She **said / told** that she liked dancing.
b Didn't he **say / tell** you that I wanted to see you?
c I want to **say / tell** something about this subject.
d Just **say / tell** me what she **said / told**.
e "**Say / Tell** me about your day," she **said / told**.
f I haven't been **said / told** anything about it.

Check your answers in the dictionary extracts.

3 Complete the joke with the correct form of either *say* or *tell*.

Sherlock Holmes and Dr. Watson went on a camping trip. As they lay down for the night, Holmes **(1)** said: "Watson, look up into the sky and **(2)** ________ me what you see."
Watson **(3)** ________: "I see millions and millions of stars."
Holmes: "And what does that **(4)** ________ you?" Watson: "Astronomically, it **(5)** ________ me that there are millions of galaxies and potentially billions of planets. In relative terms, it **(6)** ________ me that we are small and insignificant. Meteorologically, it **(7)** ________ me that we will have a beautiful day tomorrow. What does it **(8)** ________ you?"
Holmes: "Somebody stole our tent."

4 Complete the questions with the most appropriate verb: *asked*, *explained*, *said*, or *told*.

When was the last time you ...

a told your friends a joke?
b ________ no to chocolate?
c ________ somebody to "cheer up"?
d ________ what you do for a living?
e ________ somebody for a ride?
f ________ sorry to a friend?
g ________ a friend to help you?
h ________ the rules of a game to somebody?
i ________ that you needed to do some exercise?
j ________ somebody that you loved them?

Work with a partner. Ask and answer the questions.

5 Check your own dictionary. What example sentences does it include to illustrate the different verb patterns for *ask*, *explain*, *say*, and *tell*?

---

ask /æsk/ verb ★★★
1 [I/T] to speak to someone in order to get information from them: *I wondered who had given her the ring but was afraid to ask.* ♦ *The police wanted to* ***ask*** *us a few* ***questions.*** ♦ **ask (sb) why/how/whether etc.** *She asked me how I knew about it.* ♦ **ask (sb) about sth** *Did you ask about the money?*
2 [I/T] to speak to someone because you want them to give you something, or do something for you: *If you need any help, just ask.* ♦ *Can I ask you a favor?* ♦ **ask (sb) for sth** *The children were asking for drinks.* ♦ **ask sb to do sth** *He asked us to move over a little.* ♦ **ask to do sth** *I asked to see the manager.* ♦ **ask (sb) if/whether** *Ask if we can go backstage.*

ex·plain /ɪk'spleɪn/ verb ★★★
1 [T] to tell someone something in a way that helps them to understand it better: **explain sth to sb** *The doctor explained the risks to me before the operation.* ♦ **+how/when/what etc.** *I will try to explain how a car engine works.* ♦ **+(that)** *He explained that he would be moving to another city.*

say[1] /seɪ/ (3rd person singular **says** /sez/; past tense and past participle **said** /sed/) verb ★★★

1 express with words	4 show sth
2 have opinion	5 imagine sth
3 give information	+ PHRASES

1 [I/T] to express something using words: *"Nice to meet you," he said with a smile.* ♦ *"When's he coming back?" "He didn't say."* ♦ *The committee* ***said yes*** (=gave permission), *so we can go ahead.* ♦ *What a strange* ***thing to say****, Carrie thought.* ♦ *I then* ***said goodbye*** *and left.* ♦ *I already* ***said sorry*** *for hurting his feelings.* ♦ **+(that)** *She said that she liked dancing.* ♦ **+how/what/who etc.** *Did he say who called?* ♦ **say sth to sb** *Tell me what he said to you.* ♦ **say sth on/about** *I want to say something about this subject.*

tell /tel/ (past tense and past participle **told** /toʊld/) verb ★★★

1 sb gives information	6 see difference
2 sth gives information	7 have clear effect
3 talk about story	8 fail to keep secret
4 order/advise to do sth	+ PHRASES
5 know sth	+ PHRASAL VERBS

1 [T] to give information to someone: *If you see anything suspicious, tell the police.* ♦ **tell sb (that)** *Didn't he tell you that I wanted to see you?* ♦ **tell sb who/what/why/how etc.** *Just tell me what she said.* ♦ **tell sb sth** *He finally told me the reason he was so upset.* ♦ **tell sb (sth) about sth** *"Tell me about your day," she said.* → SAY
2 [T] if something such as a fact, event, or piece of equipment tells you something, it gives you or shows you some information: *The flashing light tells you when the battery needs recharging.* ♦ *What does this room tell you about the person who lived here?*
3 [T] if you tell a story or a joke, you give someone a spoken account of it: *Grandpa* ***tells*** *wonderful* ***stories*** *about the old days.* ♦ **tell sb sth** *I have to tell you this joke.*
4 [T] to order or strongly advise someone to do something: *I'm not asking you – I'm telling you!* ♦ **tell sb to do sth** *I told you to be here on time this morning.* ♦ **tell sb what/how/when etc.** *I told him what to do, but he wouldn't listen.*

From the *Macmillan Essential Dictionary for Learners of American English.*

8

READING

1 **Have you ever traveled for any of these reasons? Discuss with a partner.**

- to broaden your experience of the world
- to run away from a broken heart
- to learn a language (or something else)
- to take a break from your career
- to visit historical sites
- to get a suntan

2 **Read this travel review. When did the author's dad propose to his mom in Venice?**

Moonlit Venice

by Steph Mortimer

This trip lived up to all my expectations. I have wanted to go to Venice ever since I discovered that my dad proposed to my mom there. I had obviously heard a lot about the place, read lots of books, and looked at hundreds of photographs. But nothing prepares you for the reality of it. It is so beautiful. Around every corner, there is another lovely building or picturesque square. The architecture is stunning. I managed to find a very good hotel not far from the famous Rialto Bridge. It's on a small central square, but was very quiet at night. (This was a relief, as I'm a very light sleeper and wake at the slightest sound – even with earplugs in!) I spent my days walking all over the city, soaking up the beauty of it all. In the evenings, I ate really good Italian food. Many of the cafés and restaurants are very expensive, but you can find cheaper places if you are prepared to walk a bit. One night, I set out to find the little square where my dad went down on one knee 55 years ago. In the moonlight, it looked so pretty and romantic. I understood why my dad had chosen that place. Venice is so special. If you have never been there I urge you to go – seeing is believing! I will be going again as soon as I can.

3 **Are these statements true or false?**

a The author has wanted to go to Venice since her parents' wedding.
b She has done her homework on Venice.
c Her hotel was located in a very busy street.
d She couldn't sleep at night.
e She ate Italian food in the evenings.
f She found the restaurant where her dad proposed 55 years ago.

Is there a place that is special for your family? Would you like to go there?

Glossary

live up to sth (phrasal verb): to be as good as what was expected or promised

manage to do sth: to succeed in doing sth

soak up: (INFORMAL) to spend time experiencing, listening to, or feeling something enjoyable

urge someone to do sth: to advise strongly

SPEAKING

1 **Work with your partner. Make a list of different places you've traveled to.**

2 **Choose five places from your list and think about how to describe where they are. Use the expressions in the box.**

It's in the	north/southwest	of (Japan).
	southern/ northeastern part	of (Peru).

	on the coast	to the north of (Vigo).
It's	in the mountains	not far from (Jalapa).
	in (Pernambuco)	between (Recife) and (Olinda).

Tell your partner where, when, and why you traveled to these places.

READING & VOCABULARY

1 Look at the photographs of popular places. Which one would you most like to visit and why? Read the description below. Which picture does it describe?

Visiting this place is a life-changing experience. If you are in this part of the world, you must include it in your itinerary. To get here is difficult, but ultimately rewarding. It involves four days of cold, pain, and exhaustion. But when the mist lifts to reveal the emerald peaks and terraced ruins of this ancient place, I promise you will forget all the hardship. The best time to visit is May through September. Although this is the busiest time, it is also the driest. Believe me, this is not a place you want to visit in the rainy season. You'll need to take strong walking boots and a torch with spare batteries. If you want to join an organized tour, you'll also need to make your reservation many months in advance, as it is a very popular destination.

d

2 Read the paragraph again. Are these sentences true or false?

- a The writer thinks this is a good place to visit.
- b Getting to the place is easy.
- c May to September is the rainy season.
- d The busiest time to arrive is also when there is the least rain.
- e You must book your place on a tour a long time before you arrive.
- f You'll need smart shoes.

3 Work with a partner. Complete the two descriptions below using words and expressions in the box.

contests spectators era ~~attractions~~ damaged constructed Italy
island sailing chased ship sea blue

The Colosseum is one of the most famous and popular tourist **(1)** attractions in Rome, **(2)** __________. It was **(3)** __________ between AD 72 and 80, and is still the largest amphitheater ever built. It could hold between 50,000 and 80,000 **(4)** __________, who came to watch the popular gladiator **(5)** __________ and other public events. Since the early medieval **(6)** __________, the Colosseum has stopped being an entertainment venue. It has been **(7)** __________ by earthquakes and stone robbers, but it remains an icon of ancient Rome and its emperors.

This beautiful place is on the northwest coast of the Greek island of Zakynthos. It was named Shipwreck Beach after a container **(8)** __________ ended up on the beach here on October 2, 1980. The M V Panagiotis was **(9)** __________ from Turkey to Italy with, it is believed, illegal goods on board. It was being **(10)** __________ by the Greek navy when stormy weather forced it into the small cove. The crew abandoned ship and ran off. The remains of the ship still lie on the beach. The beach can only be reached from the **(11)** __________ and is loved for its white sand and clear **(12)** __________ water. There are regular boat tours from other parts of the **(13)** __________.

4 Work with a partner. Talk about places in your city or country ...

- a that are unspoiled.
- b where there are wonderful beaches.
- c where the views are spectacular.
- d where young people go to hang out and be seen.
- e where you can hardly move because it's so crowded on the weekend.
- f that are popular with foreign tourists.

LISTENING

1 Look at pictures (a-d) taken on Conrad's around-the-world trip. Where do you think they were taken?

a

b

c

d

2.09 **Listen to Amy and Joe discussing the pictures on Conrad's blog and check your ideas. Number the pictures in the order they mention them.**

2 **Match the words in the box with the pictures (a-d) in Exercise 1.**

river   Buddhist temples   a built-up skyline   forests
horseman   high-rise buildings   snow-capped mountains   waterfalls

Are there any places in your country where you can see these things? Tell a partner.

GRAMMAR

1 **Complete these explanations of the modal structures from the discussion on page 74. Use *must* or *can't*.**

- **a** I think it's certain = "It __________ be Singapore ... I know he stopped off there."
- **b** I think it's possible = "It might/ may/ could be Vietnam."
- **c** I think it's impossible = "It __________ be India, because he hasn't been there yet."

> **Modals of deduction**
>
> The lights aren't on:
>
> Sam **must** be out. (= certain)
>
> He **can't** be in. (= certain)
>
> He **might**/**may**/**could** be away for the weekend or on vacation or ... (= possible)

2 **Look at the information in the table and try and name the countries (a-f) from the list in the box. Discuss your ideas with a partner.**

Angola Argentina Spain Uruguay Brazil Cuba Mexico Mozambique Peru Portugal

Country	Population (country)	Population (biggest city)	Official language	Highest mountain	Main exports
a ________	Over 45 million	About 3 million	Spanish	3,718 m	chemicals, fruit, cars
b ________	Over 10 million	Over half a million	Portuguese	2,351 m	chemicals, cork, leather
c ________	Over 208 million	Over 12 million	Portuguese	3,014 m	animal feed, chemicals, coffee
d ________	Nearly 130 million	Nearly 9 million	Spanish	5,700 m	chemicals, coffee, cotton
e ________	Over 43 million	Nearly 3 million	Spanish	6,962 m	animal oils, meat
f ________	Over 25 million	Nearly 3 million	Portuguese	2,619 m	oil, diamonds

Write sentences with *must be*, *might be*, or *can't* be to show how you decided.

Country "c" must be Brazil, because it's the country with the biggest population and they speak Portuguese there.

Have you ever been to any of these countries? Tell your partner.

3 **Grammar Extra 8, Part 1** page 142. Read the explanation and do the exercises.

PRONUNCIATION

1 2.10 **Listen and repeat the words in the box. Mark the main stress.**

the Amazon the Andes Antarctica Asia the Atlantic the Danube Europe
the Himalayas the Indian Ocean the Nile the Pacific the Pyrenees

2 **List the words in the correct column according to size (from largest to smallest).**

+ ↓ -	Continents	Mountain ranges	Oceans	Rivers
	Asia			

2.11 **Listen, check, and repeat.**

READING & LISTENING

1 Read the text conversation between two friends. What was Nick's motivation for the trip?

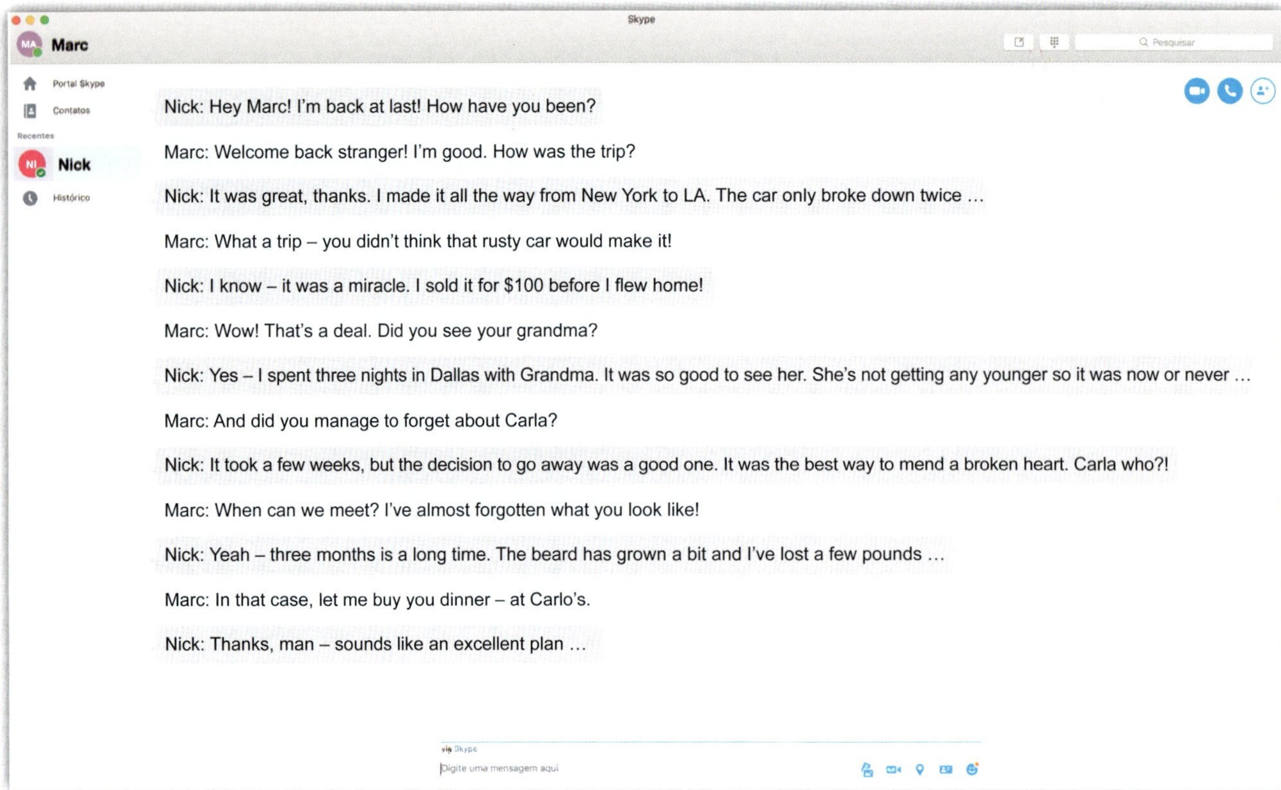

Nick: Hey Marc! I'm back at last! How have you been?

Marc: Welcome back stranger! I'm good. How was the trip?

Nick: It was great, thanks. I made it all the way from New York to LA. The car only broke down twice …

Marc: What a trip – you didn't think that rusty car would make it!

Nick: I know – it was a miracle. I sold it for $100 before I flew home!

Marc: Wow! That's a deal. Did you see your grandma?

Nick: Yes – I spent three nights in Dallas with Grandma. It was so good to see her. She's not getting any younger so it was now or never …

Marc: And did you manage to forget about Carla?

Nick: It took a few weeks, but the decision to go away was a good one. It was the best way to mend a broken heart. Carla who?!

Marc: When can we meet? I've almost forgotten what you look like!

Nick: Yeah – three months is a long time. The beard has grown a bit and I've lost a few pounds …

Marc: In that case, let me buy you dinner – at Carlo's.

Nick: Thanks, man – sounds like an excellent plan …

2 Work with a partner. Discuss these questions.

- **a** How long has Nick been away?
- **b** How much did Nick sell his car for?
- **c** How many times did Nick's car break down?
- **d** What did Marc offer to buy Nick?
- **e** Who do you think Carla is?

3 2.12 **Listen to the conversation between Nick and Marc. What do you think Marc said next?**

VOCABULARY

1 Look at this expression from the conversation above. What does it mean?

"… so it was now or never."

- **a** either now or in the future
- **b** only now and not in the future

2 Work with a partner. Use words from the box to complete some more fixed expressions.

all	tidy	come	give	peace	Sooner	~~take~~

- **a** I don't particularly like watching TV. I can ____take____ **it or leave it**.
- **b** When I go on vacation, all I want is some ____________ **and quiet**.
- **c** I vacuum my car regularly because I like it to be **neat and** ____________.
- **d** It's 200 kilometers to the coast from here, ____________ **or take** a few kilometers.
- **e** My computer is getting old. ____________ **or later**, I'll have to buy a new one.
- **f** I don't eat chocolate for weeks. Then I'll eat three bars in one day! It's ____________ **or nothing** with me.
- **g** My teenagers treat our house like a hotel. They just ____________ **and go** as they please.

Are any of the sentences true for you?

GRAMMAR

1 **This is Nick's route across the USA. Refer to the conversation on page 76 and answer these questions.**

a Where did Nick begin his journey?
b Where did Nick stop to visit his grandma?
c Where did Nick sell his car?

2 **Look at these statements about Nick's trip and choose the correct verb from the box.**

stopped bought texted ~~split~~ broke down flew drove

a Nick had ___split___ with his girlfriend before he went away.
b Before the trip, Nick had ______ an old car.
c The car only ______ ______ twice.
d Nick ______ all the way from New York to Los Angeles.
e In Dallas, Nick ______ to visit his grandmother.
f Nick ______ home from Los Angeles to New York.
g When Nick got home, he ______ his friend, Marc.

Past perfect

had + past participle

We were too late: the train **had** already **left**.

I knew I **hadn't been** there before.

Why are the events which took place before his trip described in the past perfect?

3 **Work with a partner. Complete each of these sentences with a verb in the past perfect to make up a story about Michael's journey to Venezuela.**

a Michael was looking forward to his business trip to Venezuela because ...
b He was late leaving the house because ...
c The traffic was very slow from his house to the airport because ...
d At the check-in, he had to accept a seat at the back of the plane because ...
e The departure was delayed because ...
f As the plane was taking off, he suddenly remembered that ...

Compare your ideas with other people in the class.

4 **Pairwork Student A:** page 122. **Student B:** page 126.

5 **Grammar Extra 8, Part 2** page 142. Read the explanation and do the exercises.

SPEAKING: ANECDOTE

1 2.13 **Listen to Suzi talking about a trip she has been**
Cross out the wrong information in each of her answers.

a Where did the trip start? **The Dead Sea.**
b Where did the trip finish? **St. Christopher's Monaste**
c What was the reason for the trip? **I couldn't go diving.**
d What form of transportation did you use? **A big**
e What was the weather like? **Hot and windy.**
f Who did you go with? **Seven tourists, a guide, and a drive**
g How long did it take you? **Three hours.**
h What did you do during the trip? **I looked out of the window at the ocea**
i Did you stop en route? What for? **Yes, to take pictures and buy fo**
j Would you go on the same trip again? Why? **Yes, but in my**

Correct the information. Listen again and check

2 **You are going to tell your partner about a trip you have been on.**

- Ask yourself the questions in Exercise 1.
- Think about what to say and how to say it.
- Tell your partner about your trip.

LANGUAGE FOR LIFE

1 ▶ 2.14 **Read and listen to a conversation between a couple in a car. Answer the questions.**

a Where do they want to go?
b Which number road are they looking for?
c How many times do they pass the movie theater?

Angie: Rick, do you know where we are?
Rick: Yes, of course. Why?
Angie: Because we've passed the same movie theater twice.
Rick: Oh, no.
Angie: You'd better stop and ask somebody.
Rick: OK. ... Excuse me, I'm trying to get to Sacramento. Do you know how we can get onto Route 80 from here?
Man 1: Yes, first you need to turn around and then take the first left. Go to the end of the road and you'll come to a stop sign. Take a right and you'll see Route 80.
Rick: Great, thanks. ... Did he say left or right?
Angie: I can't remember. Look, stop and ask that woman.
Rick: Excuse me, we're looking for the road to Sacramento. Could you tell me which way we need to go?
Woman: Sacramento? Go straight down here until you come to a gas station. Then turn left and follow the signs.
Rick: OK, thanks. ... I haven't seen the gas station yet.
Angie: No, neither have I, but here's that movie theater again.
Rick: Oh, no. ... Excuse me, we're lost. Do you have any idea where Route 80 is?
Man 2: Er, no, sorry.

2 **Read the conversation again and complete the useful phrases.**

Saying what you're looking for
a Excuse me, I'm trying *to get to* Sacramento.
b Excuse me, we're looking ________ Sacramento.

Asking for directions
c Do you know how ________ Route 80?
d Could you tell me which ________ ?
e Do you have any idea where ________ ?

Giving directions
f You need to turn ________ and then ________ left.
g Go to the end of the road and you'll ________ .
h Go straight down here until ________ .
i Turn left and follow ________ .

▶ 2.15 **Listen, check, and repeat.**

3 **Work with a partner. Rewrite the following questions in less direct language. Refer to the expressions (c-e) in Exercise 2 and start your questions with *Do you know ...? Could you tell me ...?* or *Do you have any idea ...?***

a Where's the nearest bank?
Excuse me. Do you know where the nearest bank is?
b How can I get to the airport from here?
c I'm looking for the bus station. Which way do I need to go?
d How can I get downtown from here?
e Where can I get a taxi?
f How can I get to the shopping mall from here?

Ask each other the questions and give appropriate directions from where you are now.

Life Skills: Problem-solving
A Flight Mystery

1 ▶ 2.16 **Listen to the story of Tim, the lost traveler. Where was he spotted last?**

2 **Look at these statements. Rank them in order, from most to least likely. Discuss with your partner.**

He must still be in the United States. ☐
He might be in the UK under a different passport. ☐
He took the wrong flight and hasn't been able to get back to the UK. ☐
He might be in trouble with the police. ☐
He changed his mind and went on vacation instead. ☐
Something bad has happened to Tim. ☐

3 **Where do you think Tim is? Work in small groups and decide on an explanation for his disappearance. Use modals of deduction (*must, can't, might,* etc.) in your discussions.**

MACMILLAN LIFE SKILLS

Dictionary labels

1 Match the dictionary labels with their definitions.

a British
b American
c formal
d informal

1 Not used in everyday speech or writing.
2 Used in American English, but not in British English.
3 Used commonly in speech, but not in writing.
4 Used in British English, but not in American English.

2 Use an appropriate label from Exercise 1 as a heading for the word lists (1-3).

1	2	3
sweets	guy	alight
pavement	nerd	beverage
rubbish bin		refrain

Check your answers in the dictionary extracts.

3 Work with a partner. Decide what each sign means and where you might see it. Use the dictionary extracts to help you.

1

2

3

4

a Foot passengers please disembark via the steps at the front of the ferry
b All cyclists must dismount here
c The use of calculators is not permissible
d Do not alight from the train whilst it is still in motion

Write less formal versions of each notice.

1 *Please don't use your calculator.*

4 Rewrite these sentences in American English.

a Last year, I took my holiday in the autumn.
Last year, I went on vacation in the fall.
b We keep our rubbish bin on the pavement in front of our house.
c I never eat sweets or biscuits between meals.
d I get angry with lorry drivers who go too fast on the motorway.
e There's a postbox near the Underground station.

Are any of the sentences true for you?

5 Check your own dictionary. What kinds of labels does it use?

alight² /əˈlaɪt/ verb [I] *formal* to get off a train, bus, or other vehicle

autumn /ˈɔtəm/ noun [C/U] *British* fall

beverage /ˈbev(ə)rɪʤ/ noun [C] *formal* a drink

biscuit /ˈbɪskɪt/ noun [C] *British* cookie

disembark /ˌdɪsɪmˈbɑrk/ verb [I] *formal* to get off a ship or plane

dismount /dɪsˈmaʊnt/ verb [I] *formal* to get off a horse or a bike

guy /gaɪ/ noun [C] ★★ *informal* a man

highway /ˈhaɪˌweɪ/ noun [C] ★ a wide road that has been built for fast travel between towns and cities

holiday /ˈhɑlɪˌdeɪ/ noun [C/U] ★★★ *British* a vacation

lorry /ˈlɔri/ noun [C] *British* a truck

motorway /ˈmoʊtərˌweɪ/ noun [C] *British* a large highway

nerd /nɜrd/ noun [C] *informal* someone who is boring and not fashionable

pavement /ˈpeɪvmənt/ noun [C] *British* a sidewalk

permissible /pərˈmɪsəb(ə)l/ adj *formal* if something is permissible, you are allowed to do it

persons /ˈpɜrs(ə)nz/ noun [C] *formal* the plural of person is people, but in formal or official language the form persons is used

postbox /ˈpoʊstˌbɑks/ noun [C] *British* a mailbox

purchase¹ /ˈpɜrtʃəs/ verb [T] *formal* to buy something

refrain /rɪˈfreɪn/ verb [I] *formal* to stop yourself from doing something

rubbish bin /ˈrʌbɪʃ ˌbɪn/ noun [C] *British* trash can

sweets /swits/ noun [C] *British* candy

Underground, the /ˈʌndərˌgraʊnd/ noun [singular] *British* the subway

From the *Macmillan Essential Dictionary for Learners of American English.*

SPEAKING & READING

1 **In pairs discuss:**

Why do people go on social media?

Do young people and adults go on different reasons?

2 **Complete the questionnaire. Then compare your answer with your partner.**

www.survey.com

Dashboard **My Surveys** **Products** **Resources** **Plans & Pricing**

One thousand Americans between the ages of 18 and 35 were interviewed for a survey about attitudes to social media. These are the questions they were asked.
Check the answers a), b), or c) for the answer which most applies to you.

WHAT DO YOU USE SOCIAL MEDIA FOR?

1 ... for politics?
- a I like to share how I vote on social media.
- b I prefer to keep my voting record private in case I offend my friends.
- c I find it boring to read about people's political views on social media.

2 ... for food?
- a I like to post successful recipes so that my friends can enjoy good food too.
- b I read food blog posts and watch demo videos but rarely cook anything myself.
- c I surf the net for good recipes when I am having friends round for a meal.

3 ... for travel?
- a I think that the internet is the best tool for researching destinations and booking trips.
- b I post blogs about my trips so that my friends and others can share my experiences.
- c I don't like to reveal where I have been in case my secret spots get ruined by tourists.

4 ... for shopping?
- a I mainly buy clothes on the net.
- b I look at favourite brands on the net, select some pieces, then go to the mall to try them on.
- c I mainly buy from stores.

5 ... for entertainment?
- a I download or stream most of my videos and movies from the net.
- b I use the net for catch-up TV.
- c I rarely use the internet for entertainment.

6 ... for news?
- a I get the news from social media rather than from the newscasts or newspapers.
- b I look at Twitter first when a news item breaks.
- c I rarely use social media for news.

Glossary

Trend (n.): gradual change

Overrun (v.): occupy in large numbers in a way that it is umpleasant.

Purchase (n.): the action of buying something

Catch up on sth (phrasal verb): to do something that should have been done before

Newscasts (n.): a news program

READING

1 **Read about the findings which came out of the survey about social media.**
Complete the results with the most appropriate word from the box.

surfed political bookings ~~entertainment~~ newspapers downloaded stores quiet

No one wants to appear superficial when using social media. Nowadays it seems most people want to make a statement when they post on the internet. Many people turn to different online environments where they can tell their friends their opinions on a great variety of issues, such as politics, food, travel, shopping, **(1)** _entertainment_, news, etc. See below for current trends in internet use.

On politics: 63% of people said that they liked to express how they voted on social media whereas 30% *didn't like* to risk causing offence to friends so preferred to keep their political opinions private. A minority, 7%, *thought* it was boring to read about other people's **(2)** ______________ views online.

On food: 27% stated that they had posted successful recipes online to share with friends, while 13% admitted that they had read food blog posts and had watched demo videos but rarely cooked anything themselves. The majority of respondents reported that they had **(3)** ______________ the net for good recipes before having friends round for a meal.

On travel: The majority of people *thought* that the best way to research destinations and make **(4)** ______________ was via the net (55%) and a lot of people (43%) *enjoyed* sharing their experiences via blogs. Only 2% preferred to keep **(5)** ______________ about their travel in case their favorite places were over run with tourists.

On shopping: The vast majority of respondents (65%) said that they had bought their clothes online. 24% explained that they had looked at their favorite brands on the net, then went to the mall to try them on before they made a purchase. Only 11% claimed that they had bought mostly from **(6)** ______________.

On entertainment: 68% said that they had **(7)** ______________ or streamed most of their videos and movies from the net. 25% *preferred* to use the net mainly to catch up on TV programs. A minority of 7% declared that they rarely used the internet for entertainment.

On news: 59% *insisted* that they got the news from social media rather than from the newscasts or **(8)** ______________. 38% said that they looked at Twitter first when a news item broke and only 3% said that they had refused to use social media for news.

2 2.17 **Listen and check. Would the survey results be different in your country?**

GRAMMAR

1 **Which of the reporting verbs in the box can't you use to complete the statement below? Why not?**

admitted claimed explained insisted replied said suggested told

*13% ______________ that they **had read** blog posts and **had watched** demo videos.*

2 **In the reported statement in Exercise 1, the verb *read* is in the past perfect. Which sentence (*a*, *b*, *c*, or *d*) did people actually say?**

a "Yes, I was reading." b "Yes, I read." c "Yes, I've read." d "Yes, I'll read."

When you report speech, you usually move the tense back (e.g. present perfect becomes past perfect). True or false?

3 **Complete these sentences in direct speech. Use the reported statements highlighted in the survey results above to help you choose the correct form of the verb.**

a "Yes, I (read) _have read_ recipes online."
b "Yes, I (surf) ______________ for good recipes before having friends for dinner."
c "Yes, I (stream) ______________ most of my videos and movies from the net."
d "Yes, I (get) ______________ the news from the net rather than from newscasts and newspapers."

4 **Grammar Extra 9** page 144. **Read the explanation and do the exercises.**

Reported statements

"She's not there."

→ He **told** us that she **wasn't** there.

"I bought some new clothes."

→ She **said** that she**'d bought** some new clothes.

SPEAKING

Find out how many people in the class ...

- are reading a novel right now.
- enjoy reading biographies and autobiographies.
- still listen to the same music that they did ten years ago.
- have a favorite place to read.
- buy and play music.
- prefer watching a movie to reading a book.
- have been to a concert recently.

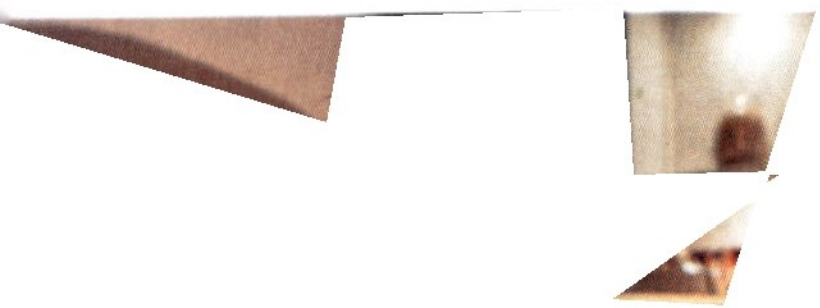

LISTENING & VOCABULARY

1 2.18 **Listen to seven conversations. What are the people talking about in each one? Write *book*, *movie*, or *music*.**

1 music, 2 ...

2 **The table contains words and expressions relating to books, movies, and music from the seven conversations in Exercise 1. Complete the table with the correct heading (*Books* / *Movies* / *Music*) for each column.**

a ______	b ______	c ______
acting cinematography special effects tearjerker	album lyrics performing live techno track	bestseller can't put it down chapters difficult to get into

Add these words to the table. Some words go in more than one column. Add words of your own.

band blues classical dance director fantasy gig hip-hop a hit horror musical novel orchestra paperback plot premiere reggae science-fiction short story soundtrack stereo system storyline subtitles

3 2.19 **Listen to these extracts from movie soundtracks. What kind of movie do you think they go with? Choose from the list below.**

action movies comedies gangster movies horror movies love stories romantic comedies science-fiction movies spy movies thrillers war movies westerns

Work in groups. Think of some movies of each of the types above. Which types of movies do people in your group like best?

READING & GRAMMAR

1 **Read this report of an interview with Taylor Swift. What does she say about her fans, her song lyrics, and romance?**

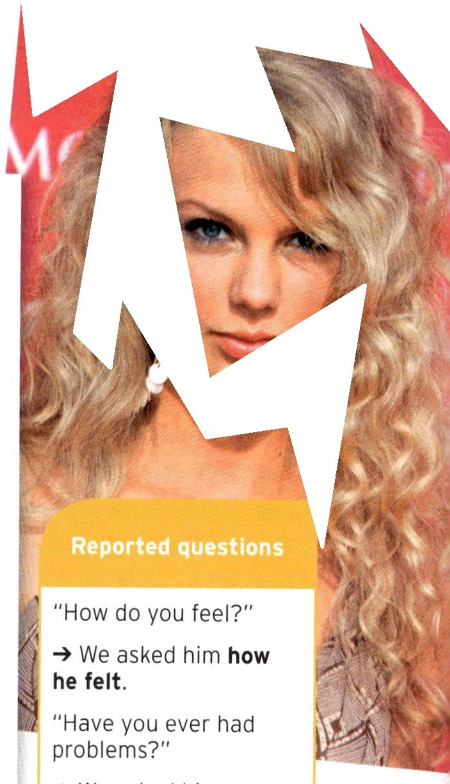

In an online interview, Taylor Swift talked about how fame had changed her life. When the interviewer asked whether Taylor still invited fans into her home, she replied that she did. She said she liked to have small gatherings at her New York apartment because it helped her to bond with her fans on a more personal level. She felt it kept her down to earth and kept her life manageable.

When the interviewer asked her whether her life was still normal, Taylor said that it wasn't normal anymore. Taylor said that fame had changed everything. But she added that she keeps very close to her old friends and family, which helps her not to lose touch with reality.

Then they talked about her songs, which deal with the problems of everyday life. They asked Taylor what she felt about her critics. She replied that she didn't mind them. Some people said she was "brave" while others said she was "over-emotional". And when they asked her what her attitude to romance was now, she said that, since moving to New York, love and heartbreak — which used to be main themes in her music — had sort of faded to the background. They asked her what her current plans were and she replied that she was planning some new shows to promote her album.

Reported questions

"How do you feel?"

→ We asked him **how he felt**.

"Have you ever had problems?"

→ We asked him **whether / if he had ever had** problems.

2 **What are the actual questions that are used in the interview? Underline the five reported questions in the report and rewrite them in direct speech.**

3 **Look at the examples in Exercise 2 and decide if the following statements are true or false when you report questions.**

a The tense usually moves back in a reported question (simple present → simple past).
b *Whether* or *if* are used to report *yes/no* questions. (*Did you go out?* → *She asked me if I'd gone out.*)
c The word order changes to subject + verb (*Who are you?* → *He asked me who I was.*).

4 **Pairwork Student A:** page 122. **Student B:** page 126.

SPEAKING: ANECDOTE

1 2.20 **Listen to Alice talking about a movie she enjoyed. Read the questions and check (✓) the answers that are correct.**

a What's the title of the movie? **Forrest Gump.** ✓
b When and where did you see it?
The other night at the movie theater.
c Who's in it? **Tom Hanks, Robin Wright, and Sally Field.**
d Who directed it? **I can't remember.**
e What is it based on? **A true story.**
f What type of movie is it? **A thriller.**
g What do you particularly like about it?
The parts where he meets famous people.
h What was the soundtrack like? **Great.**
i What kind of ending does it have? **A happy ending.**
j Would you recommend this movie? **No, I wouldn't.**

Listen again and change the incorrect answers.

2 **You are going to tell your partner about a movie you enjoyed.**

- Ask yourself the questions in Exercise 1.
- Think about *what* to say and *how* to say it.
- Tell your partner about a movie you enjoyed.

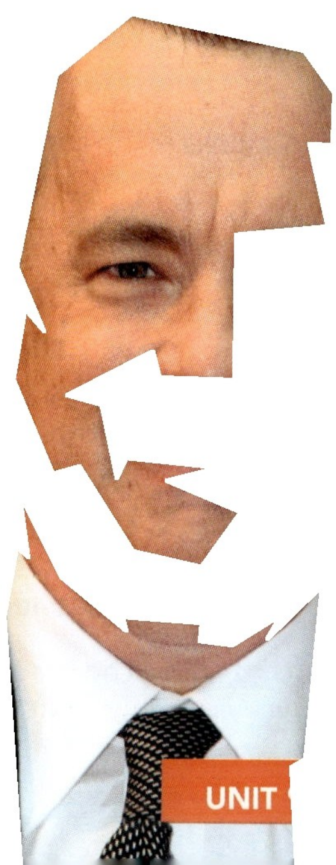

VOCABULARY & SPEAKING

1 **Read and underline the correct alternatives in the sentences below.**

bookchoice.com

book choice Home Books Reviews Contact

We asked several people the question, "How do you choose a book to read?" Here are their replies.

I judge a book by its cover. If the cover looks **(1) interesting / interested**, I buy the book. Sometimes I'm lucky, and the book is good. And sometimes I'm **(2) disappointing / disappointed**.

I always read book reviews online, and when I read about a book that sounds **(3) interesting / interested**, I write it down in my notebook.

I don't take any risks and I always read books by authors I know. I get really **(4) exciting / excited** when one of my favorite authors puts out a new book, and I buy it immediately. This way I'm never **(5) disappointing / disappointed**.

I read the first page, and if it's **(6) boring / bored**, I don't buy the book. If I want to turn over the page and keep on reading, I buy the book.

It's easy – I never read fiction, but I'm **(7) fascinating / fascinated** by biographies of famous people. I find strong women in history particularly **(8) inspiring / inspired**.

I tend to choose books written by women. Women have a better feeling for characters and the relationships between them, and that's what I find **(9) interesting / interested** in a book.

2 2.21 **Listen and check your answers. How do you choose a book?**

3 **Add the adjectives in Exercise 1 to the table below.**

To describe how people feel	To describe the thing (or person) that causes the feeling
annoyed challenged confused exhausted relaxed tired worried	annoying challenging confusing exhausting relaxing tiring worrying

4 **Tell your partner how you're feeling today. Explain why. Choose words from the table in Exercise 3 or use your own ideas.**

Choose three other adjectives and say what makes you feel like this.

On Monday evenings, I feel exhausted. I work in a bar and it's very tiring.

PRONUNCIATION

1 **Say the words in the box and add them to the table.**

~~annoying~~ challenging disappointing entertaining exciting exhausting interesting overwhelming worrying

A: ■ ▪ ▪	
B: ▪ ■ ▪	annoying
C: ▪ ▪ ■ ▪	

2.22 **Listen, check, and repeat.**

2 **Underline the stressed syllable in each word.**

READING & VOCABULARY

1 **Look at the picture and read the synopsis of *Touching the Void* by Joe Simpson. What kind of book is it? Would you be interested in reading it? Why? / Why not?**

Look inside

Touching the Void

by Joe Simpson
★★★★☆ 1,610 customer reviews

Share

E-book	Hardcover	Paperback	Audible
$ 12.29	$ 19.86	$ 15.26	$ 17.17

Synopsis

Touching the Void is the heart-stopping account of Joe Simpson's terrifying adventure in the Peruvian Andes. A few days after Joe and his climbing partner, Simon, reach the summit of the remote Siula Grande, Simon staggers into Base Camp, exhausted and frostbitten, with news that Joe is dead.

Although this is a real-life account, it is a real page-turner. The technical information about mountain climbing is fascinating, and the stunning photos of the mountains give it authenticity, but it is the characters and plotline which make it more like a novel.

The story is told through Joe's eyes: the original disaster; what happens to Joe; and how the pair deals with the psychological traumas that resulted when Simon was forced into a terrible decision. It makes not only an epic story of survival, but an amazing tale of friendship.

2 **Read these reviews of *Touching the Void* from an online bookstore. How many stars do you think each person gave the book?**

a ☆☆☆☆☆ **Cliff-hanger**
by *S Cooke*
Format: Kindle Edition | **Verified Purchase**

Although the start of the book was a bit long and drawn out, by the time I reached chapter 5, I was hooked. Although I'm not a regular reader, and it took a long time to finish it, I am glad I did. If you are looking for an emotional "cliff-hanger" (sorry for the bad joke!) then this book is for you.

Comment

b ☆☆☆☆☆ **Astonishing!**
by *Mrs R Ramsden*
Format: Paperback | **Verified Purchase**

An astonishing story! It is as tense as any thriller and Joe's writing brings their struggles on the mountain to life. From my comfortable armchair, I can't begin to imagine what it must have been like for the two climbers. A tremendous read.

Comment

c ☆☆☆☆☆ **Repetitious and monotonous**
by *Charles Dickens*
Format: Kindle Edition | **Verified Purchase**

I didn't enjoy this book at all. The early part of the book is really monotonous; a repetitious account of ice and bad weather.

Comment

d ☆☆☆☆☆ **A bit too much!**
by *AVFC*
Format: Hardcover | **Verified Purchase**

I couldn't even bring myself to read all the way through. Too much tension for my taste. Perhaps it's just not my kind of book.

Comment

WRITING

Write a review of a book. Include the following information.

- The title of the book and the author.
- The central characters.
- The type of book.
- A summary of the plot (in the present tense).
- Where it takes place.
- What you liked or didn't like about the book.

LANGUAGE FOR LIFE

1 **Work in groups of three. Discuss the advantages and disadvantages of owning a car. Note down as many points as you can.**

2 ▶ 2.23 **Listen to three friends having a discussion about owning a car. Do they mention any of the same points you noted down?**

3 **Work with a partner. Complete the conversation with one word in each space.**

Kayla: Hi, Ryan.
Julia: Hi, Ryan. What happened to you? You're late!
Ryan: Yes, I'm really sorry. I had to wait ages for a bus.
Julia: What's wrong with your car?
Ryan: I sold it! I **(1)** ___think___ there are too many cars in this city.
Julia: Well, that's true, **(2)** __________ a car is useful.
Ryan: I'm not so **(3)** __________ about that. The traffic's awful, and I can never find a parking space.
Kayla: But how are you going to get to work?
Ryan: By bicycle.
Kayla: **(4)** __________ you think bicycles are dangerous?
Ryan: Not really. They're certainly less dangerous for the environment.
Julia: Well, as far **(5)** __________ I'm concerned, *a car is essential*. I have to drive my kids to school.
Ryan: Your kids should walk to school. If you ask **(6)** __________, children don't get enough exercise.
Julia: I don't **(7)** __________ that's true! My kids do soccer, swimming, and tennis – and I need a car to get them there on time.
Kayla: I **(8)** __________ with Julia. I couldn't live without my car. I sometimes work in the evening, and I don't feel safe getting a bus late at night.
Ryan: OK, I see your point, **(9)** __________ aren't you worried about pollution?
Julia: Do you **(10)** __________ what I think? It's not my problem. I can't save the planet.
Ryan: I don't **(11)** __________. Everybody can do something!
Kayla: OK, OK, you're **(12)** __________! Now, let's change the subject. **(13)** __________ did you think of my new TV?
Julia: It's great, but I hope it's solar-powered!

Listen again and check your answers.

4 **Classify the highlighted expressions from the conversation in the following table.**

Ask for an opinion	Give an opinion	Agree with an opinion	Disagree with an opinion
Don't you think bicycles are dangerous?	I think there are too many cars …	Well, that's true, …	I'm not so sure about that.

▶ 2.24 **Listen and repeat the expressions. Copy the stress and intonation exactly.**

5 **Work in groups of three. Choose a topic below and note down all the advantages and disadvantages. Write a short conversation between three friends including some useful phrases from Exercise 4.**

petrol cars or electric cars | living abroad | living with your parents | using public transportation | working from home

Practice your conversation.

Life Skills: Negotiating
Borrowing the Car

1 **What are the golden rules of successful negotiating? Work with a partner and choose what you think are the key principles in this list.**

- direct language
- empathy
- politeness
- listening to the problems of others
- brevity
- no compromise
- flexibility
- aiming for a win/win

2 ▶ 2.25 **Listen to the beginning of the conversation. Work with a partner and decide how best Rob could negotiate to get the car. Write out what he should say.**

3 ▶ 2.26 **Listen to the rest of the conversation. Look at the list in Exercise 1. What went wrong for Rob? Discuss with your partner.**

4 **Role-play the situation between Rob and Rosa and come to a happy compromise.**

MACMILLAN LIFE SKILLS

Collocations

1 Work with a partner. Decide which verbs combine most naturally with the nouns to form collocations.

	action	advice	a comment	a decision	a mistake	an opinion
give	✗	✓				
make						
take						

Check your answers in the dictionary extracts for the nouns. Notice how strong collocations are in bold in the example sentences.

2 Work with a partner. Decide if you agree or disagree with the following statements.

a *Collocation* means the way that particular words regularly and naturally combine with each other. So *have an opinion* is a strong collocation, *own an opinion* is not.

b You should try to identify, record, and learn collocations that you find in English texts or in dictionary entries.

c Learning collocations will help you: (1) sound more natural; (2) be more precise; (3) improve your writing style.

3 Underline the correct collocation in each of these dictionary examples.

a **verb + noun**
The students all ***gave / provided / spoke*** *their opinions.*

b **adjective + noun**
Professor Wright has a ***big / high / large*** *opinion of your work.*

c **noun + noun**
Despite our ***disagreements / differences / distinctions*** *of opinion, we remained good friends.*

d **noun + preposition**
What is your opinion ***by / for / of*** *her latest novel?*

e **adverb + adjective**
It now seems ***highly / totally / completely*** *unlikely that the project will be finished on time.*

f **verb + adverb**
Everyone spoke very ***strongly / greatly / highly*** *of him.*

Check your answers in the dictionary extracts for *highly* and *opinion*.

4 Use the collocation information in the dictionary extracts for *advice* and *mistake* to complete the questions.

a Do you sometimes ask your boss or teacher ___for___ advice?
b When was the last time you o________ advice to a friend?
c Are you more likely to a________ advice from your parents or your friends?
d Have you ever i________ somebody's advice and then regretted it?
e What's the most c________ mistake you've ever made?

Ask your partner the questions.

5 Check your own dictionary. How does it show information about collocations?

ac·tion /ˈækʃ(ə)n/ noun ★★★
1 [U] the process of doing something: *Police say they will* ***take*** *tough* ***action*** *against drug dealers.*

ad·vice /ədˈvaɪs/ noun [U] ★★★ an opinion that someone gives you about the best thing to do in a particular situation: *Ask your father for advice.* ♦ *We are here to* ***give*** *people* ***advice about*** *health issues.* ♦ *I* ***took*** *his* ***advice*** (=did what he advised) *and left.* ♦ *She's* ***acting on*** *her lawyer's* ***advice.***

Words often used with advice
Verbs often used with ***advice***
- **give, offer, provide** + ADVICE: give someone advice
- **ask for, seek** + ADVICE: ask for advice
- **accept, act on, follow, take** + ADVICE: do what someone advises
- **disregard, ignore, reject** + ADVICE: not do what someone advises

com·ment[1] /ˈkɑˌment/ noun [C/U] ★★★ a written or spoken remark giving an opinion: *I've had enough of your sarcastic comments.* ♦ *Did she* ***make*** *any* ***comment*** *about Eddie?*

de·ci·sion /dɪˈsɪʒ(ə)n/ noun ★★★
1 [C] a choice that you make after you have thought carefully about something: *The committee will* ***make a decision*** *by the end of the week.* ♦ *Have you* ***come to a decision*** *yet?* ♦ **a decision to do sth** *Mrs. Osman has announced her decision to retire.*

high·ly /ˈhaɪli/ adv ★★★
1 used before some adjectives to mean "very," or "very well": *It now seems* ***highly unlikely*** *that the project will be finished on time.* ♦ *She's a* ***highly educated*** *young woman.*
2 used for saying that someone or something is very good or very important: *a* ***highly valued*** *member of the staff* ♦ *Everyone we talked to* ***spoke*** *very* ***highly of*** *him.*

mis·take[1] /mɪˈsteɪk/ noun [C] ★★
1 something that you have not done correctly, or something you say or think that is not correct: *spelling/grammar mistakes*
2 something that you do that you later wish you had not done, because it causes a lot of problems: *You're* ***making a big mistake.*** ♦ **it would be a mistake to do sth** *It would be a mistake to think that the trouble is over.* ♦ **make the mistake of doing sth** *I made the mistake of inviting Jennifer to the party.*
PHRASE **by mistake** if you do something by mistake, you do it accidentally = BY ACCIDENT ≠ ON PURPOSE: *Oh no – I sent her the wrong letter by mistake.*

Words often used with mistake
Adjectives often used with ***mistake*** *(noun, sense 2)*
- **bad, big, costly, dreadful, fatal, serious, terrible** + MISTAKE: used about mistakes that have bad results

o·pin·ion /əˈpɪnjən/ noun [C] ★★★ the attitude that someone has toward something, especially about how good it is: *What is your* ***opinion of*** *her latest novel?* ♦ *Professor Wright* ***has a high opinion of*** *your work* (=thinks your work is good). ♦ *The students all* ***gave their opinions.*** ♦ *Despite our* ***differences of opinion,*** *we remained good friends.* ♦ *The book was a waste of time,* ***in my opinion.*** ♦ ***Public opinion*** *has turned against Senator McCormac in recent months.*

From the *Macmillan Essential Dictionary for Learners of American English.*

GRAMMAR

Grammar Extra pages 140-145.

1 Underline the correct words.

- a Has anyone ever **told you** / **told** that you have beautiful eyes?
- b Do you mind **having** / **to have** your picture taken?
- c Have you ever **promised to do** / **promised doing** something and then not done it?
- d Do you enjoy **spending** / **spend** time alone on weekends?
- e Did your parents ever tell you **not do** / **not to do** something, but you did it anyway?

Work with a partner. Ask and answer the questions.

2 **Complete the text with the passive form of the verbs.**

Yesterday two men (**1** arrest) ___were arrested___ in St. Louis, after a bank manager (**2** rob) ________________ . It (**3** believe) ________________ that the thieves used a car that (**4** report) ________________ stolen two days earlier. The car (**5** find) ________________ abandoned several miles away. The two suspects (**6** take) ________________ to the police station for questioning. The money (**7** not find) ________________ yet. Anyone with information about the robbery (**8** ask) ________________ to call St. Louis police.

3 **Complete the story with the simple past or past perfect form of the verbs.**

You'll never guess what happened to me last night! After finishing work, I (**1** go) ___went___ to the gym, as usual. Then I went out to a restaurant with some clients. When it was time to go, I (**2** realize) ________________ I (**3** leave) ________________ my bag at the gym – with my keys in it! Unfortunately, my wife, Kerry (**4** not be) ________________ at home because she (**5** go) ________________ to Chicago for a meeting. Anyway, I went back to the gym, but it (**6** already close) ________________ . So I went home. All the lights were off, so I (**7** decide) ________________ to try and climb through the downstairs bathroom window, which was partly open. Just as I was trying to open the window, I (**8** see) ________________ a light. It was two police officers. I explained that I (**9** lose) ________________ my keys, but they wouldn't listen. They were just going to put me in the patrol car, when Kerry (**10** open) ________________ the door. She (**11** get) ________________ back early from her meeting, and (**12** be) ________________ inside the house the whole time – watching a crime thriller on TV!

4 Underline the correct modals of deduction.

- a Tim's plane has landed, but he's not here yet. He **can't** / **may** be stuck in Customs.
- b There are some gray clouds in the sky. It **can** / **could** rain later.
- c Everyone is leaving the office. It **may** / **must** be the end of the day.
- d The lights in their apartment are all off. They're not answering the phone. They **can't** / **might** be at home.

5 **Complete the sentences in reported speech.**

- a "I'm innocent!" The man told the police that he ___was___ innocent.
- b "I'm not a bank robber." He said that he ________________ a bank robber.
- c "I wasn't in town when the robbery happened." He claimed that he ________________ in town when the robbery happened.
- d "I have never seen Smith and Jones before." He added that he ________________ Smith and Jones before.
- e "I didn't rob the bank." He insisted that he ________________ the bank.

VOCABULARY

1 Match the definitions with the words in the box.

desperate ~~hypocritical~~ insensitive obsessed photogenic unflattering

- **a** to describe someone pretending to be morally good but behaving in a way that shows that they are not sincere hypocritical
- **b** unable to stop thinking about something or someone
- **c** to describe someone who looks good in pictures
- **d** not noticing or caring about other people's feelings
- **e** making someone seem unpleasant or unattractive
- **f** needing or wanting something very much

2 Complete the sentences with the words in the box. There are two extra words.

arrested chase convicted court escorted sentenced shoplifted stolen ~~thief~~

- **a** The police caught the ____thief____ stealing a frozen chicken in the grocery store.
- **b** Police officers ________ the gang to the police station.
- **c** Yesterday, three priceless paintings were ________ from an art gallery in Denver.
- **d** Highway patrol have ________ a sixteen-year-old boy after a ten-kilometer ________ through Los Angeles.
- **e** The witness told the ________ that she had seen the man holding the knife.
- **f** After a long trial, the judge ________ the men to ten years in jail.

3 Underline the correct words.

Dear Mom and Dad,

We're having a great time here in Jamaica.
We're staying in a cabin on the **(1) sandy / southern** part of the island, overlooking the **(2) beach / white sands** of the beach below. We're **(3) surrounded / overlooking** by beautiful forests and have **(4) spectacular / towering** views of the mountains. Some of the beaches are very **(5) visible / popular** with tourists, but our little beach is hidden from the road, so it's completely **(6) unspoiled / packed**. I want to stay here forever!

Love, Alexis

4 Complete the words for features of a landscape.

- **a** a nc i ent r__ __ns
- **b** B__ddh__st t__mpl__
- **c** h__gh-r__s__ b__ __ld__ng
- **d** b__ __lt-__p skyl__n__
- **e** sn__ w-c__pp__d m__ __nt__ __n
- **f** w__t__rf__ll

PRONUNCIATION

1 Look at some words from Units 7-9. Say the words and add them to the table.

~~annoying~~ ~~celebrity~~ ~~classical~~ director dramatic embarrassing experience fantasy insensitive interviewed privacy suggested

A: ▪■▪	annoying
B: ■▪▪	classical
C: ▪■▪▪	celebrity

2 Underline the stressed syllable in each word.

2.27 **Listen, check, and repeat.**

READING & LISTENING

1 Read this newspaper article and decide which sentence (a, b or c) best summarizes the story.

- a Prince Harry is complaining that the paparazzi do not take enough pictures of him.
- b Prince Harry wishes that he could photograph the rich and famous.
- c Prince Harry does not like the paparazzi.

Daily News

Thursday, June 22, 2017

HARRY SPEAKS OUT

Prince Harry has spoken out about his hatred of some of the media. In particular, Harry has talked about the paparazzi who were chasing his mother, Princess Diana, on the night she was killed in a car crash in Paris. Her sons have always been unhappy that none of the paparazzi were arrested or charged with a criminal offence.

In a recent documentary, the prince talked about how his mother's life was dominated by the constant presence of journalists and photographers. He remembers that she could not leave the house or go to the gym without a group of journalists waiting for her and following her. These people often tried to insult her so that they could capture a picture of her getting mad at them. Once, when she was driving Harry and his older brother, William, to a friend's house, she was forced to stop the car because she was surrounded by photographers.

Harry recalls that she got out of the car to speak to them and when she came back she was crying. In the documentary, Harry said that as a young boy he had wanted to protect his mother, but felt unable to do so. Perhaps unsurprisingly, the youngest prince has been involved in disputes with the media himself. He once pushed a camera into a photographer's face when he came too close. He said he valued his private life and gets particularly upset when the media invade the privacy of his family and friends. He maintains that he is happy to be photographed and interviewed when he is carrying out his royal duties and on public occasions, but that he must be allowed to have a personal life.

2 Read the text again. Are these statements true or false?

- a Princess Diana's son is unhappy with some of the media.
- b Photographers were charged with a criminal offence after Princess Diana's death.
- c Harry wanted to protect his mother.
- d Harry once stole a camera.
- e A private life is important to Harry.
- f Harry does not want any photographs taken of him.

3 2.28 **Listen to a radio call-in show. Are the callers sympathetic to Harry?**

4 Listen again and underline the correct option to complete each sentence.

- a Megan completely **disagrees / agrees** with Prince Harry's views.
- b Megan thinks **all of us / none of us** would like to be watched all the time.
- c Charlie thinks the royal family **should / shouldn't** put up with intrusion.
- d The royal family **has to / doesn't have to** be popular.
- e Steven's view is **the same as / different to** Charlie's.
- f Steven thinks the royal family should be **respected / insulted**.
- g Bryn **does / doesn't** think Steve expressed his view clearly.

5 What do you think about Prince Harry's comments? Do you think he is entitled to privacy or not? Work in pairs. Discuss your opinion with a partner.

WRITING & SPEAKING

1 Work with a partner. Look at a news reporter's notes for a story and compare them with her finished article.

John Kronau (25) arrested by NY State Police

- Frightened cashier at Troy Savings Bank.
- Handed her note: "Don't be alarmed – this is bank deposit – please take money out of envelope, put in my account."
- Later said: "It was innocent joke."
- Added: "I've never been in trouble with police before."

25-year-old John Kronau **(1)** ____was____ arrested by the New York State Police after he **(2)** ________ frightened a bank cashier at Troy Savings Bank. Kronau handed the cashier **(3)** ________ note that read, "Don't be alarmed – this is **(4)** ________ bank deposit – please take the money out of **(5)** ________ envelope and put **(6)** ________ into my account." He later claimed that it **(7)** ________ been an innocent joke and added that he had never **(8)** ________ in trouble with **(9)** ________ police before.

Complete the finished article with the words in the box.

a a been had had it the the ~~was~~

2 Choose the best headline for the article.

a BANK CASHIER ARRESTED **b** MAN ROBS BANK **c** JOKER HELD BY POLICE

3 Look again at the notes, the finished article, and the headlines. Underline the correct words in these statements (a-c).

a When you take notes you often **include** / **leave out** short words such as *a*, *the*, *be*, and *have*.
b You usually use **direct** / **reported** speech in notes and **direct** / **reported** speech in finished articles.
c In headlines you **include** / **leave out** short words such as *a*, *the*, *be*, and *have*.

4 Work with your partner. Read the set of notes below and write up the finished article to appear in the next edition of *Internet News*. Write a headline for the story.

- $5,000 stolen from grocery store (May 25), Dallas
- Local newspaper ran story, claimed thief took $7,000
- Thief called newspaper to complain and said: "Maybe store manager took extra $2,000"
- Staff at newspaper kept him busy on phone while police traced call.
- Arrested ten minutes later while still on phone talking to newspaper!

5 Discuss the questions in small groups.

a What amusing news stories have you heard recently?
b Should all news be heavy and serious, or is there a place for lightweight stories?
c Where do you get most of your news from – newspapers, TV, or the internet?
d In your opinion, what's the most important news story of the last week?

READING & VOCABULARY

1 **What is your earliest childhood memory? Ask a partner about theirs.**

2 **Read this extract from a book of childhood memories. Was the child helping her mom?**

Glossary

flap (noun): a fast movement of something in the air

kid around (phrasal verb): behave in a silly way

settle (verb): something drops to the floor or bottom

My earliest memory is of helping my mom change the bed sheets. She used to try and flap the big sheet onto the big double bed and I would roll underneath every time. I thought it was really funny and I would laugh as the sheet settled on top of me. Mom found it funny to begin with and then she would start to get annoyed.

I guess she had lots of other things to do and I had all the time in the world for kidding around! Thinking about it, I wasn't really "helping", was I? But a strong memory of my entire childhood is that my mom was someone who loved me all the time, even when she was mad at me.

Work with a partner and think of three more endings to the following sentence:

A mom is someone who ...
picks you up when you fall over.

3 **Underline the correct particle or preposition in these questions about childhood. Use a dictionary if necessary.**

- a Who **brought** you **up** / **down**?
- b Who **told** you **off** / **apart** when you were bad?
- c Who **worried for** / **about** you when you went out at night?
- d Who **took care of** / **for** you when you were sick?
- e Who **tucked** you **in** / **away** at night?
- f Who **yelled at** / **for** you when they were angry with you?
- g Who **sat up** / **down** waiting for you to come home?
- h Who **cleaned up** / **out** after you had played with your toys?

Think about the different people who helped to take care of you in your own childhood – parents, older brothers and sisters, babysitters, etc. Answer the questions and compare your answers with your partner.

LISTENING

1 2.29 **Listen to some children defining four things from the list below. Which things do they talk about and in what order?**

a a dinosaur
b an iceberg
c a vet
d a robber
e a museum
f fall
g a desert
h a jungle

2 **Work with a partner. Imagine you are explaining other things from the list to a six-year-old child. Write down what you would say. Ask another pair of students to identify what you have defined.**

GRAMMAR

1 **Look at the children's definitions below showing the subject of the verb in the relative clauses. Answer the questions (1-3).**

a A person that (subject) helps (verb) animals.
b It's something that (subject) lived (verb) a very long time ago.

1 In which definition can you replace the relative pronoun *that* with *which*?
2 In which definition can you replace the relative pronoun *that* with *who*?
3 Is it possible to leave out the relative pronouns in these definitions? Why?/Why not?

Defining relative clauses

an adult who **takes care of you**

a child (that) **you take care of**

a toy which **makes a noise**

a toy (that) **you play with**

2 **Work with your partner. Read the definitions (a-d) of words to do with childhood and follow the instructions (1-3).**

a A *truant* is a student who stays away from school without permission.
b A *bib* is a piece of cloth that protects babies' clothes when they are eating.
c A *pacifier* is a plastic object which you put in a baby's mouth to stop the baby from crying.
d A *nanny* is a person who you employ to take care of your children.

1 Underline the relative clauses in each definition.
2 Identify the subject and the verb in each relative clause.
3 Decide which relative pronouns you need to keep and which ones you can leave out.

What is the translation of these relative pronouns in your language?

3 **Pairwork Student A:** page 123 **Student B:** page 127

4 **Work with a partner. Put the words in the correct order to make questions about your memories of childhood. Then discuss questions 1 and 2.**

What can you remember about ...

a to / the school / that / went / you ?
the school that you went to?
b played / the toys / with / you / that ?
c that / you / to / invited / the parties / were ?
d the books / were / in / which / interested / you ?
e about / that / the things / you / worried / were ?
f the things / dream / used to / of / that / you ?

1 What type of word does each question end with?
2 Can you leave out the relative pronouns *which* and *that* in these questions? Why?/Why not?

Work with your partner. Ask and answer the questions (a-f).

5 **Grammar Extra 10, Part 1** page 146. Read the explanation and do the exercises.

READING

1 **Which of the following statements about childhood do you agree with? Discuss with a partner.**

a School days are the best days of your life.
b Children don't have as much fun these days as they did 40 or 50 years ago.
c There is too much emphasis on tests and exam results these days.
d Children are becoming more independent at a young age.
e It's good for children to be bored sometimes.
f Parents should never lie to their children.

2 **Read this text and choose the best title.**

Kids Need To Play | Schools of Tomorrow | Chinese Education

mblog.com

M blog

Thursday, May 25, 2017

I grew up in the United States in the 1950s and I consider myself lucky. It was a time when kids were given a lot of freedom. We went to school, but it wasn't the big deal it is today. Teachers didn't watch over us all the time, and if they saw us behaving badly, they rarely intervened. We wrestled in the dirt, climbed trees in the woods, and had snowball wars in winter – none of which would be allowed today. Out of school, we had our chores, and some of us had part-time jobs such as paper rounds (which gave us a sense of maturity and money of our own) but, most of the time, we were free – free to play for hours each day after school, all day on weekends, and all summer long. Homework was non-existent in elementary school and minimal in high school. There seemed to be an understanding that children need lots of time and freedom to play — if children play, they will develop a wide range of skills.

How times have changed. Just today, the Education Secretary has announced plans to make school days longer and school holidays shorter. The hope is that if students are in school longer, it will raise test scores

to the level of those in China, Singapore, and other East Asian nations. But things may be changing in those Asian countries. The Chinese Ministry of Education thinks children should have less time in school and less homework. The report also said that test scores should be focused on less. Because students spend nearly all their time studying, they don't have much time to be creative or follow their passions. They don't develop physical and social skills in the same way as kids did in the past. In addition, some schoolchildren these days suffer from extraordinarily high levels of anxiety, depression, and stress disorders, which appear to be linked to academic pressure. Unless educators think again, students will continue to miss out on valuable play time.

3 **According to the article which version of these statements is correct?**

a The author is in favor of **free play** / **child labor**.
b When the author was young, teachers **frequently** / **rarely** intervened.
c **Climbing trees** / **Doing homework** wouldn't be allowed today.
d The author thinks part-time jobs give children **a sense of maturity** / **a feeling of stress**.
e The Education Secretary wants to make **school days** / **holidays** shorter.
f Academic pressure can lead to **anxiety** / **happiness**.

What were your school days like? Do you think there was too much work and not enough play? Discuss with a partner.

PRONUNCIATION

1 2.30 **Listen to the words and identify the silent letter in each group.**

- a know knee knife
  Silent letter = k
- b white hour ghost
- c doubt debt bomb
- d castle listen often
- e whose wrist sword
- f psychologist pneumonia psychiatrist

2 **Listen again and repeat.**

GRAMMAR

Real conditionals

If it**'s** fine on Sunday, we**'ll go** for a picnic.

If you **want** to join us, **bring** some food.

Jon **won't come** unless you **ask** him.

unless = if ... not

1 **Read this extract from the article on page 94.**

Unless educators think again, students will continue to miss out on valuable play time.

Complete the second sentence so that it has the same meaning as the extract above.

If educators ________________ think again, students will continue to miss out on valuable play time.

2 **Read these rules about real conditional sentences. Are they true or false?**

- a Real conditional sentences have two clauses: an *if*-clause and a main clause.
- b They talk about "real" or possible situations including threats, warnings, and promises.
- c You usually use a present tense in the *if*-clause – you never use *will*.
- d You usually use *will*, *can*, *might*, etc. or an imperative form in the main clause.
- e *Unless* means the same as *if ... not*.

3 **Work with a partner. Read the following sentences said by a parent to a child and discuss the meanings. Underline the correct alternatives.**

- a If **you're** / **you'll be** very good, I might buy you an ice cream cone.
- b If **you fall off** / **you'll fall off** that wall, don't come crying to me.
- c If **you'll call** / **you're calling** your friends this evening, don't stay on the phone too long.
- d **If** / **Unless** you hurry up, you'll be late for school.
- e If **you haven't finished** / **you've finished** your homework, you can't watch TV.
- f If **you finished** / **you are finishing** your dinner, you can leave the table.
- g **If** / **Unless** you're going to stay out late, take a front door key.
- h If **you're going to play** / **you'll play** that awful music, shut your door.

What age (0-18) do you think the child would be if a parent was saying these things?

4 **Grammar Extra 10, Part 2** page 146. Read the explanation and do the exercises.

VOCABULARY & SPEAKING

1 **Correct the statements (a-f).**

- a If the boss ~~will be~~ is away, nobody will do any work.
- b If you will get something easily, you won't be sorry to lose it.
- c Unless you will consider something carefully, you might fail.
- d Unless you will concentrate, you won't succeed.
- e If you will fail the first time, you might not want to try again.
- f Unless you will make an effort, you won't succeed.

1. You snooze, you lose.
2. No pain, no gain.
3. Once bitten, twice shy.
4. Easy come, easy go.
5. Look before you leap.
6. When the cat's away, the mice will play.

Match each statement (a-f) to a common English proverb (1-6).

2 **Work with a partner. Think of other proverbs you have in your own language(s). How would you say them in English using *If* ... or *Unless* ...?**

LISTENING & GRAMMAR

1 ▶ 2.31 **Listen to a TV show about bringing up children and choose the best definition for pushy parents.**

a Parents who are very liberal and give their children lots of freedom.
b Parents who are very ambitious for their children to be the best, whatever the cost.
c Parents who are very strict and don't allow their children to play or have friends.

2 **Listen again and underline the correct alternative.**

a George and Rachel **agree** / **disagree** about how to bring up their daughter.
b Hayley is **four** / **five** years old.
c Rachel wants Hayley to be a **rock** / **movie** star.
d Hayley has singing lessons and acting classes every **week** / **summer**.
e On weekends Hayley goes to **parties** / **auditions**.
f George thinks his wife is **obsessed** / **reasonable**.
g **George** / **Rachel** is the "pushy parent."

3 **The studio audience asked George and Rachel some questions. Look at the answers.**
Write G if you think it's George's opinion and R if you think it's Rachel's.

a How does Hayley feel?
"She enjoys life." ☐
"She's too young to know." ☐
b What are you going to do when Hayley starts school?
"Continue doing auditions." ☐
"Stop doing auditions. Our child isn't a business." ☐
c Are you depriving Hayley of a normal childhood?
"Yes." ☐ "No." ☐
d Do you have any other children and how are they affected?
"Yes, our son misses his mom." ☐
"Yes, our son is proud of his little sister." ☐
e How stressful is it to be a movie star?
"Very stressful." ☐
"We can cope." ☐

▶ 2.32 **Listen and check.**

4 **The questions in Exercise 3 are direct questions, but the audience actually asked indirect questions. Complete their indirect questions using the question frames below.**

a Do you know ... *how Hayley feels?*
b Can you tell me ...
c Do you think ...
d Could you tell me ...
e Do you have any idea ...

Indirect questions

How **does she feel**? →
Do you know how **she feels**?

Is she happy? →
Can you tell me **if/ whether she's** happy?

▶ 2.33 **Listen and check.**

5 **Work with a partner. Answer these questions about the construction of indirect questions.**

a Do you use *do/does/did* in indirect questions?
b Is the word order (subject + verb) the same as in affirmative sentences?
c Do you use *if/whether* for *yes/no* questions?

6 **Work with your partner. Put the ends of these indirect questions in the correct order.**

a Do you think ... were / your parents / pushy parents ?
your parents were pushy parents?
b Do you know ... in the same city / if / were born / your parents ?
c Do you have any idea ... your parents / how / met ?
d Do you think ... children / too much time / spend / on digital devices / these days ?
e Can you tell me ... are / what / your ambitions for your children ?

Ask your partner the questions.

VOCABULARY

1 **Rewrite the sentences using *make* or *let*.**

a I'm not **forcing her to do** anything against her will. → I'm not …
b She's a kid – **allow her to play, allow her to have** friends. → She's a kid …

Which comment did Rachel make? Which comment did George make?

Choose 1 or 2 to complete the rule.

The correct verb pattern for *make* and *let* is:
1 *make/let* + somebody + *to*-infinitive.
2 *make/let* + somebody + infinitive without *to*.

2 **Complete the sentences with two words from the box so that they make sense. You can use the negative.**

let	made	me	us

a My parents ___let me___ wear jewelry to school.
b My parents ________ do the dishes.
c Our teachers ________ use their first names.
d My sister never ________ borrow her clothes.
e My parents ________ keep my room clean.
f My brother sometimes ________ borrow his MP3 player.
g My parents ________ dye my hair.
h Our gym teacher ________ play outside in bad weather.

How many sentences are true for you? Change the sentences into questions. Ask a partner.

Did your parents let you wear jewelry to school?

No, they didn't. Did yours?

SPEAKING: ANECDOTE

1 2.34 **Listen to Rafi talking about an activity he used to do when he was a child. Underline the correct information.**

a What was the activity?
Martial arts. / Art classes.
b Why did you choose that activity?
I liked kung fu movies. / My friends did it.
c Was it your idea or your parents' idea?
It was my parents' idea. / My idea.
d Did you enjoy it? **No, I hated it. / Yes, I was obsessed with it.**
e How often did you do it? **Once a week. / Two or three times a week.**
f Where did you do it? **At a gym. / At school.**
g How did you get there and back?
My parents drove me there. / I rode my bike.
h Do you still do it now? **Yes, I do. / No, I gave it up.**
i Would you encourage your own children to do the same thing? **No, absolutely not! / Yes, definitely.**

2 **You are going to tell your partner about an activity you did when you were a child.**

- Ask yourself the questions in Exercise 1.
- Think about *what* to say and *how* to say it.
- Tell your partner about your activity.

LANGUAGE FOR LIFE

1 2.35 **Read and listen to four people describing their favorite gadget. Match the conversations (a-d) with the pictures (1-4).**

a

A: It's one of those things you use to massage your head and it feels amazing.

B: What does it look like?

A: It's made of metal and it looks like a big spider with long legs.

b

C: It's a kind of fan that sprays water in your face.

D: What's it for?

C: It's for cooling yourself down when it's really hot.

c

E: Have you seen this fantastic gadget?

F: What do you do with it?

E: You use it to peel a pineapple. You put it on top of the pineapple and turn it until it reaches the bottom. Then you pull it out, and you have a perfect cylinder of pineapple.

d

G: Oh, no, there's an enormous spider in the bathtub! Go and get the spider catcher.

H: What does it look like?

G: It's round with a long handle.

1

2

3
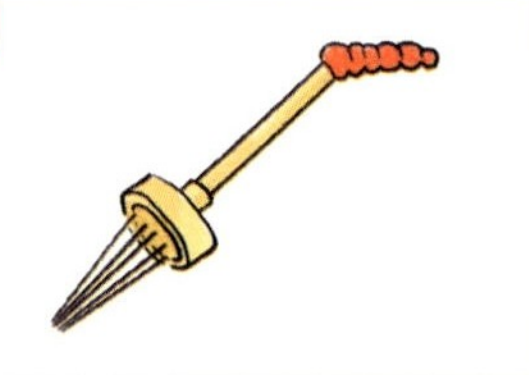

4

2 **Complete the table with the highlighted phrases from the conversations in Exercise 1.**

Purpose: what's it for	Appearance: what it looks like	Material: what it's made of
a *It's one of those things you use to massage your head.*	d It looks like a big spider.	f It's made of ________
b It's for ________	e It's ________	
c You use it to ________		

2.36 **Listen and repeat the expressions.**

3 **Look at the words and phrases in the box. Find three more ways to complete each of the useful phrases *b*, *c*, *e*, and *f* in Exercise 2. Use your dictionary if necessary.**

> cardboard light the gas long and thin plastic recharge your cell phone rectangular ~~removing stains~~ small and square stainless steel ~~storing things~~ straightening your hair unblock toilets

b *It's for removing stains / storing things / …*

4 **Describe your own favorite gadgets to your partner.**

Life Skills: Giving Feedback
Parenting

1 2.37 **Listen to two parents of 3-year-olds talking about giving feedback to their child. Which one had the most positive outcome? Why?**

2 **Complete this list of tips for giving feedback with words from the box.**

> at the right time effect positive behavior possible

Giving feedback should …

- be about **(1)** ________ not personality.
- describe the **(2)** ________ of the person's behavior on you.
- be **(3)** ________, so don't delay for too long.
- be as specific as **(4)** ________.
- be **(5)** ________ and clear.

3 **Discuss:**

How do/did your parents give you feedback? Is/Was it effective?

How different is it with kids today?

MACMILLAN LIFE SKILLS

Word families

1 **Work with a partner. Which word in each list does not exist? Cross it out.**

a disqualify misuse overcooked undernational
b unused misqualify undercooked unemployment
c inadvisable overnationalistic reusable unqualified

Check your ideas in the dictionary extracts. Check (✓) the words you know.

2 **Look again at the dictionary extracts. How do the prefixes in the box change the meanings of the base words?**

dis mis over re un/in under

Match each prefix with its approximate meaning (a-f).

a not = ______
b too much = ______
c wrongly = ______
d no longer = ______
e again = ______
f not enough = ______

3 **Guess the meaning of the following words.**

a discontinue
b misprint
c oversleep
d redo
e unaware
f underpay

Check your answers in your own dictionary.

4 **Copy the table and complete it by putting the words from the dictionary extracts in the appropriate columns according to their word class.**

Verbs	Adjective	Noun	Noun (person)
advise	*advisable*	*advice*	*adviser*
cook			
employ			
	national		
qualify			
use			

Match the parts of speech (a-d) with the lists of typical suffixes (1-4).

a verb
b adjective
c noun
d noun (person)

1 able (ible), al, ed, ful, ic, less
2 age, er, ing, ion, ism, ity, ment
3 ee, er (or)
4 ify, ize (ise)

5 **Choose a word from Exercise 4 to complete each sentence.**

a I'm not a very good (cook) ______ . I don't even know how to boil an egg.
b I hate the (national) ______ feelings that events like the Olympic Games encourage.
c Everyone needs a financial (advise) ______ . They can save you a lot of money.
d I think that experience is more important than a lot of (qualify) ______ .
e I try to (use) ______ any water bottles that I buy instead of just throwing them away.
f I've never been (employ) ______ . Since I started working, I haven't stopped.

Are any of the sentences true for you?

6 **Check your own dictionary. How does it present word families?**

Word family: advise
Words in the same family as ***advise***
- **advice** *n*
- **advisable** *adj*
- **adviser** *n*
- **advisory** *adj*
- **inadvisable** *adj*

Word family: cook
Words in the same family as ***cook***
- **cooked** *adj*
- **overcooked** *adj*
- **cooking** *n*
- **undercooked** *adj*

Word family: employ
Words in the same family as ***employ***
- **employed** *adj*
- **employment** *n*
- **employer** *n*
- **unemployed** *adj*
- **unemployment** *n*
- **employee** *n*

Word family: national
Words in the same family as ***national***
- **nation** *n*
- **nationalize** *v*
- **nationalism** *n*
- **nationality** *n*
- **international** *adj*
- **nationalized** *adj*
- **nationalistic** *adj*
- **multinational** *adj,n*

Word family: qualify
Words in the same family as ***qualify***
- **qualification** *n*
- **qualified** *adj*
- **disqualified** *adj*
- **qualifier** *n*
- **unqualified** *adj*
- **disqualify** *v*

Word family: use
Words in the same family as ***use***
- **usage** *n*
- **used** *adj*
- **useful** *adj*
- **useless** *adj*
- **reusable** *adj*
- **user** *n*
- **unused** *adj*
- **misuse** *n, v*
- **reuse** *v*

From the *Macmillan Essential Dictionary for Learners of American English.*

LISTENING & VOCABULARY

1 **Work with a partner. Think about an older person you admire.**

a How long have you known them?
b What is special about them?
c What one thing would you like to learn from them?

Are your answers similar?

2 2.38 **Read and listen to a radio show about two amazing older people. Match each one to the presenter's comments.**

a You look like someone fifty years younger!
b You must have been completely exhausted!

1

2

Jen: Morning everyone, and welcome to People's Hour. Today, we are talking about age. Let's meet two extraordinary people who are really living life to the max! Firstly, Georgina Harwood: Georgina, you may be 100, but you could just as **(1) unfortunately / easily / obviously** look like someone fifty years younger!

Georgina: Good morning, Jen!

Jen: Now, Georgina, tell us what you did to celebrate your 100th birthday?

Georgina: So, I decided to do a sky dive. I wasn't sure anyone would come and support me, but **(2) easily / luckily / unfortunately** for me, 15 members of my extended family came to watch.

Jen: How did you prepare for the jump?

Georgina: Well, I prepared very **(3) unluckily / completely / thoroughly**. I exercised every day for three months before the dive. And I listened very **(4) completely / carefully / easily** to my instructor.

Jen: Have you always been a risk-taker?

Georgina: I guess so. If I wasn't a risk-taker, I wouldn't be here today – it keeps me stimulated and active.

Jen: And how did you feel during the dive itself?

Georgina: I felt **(5) completely / fortunately / luckily** free and totally relaxed. Of course, it did help being held firmly in the arms of my lovely instructor Dave!

Jen: Any regrets?

Georgina: None, but I thought if I didn't do it, I would **(6) absolutely / probably / carefully** spend the rest of my life regretting it.

Jen: Thank you, Georgina. Now, my next guest is on the line from Japan, Mr Yuichura Miura. Yuichura, please tell us about your big achievement?

Yuichura: Hello, Jen, I can proudly say that I am the oldest person to have climbed Mount Everest.

Jen: And how old were you when you did it?

Yuichura: I was 80, and that was several years ago.

Jen: Congratulations! But you must have felt **(7) unfortunately / fortunately / completely** exhausted afterwards?

Yuichura: Yes, I was tired, but if I hadn't been **(8) fairly / completely / carefully** fit, I don't think I would have made it.

Jen: "Fairly fit" must be an understatement, Yuichura! After climbing Everest, did you take a well-deserved break from climbing?

Yuichura: Yes, I did for a while. My wife **(9) completely / really / particularly** wants me to give up climbing for good. **(10) Luckily / Personally / Absolutely**, I am keen to continue for as long as I can. If I stop, I might never climb again!

3 **Underline the appropriate "attitude" verbs.**

4 **Listen again and check.**

PRONUNCIATION

1 **Practice saying the attitude adverbs in the box and then add them to the table. Underline the stressed syllable.**

~~actually~~ apparently definitely fortunately incredibly naturally obviously positively practically predictably regularly surprisingly

A: ■ ▪ ▪	actually
B: ■ ▪ ▪ ▪	
C: ▪ ■ ▪ ▪	

2 2.39 **Listen, check, and repeat.**

VOCABULARY

1 **Look at this simple sentence structure. In which position (1-4) is it possible to put the adverb of manner *carefully*?**

subject verb object

(1) Georgina **(2)** listened to **(3)** the instructor **(4)**.

2 **Rewrite these sentences in the correct order.**

a prepared / very / I / thoroughly
b free / completely / felt / I
c You / exhausted / must / have / felt / completely
d really / She / wants me / climbing / give up / to

GRAMMAR

1 **Work with your partner. Look at the unreal conditional sentence about Georgina Harwood. Check (✓) the "real situation" (*a*, *b*, or *c*) that the sentence is based on.**

"If I wasn't a risk-taker, I wouldn't be here today ..."

a She's here today. She is a risk-taker.
b She wasn't here. She wasn't a risk-taker.
c She will be here. She will be a risk-taker.

Underline the correct alternative.

When you want to talk about unreal or imaginary situations in the present:
use (1) **the simple past** / ***would* + infinitive** in the *if*-clause;
use (2) **the simple past** / ***would* + infinitive** in the main clause.

Unreal conditionals (1)

Real situation:
I **can't** sing. I'**m not** in a band.
time (present) = tense (present)

Unreal or imaginary situation:
If I **could** sing, I'**d be** in a band.
time (present) ≠ tense (past)

if-clause: simple past

Main clause: *would/wouldn't* + infinitive

2 **Write unreal conditional sentences based on the real situations below. Start each sentence with *If* ...**

a I don't have a car. I can't drive to work.
If I had a car, I'd be able to drive to work.
b I can't cook. I don't invite my friends over for dinner.
c I don't live abroad. I see my family very regularly.
d I go out every night. I'm always tired.
e I don't have time. I don't do my English homework.
f I have to learn English. I can't learn another language.

Are any of these conditional sentences true for you? Discuss with your partner.

3 **Pairwork Student A:** page 123 **Student B:** page 127

READING

1 **Work in groups. Look at the picture, but don't read the poem. Invent an identity for the person in the picture.**

- **a** What's her name?
- **b** How old is she?
- **c** Where does she live?
- **d** What's her family background?
- **e** What has she done in her life?
- **f** Is she happy?

Compare your ideas with other people in the class.

Glossary

PCT: Pacific Crest Trail

whine (verb): make a complaining noise

nettle (noun): wild plant with pointed leaves that sting when touched

If…

If I could live my life over again
I would chill out.
I'd be less sensible, less careful.
I would take more risks.
I would take more trips and climb more
mountains,
Dive from the sky and fly down volcanos on a
tray.
I would drink and eat more.
I would leave a bad job in the city and roam
wild.
I would hike the PCT, hear more birdsong, and
soak up the landscape.
I would notice the good, not pick out the bad.
And take ten deep breaths at the beginning of
each day.
I would live in the moment, every moment.
I would be more carefree. I would think more of others
but Worry less what others thought.
I would say "I love you" more and "sorry" too.
I would chat more and snapchat less.
There would be more time for fun and less for fear.
I would take more time to stand and stare,
I would laugh and joke and smile, not frown or whine.
I would seize the day and grasp the nettle and all those other things
You're meant to do.
I would walk barefoot. I would pick more flowers.

2 2.40 **Read and listen to the poem and decide whether it fits the character you have invented. How does the person in the poem feel about her life?**

GRAMMAR

1 **Complete these sentences for a person expressing regrets. Use the words in the box.**

adventurous ~~anxious~~ enjoy fun over risks sensible seriously

a I wish I'd been less ____anxious____.
b I wish I'd been more ____________.
c I wish I'd taken more ____________.
d If only I'd had more ____________.
e I wish I hadn't been so ____________.
f I wish I hadn't taken life so ____________.
g If only I'd done more of the things I ____________.
h I wish I had my life to live ____________.

Wishes and regrets

Facts (present/past):

I **can't swim**. I **didn't take** lessons at school.

Wishes or regrets (past / past perfect):

I wish **I could** swim.

If only **I had taken** lessons at school.

2 **Write the corresponding fact for each regret expressed in Exercise 1.**

a I was anxious.

Underline the correct alternative.

a When you want to express a wish or regret about a present fact, you use a **present** / **past** tense after *wish* / *if only*.
b When you want to express a wish or regret about a past fact, you use a **past** / **past perfect** tense after *wish* / *if only*.

3 **Work with a partner. Write a wish or regret for each of these facts.**

a I couldn't go to the latest Coldplay gig.
I wish / if only I'd been able to go to the latest Coldplay gig.
b I didn't learn English at school.
c I'm not married.
d I don't know how to play chess.
e I can't play the guitar.
f I'm going on a training course next week.
g I'm studying for exams right now.
h I couldn't swim when I was a child.

Are any of the facts, wishes, or regrets true for you? Discuss with your partner.

4 **Grammar Extra 11, Part 1** page 148. Read the explanation and do the exercises.

SPEAKING

1 **Work with your partner. Think about the possible story behind each of these pictures. Talk about each of those situations. Use: *I wish* ... or *If only* ...**

a

b

c

d

e

f

2 **Have you made any bad decisions today/this week/this year/in your life so far? Talk about them with your partner.**

I wish I hadn't gone to bed so late last night. I feel really tired today.

READING & SPEAKING

1 **Imagine you could go back in time and you met your 15-year-old self. What would you say to them? What advice would you give? Discuss with a partner.**

2 **Read the article about Peter Emshwiller, who has used clever video technology to "interview" a younger version of himself. Why is the younger Peter disappointed?**

If you could really talk to your younger self, what would you say? When he was 18, Peter Emshwiller filmed himself asking his older self questions. He also recorded all the possible reactions to the questions, from polite nods to joy, sadness, annoyance, surprise and horror. Forty-eight years later, Emshwiller, now 66, created a film where he answers the questions asked by his 18-year-old self. The film is called *Later That Same Life*. It's a fascinating film.

One of the first questions the Young Peter asked was whether his future self was "exceedingly rich". Old Peter just laughed and shook his head. Young Peter also wanted to know how things had gone for his family, and in a moving moment, Old Peter simply advised his younger self to spend as much time as he could with his family, especially his father. When he was asked whether he was now a superstar, Older Peter said "no". In fact, Old Peter became a little defensive, saying that he didn't always have to live up to his dreams. Maybe Old Peter was feeling defensive because he felt disappointed, too. If he had taken a different path, perhaps he would have become a superstar. He would have pleased his younger self.

3 2.41 **Listen to the last few minutes of the interview and write the final paragraph of the article, reporting what final questions young Peter asked his older self.**

4 **Work in small groups to write the questions for an interview with yourself in 40 years' time.**

GRAMMAR

1 **Work with a partner. Look at the unreal conditional sentence from the article on page 104. Check (✓) the real situation (*a*, *b*, or *c*) that the sentence is based on.**

If he had taken a different path, perhaps he would have become a superstar.

a He doesn't take a different path. He doesn't become a superstar.
b He didn't take a different path. He didn't become a superstar.
c He won't take a different path. He won't become a superstar.

Underline the correct alternative.

When you want to talk about "unreal" or imaginary situations in the past:
use (1) **the past perfect / would +** have **+ past participle** in the *if*-clause;
use (2) **the past perfect / would +** have **+ past participle** in the main clause.

Unreal conditionals (2)

Real situation:

I **didn't have** a map.

I **got** lost.

time (past) = tense (past)

Unreal or imaginary situation:

If I'**d had** a map, I **wouldn't have gotten** lost.

time (past) ≠ tense (past perfect)

if-clause: past perfect

Main clause: *would/wouldn't* + *have* + past participle

2 **Write unreal conditional sentences based on the real situations below. Start each sentence with *If* ...**

a I didn't see you yesterday. I didn't say hello.
If I'd seen you yesterday, I'd have said hello.
b I stayed up late last night. I overslept this morning.
c I couldn't find a parking space. I arrived late for the class.
d My sister traveled around the world. She met her future husband.
e I didn't learn to drive when I was 18. I didn't have a car in college.
f It rained yesterday. I didn't go for a walk.

Are any of these conditional sentences true for you? Discuss with your partner.

3 **Grammar Extra 11, Part 2** page 148. Read the explanation and do the exercises.

READING & SPEAKING

1 **Work with a partner. Look at these four key words from three different stories. What do you think each story is about?**

1 parking garage, car, money, dropped
2 laptop, posting, kissing, social media
3 restaurant, courses, wrong, check(2X)

2 **Read and complete the texts by matching the words from Exercise 1 to each story. Discuss what you would have done in each situation.**

a

I was walking through the shared **(1)** parking garage at work the other day when I saw a pile of 50 dollar bills on the ground beside a large black luxury car. The **(2)** ________ was a top of the range model with a personalized license plate. It looked like it belonged to some billionaire or a mafia boss or something. If the **(3)** ________ had been **(4)** ________ by the owner of the car, I figured he probably wouldn't notice, as he was obviously really rich. There was no one else in the parking garage.

b

I made a shocking discovery last night. I was at my **(5)** ________, with my social media page open, when I noticed a **(6)** ________ from a guy in my group of ex-college friends. That was OK, but the problem is that in the background of one of the photos from their recent boys' trip, I saw my best friend's boyfriend **(7)** ________ another girl. My friend is not on Facebook in fact she's not on **(8)** ________, so she may not see the picture or find out about her boyfriend unless someone tells her.

c

Ed and I went to our local Chinese **(9)** ________ the other day with a couple of friends. We had a lovely meal with three **(10)** ________, drinks, and coffees. When we got the **(11)** ________ it seemed very reasonable, and Ed paid. It was only when we got home and I looked at the check that we realized that we had been given the **(12)** ________ **(13)** ________. It was meant for the table next to ours and was about half the amount it should have been.

2.42 **Listen and find out what the people did. Do you think they did the right thing?**

LANGUAGE FOR LIFE

1 Look at the useful phrases (1-7) for telephoning. In each case, cross out the phrase that is unusual or incorrect.

1 Hello. / Good morning. / ~~Speak me~~.
2 Is (name) there? / I'd like to speak to (name), please. / Is there (name)?
3 Are you (name)? / Is this (name)? / Who's calling, please?
4 Just a moment, please. I'll try to put you through. / Hold on, I'll go and get her. / One instant.
5 I am me. / It's me. / (name) here.
6 What are you up to later? / What do you do later? / Are you available later on today?
7 I'll look forward to seeing you tomorrow. / To tomorrow. / See you tomorrow.

2 Read two phone calls made by Phil Jones: one to his friend, Maddy, and the other to his bank. Complete each conversation with the most appropriate useful phrases from Exercise 1.

Conversation A

Janet: **(1)** ______________
Phil: Oh, hi. **(2)** ______________
Janet: **(3)** ______________
Phil: Yes. Hello, Janet. How are you?
Janet: Fine, thanks. **(4)** ______________
Maddy: Hello.
Phil: Hi! **(5)** ______________
Maddy: Hi there! What have you been doing?
Phil: Oh, just working. Listen, I can't talk now. **(6)** ______________
Maddy: I have to work this evening, but I thought we could go to the movies tomorrow.
Phil: OK, I'll come over about seven.
Maddy: **(7)** ______________
Phil: Bye.

Conversation B

Receptionist: **(1)** ______________ Northminster Bank. Can I help you?
Phil: Yes, **(2)** ______________
Receptionist: **(3)** ______________
Phil: My name's Philip Jones.
Receptionist: OK. **(4)** ______________ ... Oh, Mr. Jones, I'm afraid he's on the other line. Would you like to hold?
Phil: Sure.
Bank clerk: Anthony Moore.
Phil: Hello. **(5)** ______________
Bank clerk: Oh, yes, Mr. Jones. Thank you for getting back to me so quickly. There seems to be a problem with your account.
Phil: Oh? What kind of problem?
Bank clerk: Well, you've overdrawn your account by more than $500. You really need to come to the bank to discuss it. **(6)** ______________
Phil: I'm busy today. Would tomorrow be convenient for you?
Bank clerk: Yes, that's fine. Ten thirty?
Phil: Yes, ten thirty's fine for me.
Bank clerk: Well, thank you for calling. **(7)** ______________
Phil: Goodbye.

2.43 **Listen and check.**

3 2.44 **Listen and repeat the expressions from Conversations A and B.**

4 Work with a partner. Choose one of the situations below and write a telephone conversation.

a Phil calls his friend Jeff and arranges to meet him this evening.
b Phil calls Smiths Insurance and arranges a meeting with Mrs. Bella Watson

Practice your conversation.

Life Skills: Creativity & Imagination
Brainstorming

1 2.45 **Listen to the notes about brainstorming. Have you ever used brainstorming to come up with new ideas?**

2 Work with a partner. In one minute, brainstorm all the English words you can about your cell phone. Write them under these headings:

features looks materials uses

3 Work in groups. You are the creative team in an advertising agency. Your client wants you to come up with an innovative approach to selling their new cell phone. Hold a brainstorming meeting. What ideas did you come up with?

MACMILLAN LIFE SKILLS

Idiomatic expressions

1 **Look at the dictionary extracts defining some fixed idiomatic expressions – sometimes known as "binomials." Replace the underlined phrases in the sentences (a–e) with a suitable binomial.**

a His English is coming along very quickly.
b There aren't many sandwiches left, so you won't be able to make a careful selection of what you want.
c It's all there in written form.
d Her clothes were lying scattered in several different places on the floor.
e We see each other sometimes, but not often.

Check your own dictionary. Which word do you need to look up to find the expression?

PHRASE **in black and white** in a written or printed form

PHRASE **here and there** in or to several different places

PHRASE **by/in leaps and bounds** used for saying that something improves quickly or increases a lot

PHRASE **(every) now and then/again** sometimes, but not regularly or often

PHRASE **pick and choose (sth)** to choose the things you prefer, rather than simply accepting what you are given

2 **There is one mistake in each of the underlined idiomatic expressions in the sentences (a–f). Look at the relevant dictionary extract and correct the mistake.**

a Di has a young family and runs her own business. She certainly has her fingers full.
b Hugo is hopeless with money. He's over his neck in debt.
c Petra sometimes makes mistakes, but her heart is in its right place.
d Sue is always wearing fantastic clothes. She has one eye for fashion.
e Tim's business isn't making much money, but he keeps his head above the water.
f Boris got a fantastic job straight after college. He really landed on his foot.

Do any of your family, friends, or colleagues fit these descriptions? Tell a partner about them.

PHRASE **sb's heart is in the right place** used for saying that someone tries to do good things even though it does not always seem like this

PHRASE **keep your head above water** *informal* to manage to live or keep a business working even though you are not earning much money

PHRASE **have your hands full** to be extremely busy

PHRASE **land on your feet** to be lucky and get into a good situation after being in a difficult one

PHRASE **have an eye for** to have a natural ability for seeing or noticing something

PHRASE **up to your neck in sth** *informal* involved or busy with something

3 **Use the words in the box to complete the idiomatic expressions (a–f) describing feelings and emotions.**

arms	dumps	minds	moon	stitches	weather

a to be in ____________
b to be of two ____________
c to be over the ____________
d to be up in ____________
e to be under the ____________
f to be down in the ____________

Check your ideas in the dictionary extracts. Think about the last time you felt any of these emotions. Ask your partner.

When was the last time you were over the moon?

PHRASE **up in arms** angry and complaining about something

PHRASE **(down) in the dumps** *informal* feeling unhappy

PHRASE **be of two minds (about sth)** to not be certain about something, or to have difficulty in making a decision

PHRASE **be over the moon (about sth)** *British informal* to be very happy about something

PHRASE **in stitches** *informal* laughing a lot

PHRASE **under the weather** *informal* not feeling well

From the *Macmillan Essential Dictionary for Learners of American English*.

4 **Check your own dictionary. Look up your six favorite idiomatic expressions on this page and answer the questions.**

a Which word do you look for first?
b How are the idiomatic expressions organized?
c What examples are given?

READING

1 **Which of these statements are similar to your views? Talk about your sense of style with a partner.**

- a I love modern fashion and I always keep up with the trends.
- b People shouldn't care so much about their appearance.
- c I like wearing unusual patterns and colors.
- d I wear whatever is comfortable and I don't care what it looks like.
- e I save up for designer brands.
- f I often shop for handmade clothes.
- g I like to stand out in a crowd.

2 **Read the article below. Which of the statements in Exercise 1 might be said by someone who likes vintage clothing?**

Vintage Style

For some people, the idea of searching through old clothes is really not appealing at all. For others, it is heaven. These people prefer to describe old clothes as *pre-loved*, *recycled*, or *vintage*. In these days of mass production and cheap fashion, some people look for clothes that have been tailored or sewn by hand. Lovers of vintage clothing say that the cut and fit of clothes from the 1940s and1950s is better than today's clothes. The clothes were made to last and not to be thrown away after one season's wear. Some of the most popular items are, for women, pretty dresses with floral patterns; silk blouses with covered buttons; skirts and jackets in good quality fabric; cashmere sweaters; and shapely 1940s swimwear. Men usually look for handmade jackets and coats; smart high-waisted trousers that can be worn with suspenders; collarless cotton shirts; and waistcoats. If you are curious about this style of clothing, you will find plenty of choice. Market stalls or charity shops are not the only places to look — you can also find a lot of interesting clothing online now. Check out the clothing bloggers who give useful advice on where to find interesting pieces and how to wear them.

3 **Underline the correct information according to the article.**

- a Old clothes are sometimes described as **recycled** / **retired**.
- b In earlier decades clothing was made to be **thrown away** / **worn** for a long time.
- c **Trousers** / **dresses** can be worn with suspenders.
- d If you want vintage clothing, there is **very little** / **plenty of** choice these days.
- e Bloggers can offer **useless** / **useful** advice.

4 **Look at the two photographs. With a partner take it in turns to describe what the people are wearing.**

Think of a person you know who has an interesting sense of style. Describe them to your partner.

5 **Pairwork** **Student A:** page 123
Student B: page 127

VOCABULARY & LISTENING

1 **Look at the items of clothing and complete the descriptions below. Use your dictionary if necessary.**

a fabulous Mexican snakeskin *cowboy boots*
b a stylish pinstriped ______
c old baggy ______
d a plain green cotton ______
e a red low-waisted ______
f a wide black leather ______
g high red leather ______
h old black skinny ______
i a short-sleeved checked ______
j a long-sleeved black and white striped ______
k a beautiful long purple silk evening ______
l a bright orange turtleneck ______

1 
belt

2 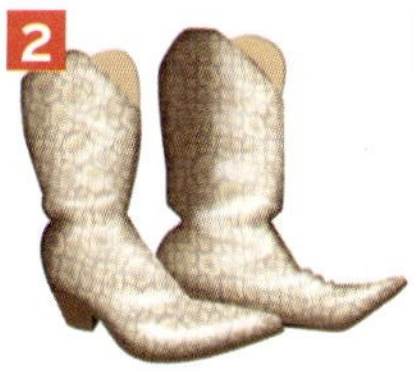
cowboy boots

3 
boots

4 
shirt

5 
dress

6 
miniskirt

7 
sweatshirt

8 
suit

9 
jeans

10 
sweater

11 
jeans

12 
top

2 2.46 **Listen to four people (Al, Fran, Jay, and Brooke) talking about clothes. Identify their favorite items from the list in Exercise 1. Which of the items of clothing in Exercise 1 do you like/dislike?**

1 

2 

3 

4 

GRAMMAR

1 **Put the adjectives describing Al, Fran, Jay, and Brooke's favorite clothes in the correct columns.**

Opinion	Size / Shape	Age	Pattern / Color	Origin	Material / Style	NOUN
1 *fabulous*				*Mexican*	*snakeskin*	*cowboy boots*

2 **Put the adjectives in the right order to describe these clothes.**

a a/an / linen / dark blue / elegant / jacket
an elegant dark blue linen jacket
b a / V-neck / black / brand-new / T-shirt
c a/an / silk / white / expensive / blouse
d a / beige / woolen / plain / sweater
e a/an / fur / old / Russian / hat
f blue / scruffy / suede / shoes

Use three adjectives to describe the most interesting item of clothing in your closet.

READING

1 **Read the description of people waiting for a job interview. Are the following statements true or false?**

- a All the other people in the waiting room are candidates.
- b One of the candidates is wealthy.
- c Three of the candidates are wearing white shirts.
- d The interviewer is younger than the candidates.

You are waiting for a job interview. Your first interview since leaving college. You are nervous. There are three other people in the waiting room. Your appointment is for 3pm. It is 2.30 and you wonder whether the other people will go in before or after you, and who will be successful.

Will it be the guy with a scar across the left eyebrow and sitting with his legs casually crossed? He is between 25 and 30 years old, just under six feet tall, average build, wearing a white, open-necked shirt and smart, grey pants. You notice he is wearing an expensive wristwatch. He has brown eyes and hair, and he also has a tan, probably just got back from vacation in the Caribbean. He is relaxed and confident, at least he appears to be.

Or will it be the woman with the preppy glasses, wearing a floral vintage dress and sensible sandals? She looks more mature than the other candidates, but that might just be her clothes. She is looking round at you and reading something from a file – she is clearly doing her preparation.

The third person is a younger woman, your sort of age, with blonde curly hair. She is wearing blue jeans with a white shirt and a smart navy blazer. It looks cool but maybe not right for an interview? She is biting her nails while staring at her cell phone.

Just then, the lady in the vintage dress stands up and introduces herself: she is the interviewer! She has been observing you for the last half hour. She invites you to follow her into the next office and the interview begins.

2 **Complete these sentences with information about yourself.**

- a I am ________________ years old.
- b I've got ________________, ________________ hair.
- c I would wear ________________ and ________________ for an interview.
- d I come over as ________________ in an interview.

3 **Work with a partner. Discuss the questions.**

- a What kinds of things do you notice about a person when you meet them for the first time?
- b What can you tell about a person from a first meeting?
- c Are your first impressions of people usually right?

PRONUNCIATION

1 **Look at these words with different vowel combinations. Link the words with the same vowel sounds.**

a	/i/	medium	bald	author
b	/u/	plain	beige	fur
c	/ɜr/	tall	blue	hair
d	/ɔ/	third	green	jeans
e	/eɪ/	two	their	suede
f	/er/	wear	worse	suits

2 2.47 **Listen, check, and repeat.**

VOCABULARY & WRITING

1 Complete the information about the man in the description on page 110.

Age: between 25 and 30	Height: ______	Build: ______
Eyes: ______	Hair: ______	Distinguishing features: ______

2 Match the words and phrases in the box to the categories in Exercise 1. Use your dictionary if necessary and find at least one other suitable word for each category.

bald blond streaks deep-set freckles a goatee hazel in her early thirties in her mid-twenties in his late teens just over 1 meter 80 medium messy a mole overweight receding red sideburns shoulder-length slim stocky a tattoo well-built

3 Read descriptions (a-c) of different roles the movie star Johnny Depp has played. Match the descriptions to the movies.

a He has a mustache and a goatee and messy black shoulder-length hair. His eyes are dark brown and he wears black eyeliner. He has a tattoo on one of his arms.

b He's tall and skinny with large deep-set eyes and a sad expression on his thin face. His hair is messy, and there are scars on his cheeks.

c He has wavy black hair with a gray streak in the front and long bushy sideburns. He has dark shadows under his eyes and lines on his forehead.

Now match each of the movies to the year of its release: 1990, 2003, 2007.

4 Write a description of a movie character. Read it aloud. Your partner guesses who it is.

SPEAKING: ANECDOTE

1 2.48 **Listen to Martin talking about a person he met for the first time recently. Put a cross (✗) by the answers that are wrong.**

a Where were you when you met this person? **At a friend's engagement party.**
b Was the person a man or a woman? **It was a woman.**
c Who introduced you? **She introduced herself.**
d What was your first impression? **I thought she was funny and very confident.**
e What did she look like? **She was tall with long curly black hair.**
f Did you notice anything special about her? **She was wearing a turquoise ring.**
g What did you talk about? **We talked about Mexico.**
h Did you find anything in common? **We'd both been to the same place on vacation.**
i Have you seen the person again? **Yes, I have.**

Correct the wrong answers. Listen again if necessary.

2 You are going to tell your partner about somebody you met for the first time recently.

- Ask yourself the questions in Exercise 1.
- Think about *what* to say and *how* to say it.
- Tell your partner about the person.

LISTENING

1 **Look at the pictures of Tony Goodwin and Marilyn Cook who took part in a TV show called *Ten Years Younger*. Discuss these questions with a partner.**

a How old do you think Tony and Marilyn are?
b What differences can you see between the *Before* and *After* pictures?

2 2.49 **Listen to two friends, Annie and Betty, discussing the TV show and check whether your ideas in Exercise 1 were right.**

3 **Make sentences with these words and phrases to describe what Tony and Marilyn had done.**

Tony had his Marilyn had her	clothes eyelids hair make-up teeth	cut and colored. chosen by a stylist. done by an expert. lifted. whitened.

Listen again and check. Do you know people who look young for their age? Tell your partner about them.

have *something* done

She's **had** her hair **cut**.

She **hasn't had** it **colored**.

Has she **had** it **styled**?
Yes, she has.
No, she hasn't.

GRAMMAR

1 **Work with your partner. In each of these sentences, who cut Tony's hair?**

a Tony cut his hair.
b Tony had his hair cut.

2 **Work with your partner. Complete the table below with the correct verb forms.**

	Do it yourself	Have it done
a	I like washing my hair.	I like **(1)** *having* my hair washed.
b	I never color my hair.	I never **(2)** ________ colored.
c	I'm cutting my hair next week.	I **(3)** ________ next week.
d	I **(4)** ________ last month.	I had my teeth cleaned last month.
e	I pierced my ears.	**(5)** ________ .
f	**(6)** ________ .	I want to have my bathroom repainted.

Cross out unlikely or unusual sentences. Check (✓) any sentences that are true for you.

3 **Have it done or do it yourself? Complete the questions as in the example.**

a If your car was dirty, would you (wash) ________ ?
... would you have it washed or would you wash it yourself?
b If your winter coat was dirty, would you (clean) ________ ?
c If your bicycle had a flat tire, would you (repair) ________ ?
d If your house needed redecorating, would you (do) ________ ?
e If your kitchen knives were blunt, would you (sharpen) ________ ?
f If your new pants were too long, would you (hem) ________ ?

Work with your partner. Ask and answer the questions.

4 **Grammar Extra 12** page 150. Read the explanation and do the exercises.

VOCABULARY & SPEAKING

1 **Match the verbs in box A with the noun phrases in box B to describe the kinds of things people do before they leave the house in the morning.**

A	
do	get
have	make
put	read
take	turn

B			
the bed	breakfast	the children ready	some coffee
the computer on	a cup of tea	the dishes	dressed
my email	my exercises	my homework	my make-up on
the newspaper	the radio on	a shower	the TV on

2 **Getting dressed is one of the routine things we must do every morning. Think about how you go about getting dressed quickly.**

a How do you decide what you are going to wear? Do you plan the night before what clothes you will wear?

b Do you try on several outfits before making a decision?

c How often do you make the wrong choice in clothes?

Compare with a partner. What are the differences?

READING & VOCABULARY

1 **Read through these two descriptions. Underline the correct alternatives.**

How I Shop for Clothes

Person A: I really enjoy shopping for clothes. I do it in a very organized way. Twice a year I go **(1) through / out of** my wardrobe and get rid of all the things I haven't **(2) worn / seen** in the past six months. Then I do some research into the latest "looks" for the next season and make a list of all the things I need. I then head out to my favorite stores. I go to the same place for my basic wardrobe items like pants, jackets, and shirts, because I know that the quality is good and the cut **(3) matches / suits** me. I usually buy a complete outfit so that I don't get home with, say, a great new jacket and find I have nothing that **(4) goes / wears** with it. When I need an outfit for a special occasion I go to a lovely place called Xtra Style. There they stock fabulous designer items and I can **(5) try on / take off** as many things as I like and the assistants always have plenty of time to help me find the right thing.

Person B: I like to be well-dressed, but I do not like **(6) trying on / going to** clothes shops. As soon as I get into a store I get really confused by all the choice and immediately just want to go **(7) in / home** again! I often come home with nothing. So, these days I buy all my clothes online. It's fantastic! I can **(8) sit / get** down with a cup of coffee and spend as long as I like browsing my favorite stores. I order items in different sizes and colors and try them **(9) on / off** in the comfort of my own home. I love getting my purchases delivered to my door, it always feels exciting to open **(10) up / out** the packages. If I need a second opinion about how something **(11) looks / wears** on me, I can ask my daughter. She is always honest about what **(12) suits / matches** me. The only downside is having to send **(13) back / away** the items that I don't want, but that's still better than the torture of a shopping trip ...

2.50 **Do you think these are descriptions of a man or a woman? Listen and check.**

2 **Complete the questions with the verbs in the box.**

fit   get dressed   look good on   match   try on   wear

a What colors ______________ you?

b How long does it take you to ______________ ?

c Do you like to ______________ lots of different clothes in stores?

d Do you usually ______________ a watch?

e Do your brother or sister's clothes ______________ you?

f Do you try to wear tops that ______________ your eye color?

Work with your partner. Ask and answer the questions.

3 **Work with your partner. How would you get ready for some of these occasions?**

- a job interview
- a wedding
- a first date
- a long flight
- an evening at the theater
- a Saturday night out with your friends
- a day at the beach
- a Sunday afternoon walk around town

A job interview: I'd take a shower. I'd put on a clean shirt and a suit. I'd ...

LANGUAGE FOR LIFE

1 **Work with a partner. Which of the things in the box do you think people are most likely to talk about at a wedding?**

a politics b the weather c the bride and groom d each other's clothes
e world peace f the enjoyable occasion g current divorce rates h the food

2 2.51 **Read and listen to five conversations at a wedding. Match each conversation with a topic from Exercise 1.**

1
A: Oh, she looks so beautiful.
B: She does, doesn't she? He's a lucky, lucky man.
A: He is.

2
C: What a beautiful day!
D: It is. So sunny. And really warm for this time of year.
C: I know. I don't think I need my jacket.

3
E: What a beautiful dress.
F: Oh, this? I've had it for ages.
E: Well, blue really looks good on you. It brings out the color of your eyes.
F: Do you think so? Thank you. And that's a very nice hat.
E: Oh, I'm glad you like it. I got it on sale – it was a bargain.
F: Was it? Well, it looks like a million dollars.

4
G: This dessert is delicious.
H: It is, isn't it?
G: Don't you want your strawberry?
H: Yes, I do. I was just saving it. Don't take it!

5
I: Thank you so much for a wonderful day. We've had a great time.
J: You're welcome. I'm glad you could make it.
I: Oh, we wouldn't have missed it for the world. Right, Arthur?
K: Mm? Oh, no, we wouldn't. Absolutely. Thank you for inviting us.
J: Oh, don't mention it. Well, have a safe trip home.
I: We will. Goodbye.

3 **Complete the sentences with the useful phrases from the conversations in Exercise 2.**

Making positive comments
a "Oh, she looks so beautiful."
b "________ day!"
c "This dessert ________."

Giving and receiving compliments
d "What a beautiful dress!" "Oh this? I've had it for ages."
e "Blue ________." "________ think so? Thank you."
f "________ nice hat." "I'm ________."

Thanking and accepting thanks
g "Thank you so much for a wonderful day." "You're welcome."
h "________ inviting us." "Don't ________."

2.52 **Listen, check, and repeat.**

4 **Work with your partner. Write a conversation between two people at a wedding.**

Choose from the following options.

- the bride's mother and the groom's mother
- the bride's grandmother and a bridesmaid
- the groom and his best man

Practice your conversation.

Life Skills: Influencing
Shopping

1 **Work with a partner. Think about what influences your decisions when you go shopping. Select the top three from the list below.**

Word of mouth
Press reviews
Internet bloggers
TV advertising
Celebrity endorsements
Friend recommendation

2 **Choose an item of clothing or an accessory you own, and make notes on how you could persuade someone to buy it.**

Word of mouth (e.g. *I heard it was popular* ...)
Internet blogger (e.g. *MyFashDiary calls it one of the* ...)
TV advertising (e.g. *The ad features a famous model* ...)
Celebrity endorsements (e.g. *Alexa Chung was seen wearing* ...)
Friend recommendations (e.g. *Sarah think it's* ...)

3 **Now try to influence your partner to buy an item of clothing. Use your notes from Exercise 2 to persuade your partner to buy the item.**

MACMILLAN LIFE SKILLS

Exploring meanings

1 Work with a partner. Look at the dictionary extract for *suspect* and discuss the questions.

a How many dictionary entries are there for the word *suspect*?
b Is *suspect* more commonly used as a noun, a verb, or an adjective?
c What is the difference in pronunciation between *suspect* as a verb, and *suspect* as a noun or adjective?
d How many meanings are explained for the verb *suspect*?
e Which is the most common meaning of the verb *suspect*?

2 Look at the sentences (a-e). Identify the correct dictionary entry and the correct meaning of *suspect*.

a Do you really **suspect** him of taking your money? = entry 1 (verb), meaning 2
b Dave is a **suspect** in the case of the missing money.
c The officer **suspected** that Burns had been involved all along.
d A **suspect** object has been disposed of at JFK airport.
e His motives were **suspect**. He seemed too good to be true.

3 Homographs are words that are spelled the same but have a different meaning and sometimes a different pronunciation. Match the example sentences with the correct pronunciation.
Use the dictionary extracts to help you.

1
a Just a **minute**, I'm on the phone. — 1 /maɪ'nut/
b The cake she gave me was **minute**! — 2 /'mɪnɪt/

2
a Do you shake hands in China, or **bow**? — 1 /baʊ/
b I love that pink **bow** in her hair. — 2 /boʊ/

3
a I've seen The Killers **live** in concert twice. — 1 /lɪv/
b Where do you **live**? — 2 /laɪv/

Use your own dictionary and look up the different meanings and pronunciation for six more homographs in the box.

close lead perfect row tear refuse

4 Look at the dictionary entry for the adjective *soft*. It shows seven different meanings.
Match the sentences (a-g) with the meanings (1-7).

a I love the **soft** purring noise of a sleeping cat.
b People who seem scary are actually often really **soft**.
c Pasta should be eaten "al dente" – not overcooked and **soft**!
d In a bedroom, **soft** pastel shades are better than bright, primary colors.
e It's better to wash your clothes in **soft** water rather than hard water.
f Cashmere is a **soft** material. In fact it's the softest material for clothes.
g Most parents are too **soft** with their children. Bring back discipline!

Which of the above statements do you agree with? Discuss with your partner.

bow¹ /baʊ/ verb **1** [I] to bend your body forward from the waist in order to show respect for someone **2** [I/T] to bend your head

bow³ /boʊ/ noun [C] **1** a weapon made from a curved piece of wood. It is used for shooting ARROWS. **2** a knot that has two circular parts and two loose ends: *The ribbon was tied in a bow.* **3** an object that you use for playing instruments such as the VIOLIN

live¹ /lɪv/ verb ★★★
1 [I] to be alive, or to stay alive: *Aunt Joan **lived to be** 86.* ♦ *Hippodamus **lived in** the early fifth century B.C.* ♦ **live to do sth** (=live long enough to do it) *He lived to see the first talking pictures.*
2 [I] to have your home in a particular place: *Paris is a nice place to live.* ♦ *They **lived in** a studio apartment in Manhattan.*

live³ /laɪv/ adv **1** if something is broadcast live, it is happening at the same time as you are watching it or listening to it **2** if something is performed live, it is performed in front of an audience

min•ute /'mɪnɪt/ noun [C] ★★★
1 a period of 60 seconds. There are 60 minutes in one hour: *I'll meet you downstairs in ten minutes.* ♦ *A bus leaves at five minutes after the hour.*

mi•nute /maɪ'nut/ adj **1** very small: *The soil contained minute quantities of uranium.* **2** very careful and detailed: *a minute examination of the evidence*

soft /sɔft/ adj ★★★

1 not hard/firm	5 not strict enough
2 not rough/stiff	6 kind/sympathetic
3 quiet/nice	7 about water
4 pale/gentle	

1 a soft substance is easy to press or shape and is not hard or firm: *soft cheese* ♦ *The soil is fairly soft after the rain.*
2 a soft material or surface is nice to touch and not rough or stiff: *I want to get a nice soft carpet for the bedroom.* ♦ *Her skin **felt soft** to his touch.*
3 a soft sound is quiet and nice to listen to: *The engine noise was no more than a soft hum.*
4 a soft light or color is pale, gentle, and nice to look at: *Her bedroom was decorated in soft shades of pink and blue.*
5 not strict enough with other people and allowing them to do things they should not do: *You're **too soft** – I wouldn't let them behave like that.* ♦ *They accused the governor of being **soft on** crime.*
6 kind and sympathetic: *He must have **a soft heart** beneath that stern exterior.*
7 soft water does not contain many MINERALS (=natural substances) and is easy to use with soap

sus•pect¹ /sə'spekt/ verb [T] ★★
1 to believe that something is true: **+(that)** *Police suspected that she had some connection with the robbery.*
2 to think that someone might have done something bad: *He wrote a letter naming the people whom he suspected.* ♦ **suspect sb of sth** *men suspected of involvement in the bombing*
3 to think that something might be bad: *Carl seemed very kind, but she suspected his motives.*

Word family: suspect
Words in the same family as **suspect**
- **suspected** *adj*
- **suspicion** *n*
- **suspicious** *adj*
- **suspiciously** *adv*
- **unsuspecting** *adj*

sus•pect² /'sʌˌspekt/ noun [C] **1** someone who might have committed a crime: *a murder suspect* **2** something that might have caused something bad

sus•pect³ /'sʌˌspekt/ adj **1** something that is suspect might not be good, honest, or reliable: *suspect motives* **2** a suspect object might be dangerous or illegal: *a suspect package*

From the *Macmillan Essential Dictionary for Learners of American English.*

Check your own dictionary. How does it show the information for words that belong to more than one word class and/or have more than one meaning?

GRAMMAR

Grammar Extra pages 146-151.

1 Cross out *who/which/that* when it can be left out.

a *India* is the country ~~which~~ I'd most like to visit.
b There are only a few *sports* **that** really interest me.
c I still have the first *CD* **that** I ever bought.
d I don't like people **who** *don't tell the truth.*
e The person **who** I spend most time with is *my friend Ben.*

Change the words in italics to make true sentences. Compare with a partner.

2 Complete each sentence so that it means the same as the sentence before it.

a If you don't wear a jacket, you'll catch a cold. = Unless you wear a jacket, you'll catch a cold.
b We'll have to go unless they arrive in the next five minutes. = If they ______
c If they don't work, they'll fail the exam. = Unless they ______
d He won't come to the party unless you ask him. = If you ______
e You won't be able to buy that car if you don't save your money. = Unless you ______

3 Write the words in the correct order to make questions. Change to contracted forms where possible.

a know / you / what / doing / Do / are / next weekend / you ?
Do you know what you're doing next weekend?
b you / Can / you / your shoes / me / bought / tell / where ?
c think / you / politics / interesting / topic / is / an / Do ?
d you / born / me / you / where / were / Could / tell ?

Work with your partner. Ask and answer the questions.

4 Complete the unreal conditional sentences.

a If I (be) ___were you___, I (drive) ___'d drive___ more carefully.
b If I (study) ______ harder for yesterday's exam, I (pass) ______ .
c We (learn) ______ a lot from animals if they (can) ______ talk.
d If I (not fall) ______ asleep, I (see) ______ the rest of the movie.
e I (can) ______ call Cleo now if I (have) ______ my cell phone.
f I (not buy) ______ this car if I (know) ______ it was so unreliable.

5 Underline the correct alternative.

a I wish I **could have done** / **can do** more with my life.
b If only I **am** / **was** more interested in money.
c I wish I **were** / **had been** ten years younger.
d If only I **didn't start** / **hadn't started** smoking.
e I wish I **have** / **had** more free time.
f If only I **was** / **had been** born in the USA.

Which statements are true for you? Discuss with your partner.

6 Look at the pictures and underline the correct verb forms.

a

b

c

d

a He **had his hair cut** / **cut his hair**.
b He **had his hair cut** / **cut his hair**.
c She's **fixing her car** / **having her car fixed**.
d She's **fixing her car** / **having her car fixed**.

VOCABULARY

1 Complete the story with the words in the box.

about me　at me　me in　me off　me up　~~of me~~

Sadly, my mom and dad died when I was very young, and I went to live with my grandparents. They took care **(1)** ___of me___ and I always felt really loved. At night, my grandma always used to tuck **(2)** ________ . When I was older, if I stayed out late, they would worry **(3)** ________ , and then, when I got home, they would tell **(4)** ________ but they never yelled **(5)** ________ . I think they brought **(6)** ________ well and made me the man I am today.

2 Complete the text with the correct form of *make* or *let*.

I went to boarding school. The teachers were really nice. They **(1)** ___let___ us wear any style of clothing we wanted and they **(2)** ________ us use their first names, too. Of course, there were still rules. They **(3)** ________ us keep our rooms neat and they **(4)** ________ us do our homework every evening. Overall, though, I would say they were very liberal. They even **(5)** ________ one girl color her hair pink!

3 Complete the sentences with the adverbs.

~~Apparently~~　Basically　definitely　Hopefully　incredibly　very much　very well

a ___Apparently___ , Jane is having an affair with Tom.
b Fay is ________ smart. She knows everything!
c Ruth can play the saxophone ________ .
d ________ , I'll pass my exams and get a good job.
e I'm ________ going out tonight. I need some fun!
f I don't really enjoy academic work ________ .
g ________ , I think I'm fantastic!

4 Put the words in the box in the correct group (a–c).

~~baggy~~　~~blouse~~　boots　checked　~~cotton~~　leather　linen　long-sleeved
plain　silk　striped　suede　suit　sweater　top

a **material**: *cotton, ...*　b **shape/design/pattern**: *baggy, ...*　c **clothes**: *blouse, ...*

PRONUNCIATION

1 Look at some words from Units 10-12. Say the words and add them to the table.

~~adventurous~~　apparently　~~audition~~　~~awful~~　Christmas　develop　~~dinosaur~~　elegant
exercise　expensive　language　pajamas　psychiatrist　ridiculous　talented　vintage

A: ■ ▪ ▪	*dinosaur*
B: ■ ▪	*awful*
C: ▪ ■ ▪	*audition*
D: ▪ ■ ▪ ▪	*adventurous*

2 Underline the stressed syllable in each word.

2.53 **Listen, check, and repeat.**

READING & LISTENING

1 **Online magazine *Blogspot* invited people to describe their lives in about 100 words. Read these three entries. Complete the sentences with the correct name.**

a ________________ will miss her dog.
b ________________ enjoys sailing.
c ________________ was laid off.

blogspot.com

Blogspot

HOME ABOUT BLOG CONTACT search

Gill – I work as a teacher in a high school. I teach Chemistry, Biology, and Physics. I love my job even though it's very tiring and not well paid. I think I'm happier now than I was 20 years ago, when I was in my teens. I used to worry all the time about how I looked and whether I would ever find a boyfriend! I think I'll be even happier when I can retire and do all the things I enjoy, like hiking and sailing. I just hope I stay fit and healthy enough to have a long and active retirement.

David – I have been having a difficult time recently. Unfortunately, I was laid off six months ago and I haven't managed to find another job. It's not that easy when you're in your fifties. Just recently I decided that I need to approach the problem in a different way. I am going to train to be a self-employed driving instructor. That way I will be my own boss and no one can fire me! It has been a very tough year for me and my wife, but I know things are going to get better. I am optimistic about the future.

Carrie – I'm going to college in the fall and I am really excited. I will be studying Engineering and hope to work in the auto industry when I graduate. I have always loved cars. When I was three, my parents bought me a cute little red pedal car and they say that I loved it so much I ate my meals in it! My best friend, Zara, is going to the same college, so we are going to be roommates. I'm looking forward to moving away from home and becoming more independent, but I'll miss my dog ... and my parents!

2 **Read the texts again. Are these sentences true or false?**

a Gill has happy memories of her teenage years.
b David is married.
c Carrie has a best friend called Clare.
d David has had an easy time recently.
e Gill is looking forward to her retirement.
f Carrie doesn't want to leave home.

3 2.54 **Listen to retired businessman Colin talking about his life. What does he regret about his past?**

4 **Listen again and number the events of Colin's life in order, 1–7.**

1 *e*, 2 ...

a He got married.
b He worked in a factory.
c He became a cab driver.
d He started his own business.
e He went to live with Ida and Bud.
f He played by the railroad tracks.
g He had two children.

WRITING & SPEAKING

1 Read Karen's email to an old school friend. Complete the text with the linking words in the box.

After although and ~~but~~ so unfortunately When While who

mail.com

Compose	To: anitamanning@heatmail.com
Inbox	Cc:
Drafts	Subject:
Sent	From: kwilson@madisonhigh.org
Spam	
Trash	

Dear Anita,

It was great to get your email through schoolfriends.com. How many years is it since we last saw each other? I don't want to think about it!

A Life's had its ups and downs, **(1)** ___but___ generally things have turned out OK for me.

B **(2)** __________ high school, I went to college in Baltimore, and studied drama. **(3)** __________ I graduated, I got a job with a small theater group which worked with children in schools all over the country. I traveled a lot, and loved it.

C **(4)** __________ I was working at a school in Detroit, I met and married Mike, **(5)** __________ was an English teacher. I left my job, and we had two children, Perry and Dylan, who are now 13 and 15. But **(6)** __________, Mike and I split up six years ago. Perry and Dylan live with me now, and **(7)** __________ we are divorced, Mike and I have stayed friends.

D I didn't have a lot of money as a single parent, and life was tough for a while. But a few years ago I wanted to start working again, **(8)** __________ I retrained as a drama teacher. I love my job **(9)** __________ guess where I'm working now? That's right, Madison High, our old school!

E I'm getting married in June to a man named Felipe. He's retiring in a few years, and we're planning to go traveling in Europe and Asia when the boys move out. It would be great to meet up sometime. I wish I'd kept in touch with more friends from high school. Do you ever see Michelle or Rachel? I'd love to know what they're doing now.

Best regards,
Karen

2 Match the questions (1-5) to the paragraphs (A-E) in the email.

1 What has happened in your personal life? C
2 What has happened in your school or professional life?
3 What are your hopes for the future?
4 How has your life been up to now?
5 What are you doing now?

3 Think about your own answers to the questions in Exercise 2. Make notes.

4 Tell your partner about your life up to now, what you're doing now, and your hopes for the future. Use the notes you made in Exercise 3.

> After I graduated from high school, I moved to Chile to live with my dad. We were living in Santiago. One evening I ...

5 Write an email to an old childhood friend about your life up to now, what you're doing now, and your hopes for the future.

Student A

UNIT 1: How similar are you?

You are going to ask Student B questions to find out how similar or different you are.

- Use the question beginnings and topics in the table below, or your own ideas.
- Take turns asking and answering questions.

How often do you ...	buy a newspaper? cook? drink tea? eat Thai food? get up at 6:00 a.m.?
Do you ever ...	go abroad? go to the theater? go swimming? lose your keys? stay up all night?

Write down what you have in common. *We both drink tea every day. I never cook, and neither does Student B.*

UNIT 2: What do you know about Shakira?

Complete the text.

- Student B has the same text as you but with different information missing.
- Write down the questions you need to ask Student B in order to find out the missing information.
- Take turns asking and answering questions and write the missing information in the text.
- When you have finished, check with Student B that your texts are identical.

Shakira, singer, songwriter, and dancer, was born in **(1)** ________________ in 1977. Her mother is Colombian, and her father is of Lebanese origin. She has **(2)** ________________ brothers and sisters.
When she was only four years old, she started belly dancing. It was at this early age that she decided to be a **(3)** ________________ .
She has sold a hundred million albums worldwide. In **(4)** ________________ she won five awards at the first Latin American MTV music awards.
In 2006, her single **(5)** ________________ reached number one in the US charts. Shakira has been in a relationship with the Spanish soccer player Gerard Pique since 2011, and the couple have two **(6)** ________________.
In 2014, she was listed as the 58th most powerful woman in the world by Forbes **(7)** ________________.

UNIT 3: How well do you know each other?

How well do you know Student B?

- Write Student B's name in the space provided below.
- Complete the sentences (a-f) according to what you think.
- Ask Student B questions beginning *How many ...?* or *How long ...?* to find out if you were right or wrong.

I think ________________ (Student B's name) ...	**Question**	**✓ = I'm more or less right. ✗ = I'm completely wrong.**
a has been wearing the same watch for ________________ .	How many ...? How long ...?	________
b has visited ________________ continents.		________
c has been living in the same house for ________________ .		________
d has known his/her oldest friend since ________________ .		________
e has read ________________ books in the past three months.		________
f has been using the same cell phone for ________________ .		________

UNIT 4: Phrasal verbs

You are going to rewrite sentences using common phrasal verbs.

- Replace the highlighted verbs in sentences 1-5 with phrasal verbs. In each case, choose a verb and a particle from the boxes. Use appropriate forms of the verb.
- Read out your sentences to Student B, who will check that you have used the correct phrasal verb.
- Similarly, check that Student B has used the correct phrasal verbs in his/her sentences (6-10).
- Choose three of your sentences that describe you best, and tell Student B. Add more information.

Verbs: break find go set take

Particles: for off out up up

1 When I have to travel by plane or train, I like to begin the trip early so that I have time to spare.
2 I'd like to start doing ballroom dancing one day.
3 When I eat out in a restaurant, I always choose something I never eat at home.
4 If I end a relationship with someone, I always stay friends with them.
5 I'm very interested in discovering more about my family history.
6 I get along with most people – I'm pretty easygoing.
7 When I arrange to meet someone, I never turn up late.
8 In an argument, I'm always the first to give in.
9 One day I intend to set up a business and run it myself.
10 My car is very reliable; it has never broken down.

UNIT 5: Childhood

Were you and Student B the same or different when you were children?

- Write six sentences about your life when you were a child, beginning with *I used to* ...
- Choose from the topics below or use your own ideas.

clothes and appearance food hobbies home pets vacations

I used to have curly hair. I used to hate vegetables. I used to ...

Ask Student B questions to find out how similar or different you were.

Did you use to have curly hair?

UNIT 6: Working conditions

Can you guess which job is being described?

- Choose three of the jobs from the box and write sentences about the working conditions for each one.
- Read out your sentences to Student B, who guesses which job you are describing.

This person has to get up early, often has to work with animals, should know what the weather forecast is, can spend a lot of time outside, and probably has to drive a tractor.

A farmer.

artist bus driver chef dentist DJ farmer firefighter
flight attendant gardener hairdresser nanny novelist plumber
police officer race car driver sales clerk supermodel teacher vet waiter

UNIT 7: Experiences

What experiences has Student B had?

- Write Student B's name in the space below.
- Write statements using phrases a–e that you think are true.
- Write questions to check your statements.
- Ask Student B the questions.

I think ________ (Student B's name) ...	Question	✓ = I'm more or less right. ✗ = I'm completely wrong.
a be burglarized *Isa has never been burglarized.*	*Have you ever been burglarized?*	______
b be stopped and searched by customs	________	______
c be let down by a friend	________	______
d be mistaken for somebody else	________	______
e be asked to make a speech	________	______

UNIT 8: Automatic pilot

You are going to complete a text with Student B's help.

- Student B has the same text as you but with different verbs missing.
- Complete the text with the most appropriate forms of the verbs in parentheses.
- Then take turns reading out your completed text and check your answers.

Two pilots (**1 fly**) *were flying* a passenger airline from Dallas to Mexico City, when one of the pilots **came out** of the cockpit to make some coffee. He (**3 have**) ________ problems with the coffee machine, so he **asked** his co-pilot to help him. As the co-pilot (**5 leave**) ________ the cockpit, he accidentally **closed** the door behind him and then immediately (**7 realize**) ________ that he'**d locked** them both out of the cockpit. The door (**9 be**) ________ fitted with an anti-terrorist lock which **was** impossible to open – even for the pilots. Fortunately, one of the pilots (**11 put**) ________ his Swiss army knife in his hand baggage which he **had stored** in a locker above one of the passenger seats. When he finally (**13 locate**) ________ the knife, the two pilots **managed** to break the lock. By the time the pilots (**15 break**) ________ into the cockpit, the plane **was cruising** eastwards over the Caribbean Sea.

UNIT 9: A funny story

You are going to complete a funny story with Student B's help. You have parts of the story already completed, and Student B has other parts.

- Dictate alternate lines of the story to Student B, and write down the sentences that Student B dictates to you.
- Compare your completed stories, which should be identical.

A woman was playing golf when she hit the ball into the woods. She went to look for it and found a frog in a trap.

a The frog asked her if she could release him from the trap.
b ________
c So the woman freed the frog. Then the frog admitted that there was something he hadn't told her.
d ________
e The woman replied that that was fine.
f ________
g The frog warned her that her husband would be the most handsome man in the world and all the women would chase him.
h ________
i The woman said that for her second wish she wanted to be the richest woman in the world.
j ________
k The woman insisted that she didn't mind.
l ________
m The woman replied that she wanted to have a mild heart attack.

UNIT 10: Call my bluff

You are going to read out three definitions of some common English words. The definitions with crosses (✗) are false, and the one with a check (✓) is true. Student B has to guess which definition (1, 2, or 3) is the correct one.

- Complete one false definition for each word. Use your imagination!
- Read out your definitions and see if Student B can guess which ones are correct.
- Then listen to Student B's definitions and guess which ones are correct.

a A "wimp" is ...
1. a person who ________________ . ✗
2. a person who is helpful and sympathetic. ✗
3. a person who isn't brave. ✓

b A "clog" is ...
1. a shoe that has a wooden sole. ✓
2. an animal that ________________ . ✗
3. a person who is not very smart. ✗

c A "doodle" is ...
1. a picture you draw when you're bored or thinking about other things. ✓
2. a small dog with curly hair. ✗
3. something that ________________ . ✗

d A "jingle" is ...
1. a place where ________________ . ✗
2. an illness that is most common in children. ✗
3. a short piece of music that is used in advertisements. ✓

UNIT 11: Dilemmas

You are going to guess what Student B would do in different situations.

- Read the dilemmas below, and guess whether Student B would answer 1, 2, or 3 in each case.
- Ask Student B questions to find out whether you guessed correctly.

a If you were in a subway and someone were listening to loud music from a boombox, what would you do?
1. I'd go over and ask him/her to turn it off.
2. I'd just look at him/her angrily.
3. I'd do nothing – it's up to the management to enforce the rules.

b If you needed to borrow a small sum of money, who would you ask?
1. I'd ask my parents.
2. I'd ask a friend.
3. I'd ask the bank.

c If you wanted some advice about your career, who would you ask?
1. I'd ask my parents.
2. I'd ask my teacher.
3. I'd ask people on social media.

d If you wanted someone to help you choose an outfit for a special occasion, who would you ask?
1. I'd ask my mother.
2. I'd ask a friend.
3. I wouldn't ask anybody – I'd prefer to go shopping on my own.

UNIT 12: Find the differences

Student B has a similar picture to yours.

- Do not show your picture to Student B.
- Ask and answer questions to find the differences between your picture and Student B's picture.
- How many differences can you find?

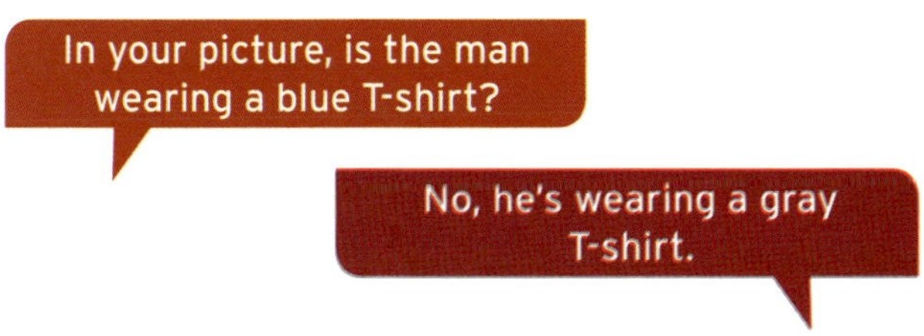

UNIT 1: How similar are you?

You are going to ask Student A questions to find out how similar or different you are.

- Use the question beginnings and topics in the table below, or your own ideas.
- Take turns asking and answering questions.

How often do you ...	buy something online? dance? drink coffee? get bad headaches? go camping?
Do you ever ...	go for a run? make new friends? ride a bicycle? take pictures? watch the sunset?

Write down what you have in common. *We both buy music online. I never dance, and neither does Student A.*

UNIT 2: What do you know about Shakira?

Complete the text.

- Student A has the same text as you but with different information missing.
- Write down the questions you need to ask Student A in order to find out the missing information.
- Take turns asking and answering questions and write the missing information in the text.
- When you have finished, check with Student A that your texts are identical.

Shakira, singer, songwriter, and dancer, was born in Colombia in **(1)** ______________. Her mother is Colombian, and her father is of Lebanese origin. She has eight brothers and sisters.
When she was only **(2)** ______________ years old, she started belly dancing. It was at this early age that she decided she wanted to be a performer.
She has sold a **(3)**______________ million albums worldwide. In 2002 she won five awards at the first Latin American MTV music awards. In 2006, her single *Hips Don't Lie* reached number **(4)** ______________ in the US charts. Shakira has been in a relationship with the **(5)** ______________ soccer player Gerard Pique since 2011, and the couple have **(6)** *two sons*. In **(7)** ______________, she was listed as the 58th most powerful woman in the world by Forbes magazine.

UNIT 3: How well do you know each other?

How well do you know Student A?

- Write Student A's name in the space provided below.
- Complete the sentences (a-f) according to what you think.
- Ask Student A questions beginning *How many ...?* or *How long ...?* to find out if you were right or wrong.

I think ____________ (Student A's name) ...	Question	✓ = I'm more or less right. ✗ = I'm completely wrong.
a has visited ____________ capital cities.	How many ...?	______
b has been using the same computer for ____________ .	How long ...?	______
c has watched ____________ hours of TV this week.		______
d has had ____________ cups of coffee so far today.		______
e has been doing his/her favorite sport since ____________ .		______
f has been listening to his/her favorite band for ____________ .		______

UNIT 4: Phrasal verbs

You are going to rewrite sentences using common phrasal verbs.

- Replace the highlighted verbs in sentences 6-10 with phrasal verbs. In each case, choose a verb and a particle from the boxes. Use appropriate forms of the verb.
- Read out your sentences to Student A, who will check that you have used the correct phrasal verb.
- Similarly, check that Student A has used the correct phrasal verbs in his/her sentences (1-5).
- Choose three of your sentences that describe you best, and tell Student A. Add more information.

Verbs: break get give set turn

Particles: along down in up up

1 When I have to travel by plane or train, I like to set off early so that I have time to spare.
2 I'd like to take up ballroom dancing one day.
3 When I eat out in a restaurant, I always go for something I never eat at home.
4 If I break up with someone, I always stay friends with them.
5 I'm very interested in finding out more about my family history.
6 I have a friendly relationship with most people – I'm pretty easygoing.
7 When I arrange to meet someone, I never arrive late.
8 In an argument, I'm always the first to stop arguing.
9 One day I intend to start a business and run it myself.
10 My car is very reliable; it has never stopped working.

UNIT 5: Childhood

Were you and Student A the same or different when you were children?

- Write six sentences about your life when you were a child, beginning with *I used to* ...
- Choose from the topics below or use your own ideas.

family music school sports toys TV

I used to fight with my sister. I used to like Nirvana. I used to ...

Ask Student A questions to find out how similar or different you were.

Did you use to fight with your sister?

UNIT 6: Working conditions

Can you guess which job is being described?

- Choose three of the jobs from the box and write sentences about the working conditions for each one.
- Read out your sentences to Student A, who guesses which job you are describing.

This person has to get up early, often has to work with animals, should know what the weather forecast is, can spend a lot of time outside, and probably has to drive a tractor.

A farmer.

artist bus driver chef dentist DJ farmer firefighter
flight attendant gardener hairdresser nanny novelist plumber
police officer race car driver sales clerk supermodel teacher vet waiter

UNIT 7: Experiences

What experiences has Student A had?

- Write Student A's name in the space below.
- Write statements using phrases a-e that you think are true.
- Write questions to check your statements.
- Ask Student A the questions.

I think ______________ (Student A's name) ...	Question	✓ = I'm more or less right. ✗ = I'm completely wrong.
a be injured playing sports *Karl has been injured playing sports.*	*Have you ever been injured playing sports?*	______
b be bitten by a snake	______________	______
c be given a gift they didn't like	______________	______
d be invited to a costume party	______________	______
e be interviewed on radio or TV	______________	______

UNIT 8: Automatic pilot

You are going to complete a text with Student A's help.

- Student A has the same text as you but with different verbs missing.
- Complete the text with the most appropriate forms of the verbs in parentheses.
- Then take turns reading out your completed text and check your answers.

Two pilots **were flying** a passenger airline from Dallas to Mexico City, when one of the pilots (**2 come out**) *came out* of the cockpit to make some coffee. He **was having** problems with the coffee machine, so he (**4 ask**) ______________ his co-pilot to help him. As the co-pilot **was leaving** the cockpit, he accidentally (**6 close**) ______________ the door behind him and then immediately **realized** that he (**8 lock**) ______________ them both out of the cockpit. The door **had been** fitted with an anti-terrorist lock which (**10 be**) ______________ impossible to open – even for the pilots. Fortunately, one of the pilots **had put** his Swiss army knife in his hand baggage which he (**12 store**) ______________ in a locker above one of the passenger seats. When he finally **located** the knife, the two pilots (**14 manage**) ______________ to break the lock. By the time the pilots **had broken** into the cockpit, the plane (**16 cruise**) ______________ eastwards over the Caribbean Sea.

UNIT 9: A funny story

You are going to complete a funny story with Student A's help. You have parts of the story already completed, and Student A has other parts.

- Dictate alternate lines of the story to Student A, and write down the sentences that Student A dictates to you.
- Compare your completed stories, which should be identical.

A woman was playing golf when she hit the ball into the woods. She went to look for it and found a frog in a trap.

a ______________
b The frog told her that he would grant her three wishes.
c ______________
d He explained that she could have three wishes, but whatever she wished for, her husband would have ten times more.
e ______________
f The woman said that for her first wish she wanted to be the most beautiful woman in the world.
g ______________
h The woman insisted that that was fine, because she would be the most beautiful woman in the world, and he would only have eyes for her.
i ______________
j The frog warned her that her husband would be ten times richer than her.
k ______________
l The frog then asked her what she wanted her third wish to be.
m ______________

UNIT 10: Call my bluff

You are going to read out three definitions of some common English words. The definitions with crosses (✗) are false, and the one with a check (✓) is true. Student A has to guess which definition (1, 2, or 3) is the correct one.

- Complete one false definition for each word. Use your imagination!
- Read out your definitions and see if Student A can guess which ones are correct.
- Then listen to Student A's definitions and guess which ones are correct.

a A "bargain" is ...
1. something you buy that costs much less than normal. ✓
2. something you take when you have a headache. ✗
3. something you ________________ . ✗

b A "doozy" is ...
1. something that is extremely unusual or special. ✓
2. a place where ________________ . ✗
3. a person who isn't very attractive. ✗

c A "plug" is ...
1. a round piece of plastic that blocks a hole. ✓
2. something that ________________ . ✗
3. a small carpet that you put in front of a door. ✗

d A "stickleback" is ...
1. a type of glue used to stick things back together. ✗
2. a small river fish that has spikes along its back. ✓
3. a gadget that you use to ________________ . ✗

UNIT 11: Dilemmas

You are going to guess what Student A would do in different situations.

- Read the dilemmas below, and guess whether Student A would answer 1, 2, or 3 in each case.
- Ask Student A questions to find out whether you guessed correctly.

a If you won two tickets to go on vacation to New York for a week, who would you take?
1. I'd take a friend.
2. I'd take my boyfriend/girlfriend.
3. I'd take a member of my family.

b If you saw your favorite actor in a restaurant, what would you do?
1. I'd stare at him/her from a distance.
2. I'd go up and ask for his/her autograph.
3. I'd pretend I hadn't seen him/her.

c If you wanted to impress someone at a party, would you tell a few white lies about yourself?
1. Never.
2. Maybe.
3. Definitely.

d If a lazy friend wanted to copy your homework, what would you do?
1. I'd say yes.
2. I'd say no.
3. I'd say yes, but I'd ask them for a favor in return.

UNIT 12: Find the differences

Student A has a similar picture to yours.

- Do not show your picture to Student A.
- Ask and answer questions to find the differences between your picture and Student A's picture.
- How many differences can you find?

In your picture, is the man wearing a blue T-shirt?

No, he's wearing a gray T-shirt.

UNIT 1: Tense review. Question forms.

Tense review

TENSES		ASPECT			
		Simple	Progressive	Perfect	Perfect progressive
Present	+	He **works**.	He **is working**.	He **has worked**.	He **has been working**.
	-	He **doesn't work**.	He **isn't working**.	He **hasn't worked**.	He **hasn't been working**.
	?	**Does** he **work**?	**Is** he **working**?	Has **he worked**?	**Has** he **been working**?
Past	+	She **worked**.	She **was working**.	She **had worked**.	She **had been working**.
	-	She **didn't work**.	She **wasn't working**.	She **hadn't worked**.	She **hadn't been working**.
	?	**Did** she **work**?	**Was** she **working**?	**Had** she **worked**?	**Had** she **been working**?

Question forms

The usual word order for questions is as follows.

Question word	(Auxiliary) verb	Subject	
______	Was	she	tired?
______	Have	they	arrived?
What	does	"collocation"	mean?
Who	are	you	meeting?
When	did	he	arrive?

Wh questions ending with prepositions

When verbs are followed by a preposition, you usually put the preposition at the end of the question.

Where *does she come from?* ***What*** *are you interested in?* ***Who*** *was she talking about?*

Common verb + preposition combinations:
complain about, talk about, think about, worry about; look at; be for, care for, hope for, pay for; suffer from; believe in, confide in, be interested in, invest in; consist of; depend on, insist on, rely on, spend on; belong to, listen to, refer to, relate to.

Subject/Object questions

Q *Who talked to you?* A *Dan talked to me.* (*Who* is the subject.)
Q *Who did you talk to?* A *I talked to Dan.* (*Who* is the object.)

When the question word is the subject of the verb in the question, you don't use *do*, *does*, or *did*. You put the verb in the third person.

Who wants to come? (NOT Who does want to come?)
Which company makes the most money? (NOT ~~Which company does make the most money?~~)
What happened? (NOT What did happen?)

UNIT 1: Exercises

1 Complete the sentences by putting the verb in the tense suggested.

a I (not study) ___didn't study___ English at elementary school. (Simple past)
b I (go) ______________ to the USA but I (never go) ______________ to the UK. (Present perfect)
c This time last year, I (take) ______________ an intensive English course in California. (Past progressive)
d I (not use) ______________ an English-English dictionary before I came to this class. (Past perfect)
e I (enjoy) ______________ watching foreign movies in the original version. (Simple present)
f I (read) ______________ a really good novel right now. (Present progressive)
g I'm very busy at work so I (not do) ______________ my English homework recently. (Present perfect progressive)

Are any of the sentences true for you?

2 The following questions and answers come from real conversations in a court of law. Complete each one with a suitable question word from the box.

How long | how many | How old | ~~What~~ | What | Where | Which | why

a
Q: (1) ___What___ is your date of birth?
A: July fifteenth.
Q: (2) ______________ year?
A: Every year.

b
Q: (3) ______________ is your son – the one living with you?
A: Thirty-eight or thirty-five, I can't remember which.
Q: (4) ______________ has he lived with you?
A: Forty-five years.

c
Q: Doctor, **(5)** ______________ autopsies have you performed on dead people?
A: All my autopsies are performed on dead people.

d
Q: (6) ______________ was the first thing your husband said to you when he woke up that morning?
A: He said, "**(7)** ______________ am I, Cathy?"
Q: And **(8)** ______________ did that upset you?
A: My name is Susan.

Work with a partner. Which exchange do you think is the funniest?

3 Write questions that match the answers.

a My sister likes talking *about movies*.
What does your sister like talking about?
b I usually go on vacation with *my family*.
Who ______________?
c I'm saving all my money for *a new car*.
What ______________?
d He comes from *the north of Brazil*.
Where ______________?
e I'm interested in *classical music*.
What kind of music ______________?
f I'm looking at *my vacation pictures*.
What ______________?

4 Complete the sentences to make them true for you.

a I watched ______________ on TV last night.
b ______________ usually gets up the earliest in my house.
c I normally have ______________ for breakfast.
d ______________ texts me the most.
e ______________ people remembered my last birthday.
f The number ______________ bus stops near my house.
g I had dinner with ______________ last night.
h ______________ people called me yesterday.

Write appropriate subject or object questions to find out the same information from your partner.

a *What did you watch on TV last night?*

Ask your partner the questions.

UNIT 2: Present perfect. Simple past. Past progressive. Comparative and superlative structures

Part 1: Present perfect. Simple past. Past progressive

Present perfect and simple past

You use the present perfect when your context is time "up to now" – i.e. you **don't** say *when*.
You use the simple past when your context is "finished" time – i.e. you **do** say *when* (or *when* is known).

Time "up to now" = Present perfect

The past Now

*I've **been** to the USA twice.* (I don't tell you when.)
*She's **finished** her book already!* (I don't tell you when.)

Typical time expressions for time "up to now":
already, before, ever, lately, many times, never, often, recently, this week, today, twice, yet.

"Finished" time = Simple past

The past 2006 2008 yesterday Now

*I **went** there in 2006 and 2008.* (I tell you when.)
*She **finished** it yesterday.* (I tell you when.)

Typical time expressions for "finished" time:
ages ago, a moment ago, on Christmas Day, in 2002, in May, last week, when I was a kid, yesterday.

Past progressive

You use the past progressive to describe a "longer" activity that was in progress when other past events happened. You usually use it in contrast with the simple past.
*I **saw** them when I **was running** in the park. They **were playing** golf when it **started** snowing.*

Part 2: Comparative and superlative structures

With short adjectives, you add *er* to form comparatives and *est* to form superlatives.
Sometimes you need to make some small spelling changes to the ending.
*nice – nic**er** – the nic**est**; big – bigg**er** – the bigg**est**; healthy – health**ier** – the health**iest***

With longer adjectives, you add *more* to form comparatives and *the most* to form superlatives.
*exciting – **more** exciting – **the most** exciting; extreme – **more** extreme – **the most** extreme*

Special cases

Irregular adjectives: *bad – worse – the worst; good – better – the best*
Some two-syllable adjectives can end in *er* and *est*.
Common examples: *happy, gentle, narrow, quiet, simple.*
*My sister is much **happier** than me. She's **the happiest** person I know.*

For some compound adjectives, you change the first part of the compound.
***good**-looking – **better**-looking – **the best**-looking*
***bad**-tempered – **worse**-tempered – **the worst**-tempered*
***long**-running – **longer**-lasting – **the longest**-lasting*

Comparative adjectives

You use comparative adjectives to compare people/things with other people/things. You can use *way, much, a little bit, a lot,* or *slightly* to modify comparisons.
*Motor racing is **way more** exciting **than** golf. A rugby field is **slightly bigger than** a soccer field.*

You use *not as ... as* to make negative comparisons. You can use *nearly* or *quite* to modify negative comparisons.
*Golf is**n't nearly as exciting as** motor racing. A soccer field isn**'t quite as big as** a rugby field.*

Superlative adjectives

You use superlative adjectives to compare people/things with all the other people/things in their group.
*The NY Yankees are **the most successful** baseball team.*

UNIT 2: Exercises

Part 1

1 Complete the sentences with the present perfect or the simple past.

- **a** I (not go) haven't been to the gym recently.
- **b** I (never break) ________________ a bone.
- **c** My mom (call) ________________ me a few hours ago.
- **d** I (not see) ________________ my friends much lately.
- **e** I (already book) ________________ next year's vacation.
- **f** I (hate) ________________ swimming when I was a kid.
- **g** My great-grandfather (do) ________________ military service.
- **h** I (not finish) ________________ this exercise yet.

Check (✓) the sentences that are true for you. Rewrite the sentences as questions. Ask your partner.

a *Have you been to the gym recently?*

2 What time is it now? Complete the sentences to say what you were doing at these times in the past.

- **a** This time yesterday ...
- **b** This time last Sunday ...
- **c** This time last week ...
- **d** This time last year ...
- **e** This time ten years ago ...
- **f** This time twenty years ago ...

3 Read the story. The verbs (1-12) are all in the past progressive. Change them to the simple past if necessary.

The most exciting experience I ever had was at Disney World in Florida. I was on vacation with my family, and we **(1) were celebrating** my parents' 25th wedding anniversary. It was a typical Florida day – the sky was blue, the sun **(2) was shining**, and everybody **(3) was having** a great time.
As I watched the roller coaster, I thought to myself, "Those people must be crazy." Just then, my brother **(4) was coming** up to me. He **(5) was holding** two passes. "I'm going on the roller coaster," he said, "and you're coming, too." I've never done anything dangerous or exciting in my life. So I don't know why I **(6) was agreeing** to go on the roller coaster, but five minutes later I **(7) was holding** onto my seat, 35 meters in the air, sure that I was about to die. The ride **(8) was seeming** to go on forever. But finally it **(9) was stopping**, and we got off. My head was spinning, but I felt really happy. Maybe I was just glad to be alive! Later, we looked at the pictures from the day. The roller coaster pictures were hilarious. Everybody **(10) was laughing** and waving their arms in the air. That is, everybody except me! I was holding on, and **(11) was screaming**. I've never been so terrified in my life, but I'm glad I **(12) was doing** it.

Part 2

1 Write the comparative and superlative forms of the adjectives in the box.

athletic	badly dressed	big	extreme	gentle
good-looking	healthy	intelligent	popular	well-paid

athletic – more athletic – the most athletic

2 Write comparative sentences using the words in parentheses.

- **a** Skydiving / extreme / ping pong (much)
  Skydiving is much more extreme than ping pong.
- **b** Soccer players / well-paid / squash players (way)
- **c** A basketball / big / a volleyball (a little bit)
- **d** Tennis / popular / judo (slightly)
- **e** Cyclists / athletic / golfers (much)
- **f** Surfers / good-looking / boxers (a lot)

Rewrite the sentences (a-f) with *nearly* or *quite* so they have the same meaning.

a *Ping pong isn't nearly as extreme as skydiving.*

3 Choose six different superlative adjectives from Exercise 1 to describe people you know.

My Uncle David is by far the healthiest person I know.

Read your sentences to a partner. Tell your partner more about each person you describe.

UNIT 3: Present perfect: simple and progressive

The present perfect always shows a connection between the past and the present. It can describe the following.

1 A *finished* action (or actions) that happened in time "up to now." You don't say *when* it happened. (Usually the simple form.)
*She**'s run** several marathons.*
***Have** you ever **swum** in the ocean?*

2 An *unfinished* action (or actions) that started in the past and continues now. (Usually present perfect progressive.)
*It**'s been raining** all day.*
*I**'ve been learning** English since 2008.*
***Have** you **been** waiting long?*

3 An *unfinished* state that started in the past and continues now. (Usually the simple form.)
*I**'ve known** Tim for ages.*
She's been here since yesterday.
*How long **have** you **had** that car?*

Dynamic and stative meanings: "actions" and "states"

Most verbs have dynamic meanings. They describe actions: something "happens." When you want to describe an unfinished action – i.e. one that started in the past and continues now – you usually use the present perfect progressive.
*I**'ve been staying** with friends.*
*What **have** you **been doing** all day?*

Note: You can sometimes use the simple form to indicate unchanging, "permanent" situations.
Compare:
I've been working here for a few weeks. (temporary)
I've worked here since I left school. (permanent)

Some verbs connected with knowledge, emotion, or possession have stative meanings. They describe states: nothing "happens." When you want to describe an unfinished state – i.e. one that started in the past and continues now – you can't use the present perfect progressive.
You have to use the simple form.
*I**'ve had** the flu for a few days.* (NOT ~~I've been having ...~~)
She's known him a long time. (NOT ~~She's been knowing ...~~)

Common verbs that often have stative meanings:
admire, adore, appear, be, believe, belong, concern, consist, contain, deserve, detest, dislike, doubt, envy, exist, fit, hate, have, hear, know, like, love, matter, mean, owe, own, possess, prefer, realize, recognize, remember, resemble, see, seem, sound, smell, surprise, understand, want, wish.

Some verbs can have both stative and dynamic meanings.
*Bob **has had** that car since it was new.* (*have* = stative meaning)
He's been having some problems with it recently. (*have* = dynamic meaning)

for* and *since
for (+ "a period of time") and *since* (+ "a point in time") are two ways of saying the same thing. You often use them with the present perfect when talking about unfinished actions or states.

You use *for* when you give the **length** of the time: ***for** a few hours* / ***for** three months* / ***for** ages*.
You use *since* when you give the **beginning** of the time: ***since** Sunday* / ***since** I graduated from college* / ***since** 2005*.

been is the past participle of *be*, but you can also use it as a past participle of *go*.
Compare:
He's been to the gym. = He went and came back.
He's gone to the gym. = He went and is at the gym now.

UNIT 3: Exercises

1 Complete the table with the words in the box.

~~2002~~ ~~a while~~ ages I was born I was ten last week March
Monday my birthday nearly six months several hours three o'clock three years

for	a while
since	2002

2 Put the verbs into the present perfect simple or progressive and complete the sentences to make them true for you.

a I (go) 've been going to the same hairdresser for ...
b I (go) ________________ to the same dentist since ...
c I (have) ________________ my TV for ...
d I (study) ________________ English since ...
e I (do) ________________ the same job for ...
f I (know) ________________ my oldest friend since ...
g I (use) ________________ the same English dictionary for ...
h I (sit) ________________ in this chair for ...

Write questions for the sentences (a-h) with *How long / you ...?*

a How long have you been going to the same hairdresser?

Ask your partner the questions.

3 Complete the sentences with *gone* or *been*.

a It's been really hot today.
b I've ________________ to the gym. I feel really tired.
c I had a headache earlier, but it's ________________ now.
d The teacher will be back soon. She's ________________ to get some books.
e My parents are away. They've ________________ abroad.
f I haven't ________________ on vacation for ages!
g I've never ________________ to Africa.
h I haven't ________________ very busy recently.

In which sentences is *been* the past participle of *go*?

Check (✓) any sentences that are true for you.

4 Complete the questions with the simple past, present perfect, or present perfect progressive.

a How many times / go to the USA?
How many times have you been to the USA?
b How long / live at the same address?
c Which elementary school / go to?
d When / learn to ride a bike?
e How many Harry Potter books / read?
f How long / go to the same doctor?
g What time / get up?
h Where / have lunch?

Ask your partner the questions.

5 Read these sentence pairs and choose the correct ending in each case. Discuss your choices with a partner.

1 a I've known my teacher **for a long time** / **very well**.
b I know my teacher **for a long time** / **very well**.

2 a I've been going to a yoga class **for years** / **this evening**.
b I'm going to a yoga class **for years** / **this evening**.

3 a I've lived in this apartment **since I was a child** / **right now**.
b I live in this apartment **since I was a child** / **right now**.

Are any of the sentences true for you?

UNIT 4: Future forms

Will ('ll), *(be) going to*, and the present progressive are three common forms used to talk about the future. Each one tells you something different about what happened at, or before, the moment of speaking.

will ('ll)

You can use *will ('ll)* to show that the future event is the result of a spontaneous decision made at the moment of speaking.

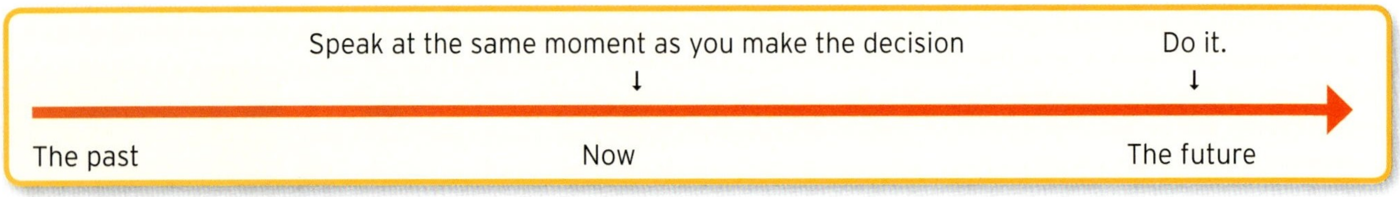

***I'll talk** to the teacher tomorrow.* (The teacher doesn't know about this. I have made my decision to talk to him while I have been speaking.)
*What **will** you **do** after college?* (My assumption is that you haven't thought about this much before or that you haven't made any plans.)

will can be used to make promises and offers.
*Don't worry. I **won't** tell anyone.*
It's hot in here. I'll turn off the heat.
*I'**ll** help you carry your bags.*

will can also be used to make predictions.
*I think we'**ll** arrive at about 10:00 p.m.*

(be) going to

You can use *(be) going to* to talk about your future plans or intentions. You have made a decision about a future event and you are talking about that decision.

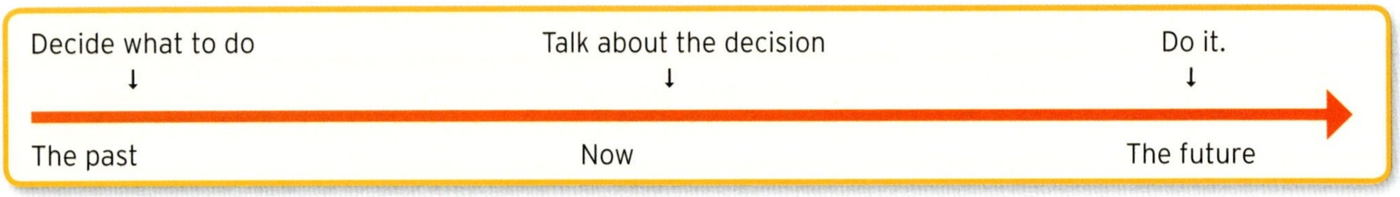

*I'**m going to** talk to the teacher tomorrow.* (The teacher does not necessarily know about this yet. But I have thought about it and I intend to talk to him.)
*What **are** you **going to** do after college?* (My assumption is that you have thought about it and may have some plans.)

(be) going to is also used to make predictions based on present evidence.
It's going to rain. (There are lots of black clouds in the sky.)
She's going to win. (She is 100 meters ahead of all the other runners.)

Present progressive

You can use the present progressive to talk about future arrangements. You have arranged a future event and you are talking about that arrangement.

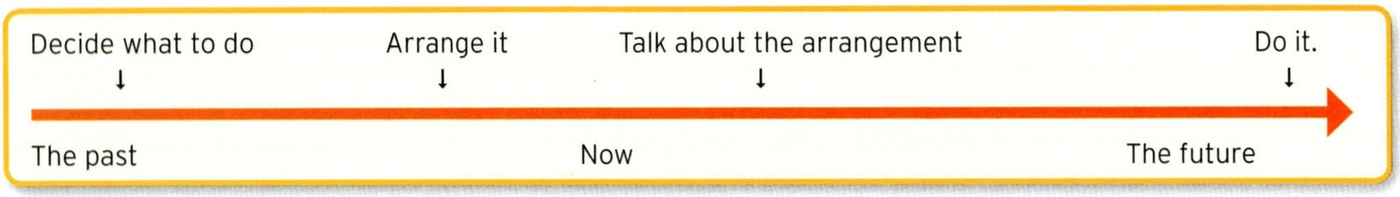

I'm talking to the teacher tomorrow. (The teacher knows about this because I called him to make an appointment.)
*What **are** you **doing** after college?* (My assumption is that you know what you are doing and you have already made some arrangements.)

UNIT 4: Exercises

1 Match each sentence (a-h) to the best explanation (1-3) according to the future form used.

- a We're having a big family party on Friday. 3
- b My cousins are coming from Florida.
- c Ben's bringing his girlfriend.
- d I'm going to invite the neighbors too.
- e Oh, no! I forgot to tell Brad and Lisa – I'll call them.
- f Mom's making all the food.
- g I'm going to do all the shopping tomorrow.
- h I'll make a list of what we need.

1 The speaker is making a decision as he/she speaks.
2 The speaker is talking about a decision he/she has made.
3 The speaker is talking about an arrangement.

2 Help your friend to prepare for a party. Write offers using *will* and the verbs in parentheses.

- a I've got so much to do! (give a hand) I'll give you a hand.
- b I've washed the glasses. (dry)
- c It's way too hot in here. (open / window)
- d I can't move this table. (help)
- e The phone's ringing. (answer)
- f There's someone at the door. (get it)

3 Read the conversations and underline the most appropriate future form.

a **A:** Conor, your room's still a mess, and Grandma **(1) 's arriving** / **'ll arrive** tomorrow.
B: OK, I told you this morning – I'm **(2) going to clean** / **cleaning** it today.
A: I want you to do it now!
B: OK, OK, I **(3) 'll do** / **'m doing** it in five minutes.

b **A:** Not again! That phone never stops ringing!
B: I **(4) 'm going to get** / **'ll get it**. Hello? Just a moment, please. Andy, it's for you.
A: OK, I **(5) 'm taking** / **'ll take** it in my office.

c **A:** You've been late four times this week and you haven't done your homework for two weeks. I'm **(6) going to call** / **calling** your parents to discuss the matter with them.
B: No, please don't. I **(7) 'm buying** / **'ll buy** a new alarm clock today and I **(8) 'll do** / **'m going to do** my homework every night from now on, I promise.

d **A:** What **(9) will you do** / **are you doing** this afternoon?
B: Oh, I **(10) 'm having** / **'ll have** lunch with Scarlett Johansson, then I **(11) 'll probably play** / **'m probably going to play** a few rounds of golf, followed by a massage, a jacuzzi, and champagne cocktails.
A: What?
B: Well, what do you think I **(12) 'll do!** / **'m doing!** I'm at work, of course!

Who is speaking? Match the people with the conversations.

1 Two work colleagues.
2 A teacher and pupil.
3 A mother and son.
4 Two friends.

4 Choose an appropriate future form to complete these sentences.

- a When I'm older I (travel) 'm going to travel around the world.
- b I (play) ________ soccer this weekend. It's an important game.
- c My friend (get married) ________ in July. It (probably be) ________ really hot.
- d I don't have any plans this evening. I think I (just stay in) ________ .
- e I (do) ________ some shopping after class. I need to get some food.
- f I (not pass) ________ my exam because I haven't studied enough.

Are any of these statements true for you?

UNIT 5: Nouns and quantity expressions

Nouns

Countable nouns

Most nouns in English are countable. They have a singular and a plural form. You can use *a/an* and numbers with them.

Regular forms:	*an apple / apples a box / boxes a city / cities a leaf / leaves*
Irregular forms:	*a child / children a foot / feet a man / men a person / people a tooth / teeth a woman / women*

You use the plural form when you are talking in general.
Children love candy and chocolate.   *I love big cities.*

a or *an*?

You use *a* before a consonant sound: ***a*** *dollar,* ***a*** *euro,* ***a*** *hotel,* ***a*** *useful knife,* ***a*** *one-way street.*
You use *an* before a vowel sound: ***an*** *umbrella,* ***an*** *egg,* ***an*** *omelet,* ***an*** *MBA,* ***an*** *hour.*

Uncountable nouns

Some nouns in English are uncountable. Most only have a singular form. You can't use *a/an* or put a number in front of them.

He played wonderful music. (NOT He played a wonderful music.)
We had fantastic weather. (NOT ~~We had a fantastic weather.~~)

Common uncountable nouns that are countable in other languages:
advice, architecture, baggage, food, furniture, hair, homework, information, knowledge, love, machinery, money, music, news, progress, research, traffic, transportation, travel, weather, work.

Plural nouns

Some nouns are always plural and don't have a singular form. You can't use *a/an* or put a number in front of them.
I have some pink jeans. (NOT ~~I have a pink jeans.~~)
Common plural nouns: *clothes, glasses, jeans, pajamas, pants, scissors, shorts, sunglasses.*

Uncountable nouns that can be countable

Some uncountable nouns can be countable depending on the meaning in context.
Glass *is a useful material.* (Uncountable: glass as a material.)
Can I have a clean ***glass****?* (Countable: an individual object.)

Quantity expressions

These are ways you can talk about quantity if you can't or don't want to use an exact number.
With countable nouns: *(only) a few / not many / a couple of / several / How many ...?*
Only ***a few*** *people came.*
How ***many*** *text messages do you get every day?*

With uncountable nouns: *(only) a little / not much / a little bit of / How much ...?*
There's a ***little*** *tea left but no milk.*
How ***much*** *information do you have?*

With countable and uncountable nouns: *none / not any / some / a lot of / lots of / plenty of*
She has ***a lot of*** *friends.*
He didn't give me ***any*** *advice.*

too much/many and *not enough*

too + *much/many* (+ noun) = more than you need.
not enough (+ noun) = less than you need.
I have ***too much*** *work and* ***not enough*** *time.*
There are ***too many*** *cars and* ***not enough*** *buses.*

UNIT 5: Exercises

1 Complete the noun phrases with:

- *a/an* and *C* for singular countable nouns
- nothing (-) and *P* for plural countable nouns
- nothing (-) and *U* for uncountable nouns.

Use a dictionary if necessary.

a advice *U*
b *an* eggplant *C*
c baggage
d furniture
e hair
f homework
g information
h jeans
i justice
j knowledge
k luck
l machinery
m orange
n pants
o progress
p rice
q spaghetti
r suggestion
s traffic
t travel
u user
v veal
w weather
x wine

2 Translate the nouns in Exercise 1. Put a cross (✗) next to any nouns that are countable in your language and uncountable in English.

Write an example sentence in your own language for the nouns with a cross. Translate your sentences into English.

3 Underline the only possible noun to complete each sentence.

a I usually wear a **jeans** / **glasses** / **watch** / **black socks**.
b Today I'm wearing a **pants** / **jacket** / **black boots** / **contact lenses**.
c I always carry a **scissors** / **sunglasses** / **comb** / **money** in my bag.
d I've transported a **furniture** / **refrigerator** / **baggage** / **sports equipment** in my car.
e I had a good **food** / **luck** / **idea** / **advice** at work today.
f My best friend has a very nice **manners** / **clothes** / **house** / **hair**.
g Last week I finished a difficult **work** / **research** / **training** / **book**.
h I heard a good **interview** / **music** / **news** / **information** on the radio this morning.

Are any of the sentences true for you?

Use some of the other nouns to write eight more sentences that are true for you. Change the grammar where necessary.

I usually wear jeans.
I always carry a pair of scissors …
I had some good food …

4 Check (✓) the nouns in the box that you can use to complete both question *a* and question *b*.

beer ✓ bread coffee cola flour honey
meat pasta rice tea yogurt

a Do we have any ________________?
b Would you like a ________________?

5 Read the problems that Sally and Jimmy had when they went out for dinner. Cross out the incorrect word in each sentence.

a There wasn't **enough** / ~~**some**~~ / **any** salt in her omelet.
b There was **some** / **a slice of** / **a few** ham in her vegetarian salad.
c **A few** / **Several** / **A little** of his fries were burned.
d There were **hardly any** / **much** / **not many** desserts they liked on the menu.
e It was really noisy because there were **so much** / **so many** / **lots of** people.
f He didn't have **any** / **enough** / **some** cash to pay for the meal.
g There were **no** / **very few** / **any** taxis outside when they left.
h He had never had **some** / **any** / **so many** problems in this restaurant before.

UNIT 6: Prepositions of time. Modals of obligation and permission

Part 1: Prepositions of time

Prepositions	Examples
AT + a specific time of day	**at** five o'clock, **at** 3:45 p.m., **at** lunchtime Some other expressions: **at** night, **at** noon
ON + a day, part of a day, or date	**on** Tuesday, **on** Friday evening, **on** January 1, **on** the weekend
IN + a period of time	**in** the evening, **in** December, **in** the summer, **in** the sixties

in, during, **and *for***

You use *in* or *during* to talk about **when** something happens inside a particular period of time.
You use *for* to talk about **how long** something lasts.
*Eva went to Texas **in/during** the summer.*
*Eva went to Texas **for** two weeks.* (NOT ... ~~during two weeks~~)

If the "period of time" is expressed as an event, activity, or experience, you use *during*.
*She called me **during** the meeting.* (NOT ... ~~in the meeting~~)
*He told me the story **during** the flight.* (NOT ... ~~in the flight~~)

Part 2: Modals of obligation and permission

It's necessary	It's not necessary	It's permitted	It's not permitted
have to must need to should	don't have to don't need to	can	can't mustn't shouldn't

***must* and *have to*: similar meanings**

Must suggests personal obligation – it's necessary because the speaker thinks it is.
Have to suggests external obligation – it's necessary because of a rule or an arrangement.
*I have a terrible toothache. I **must** go to the dentist.*
*I can't come to class tomorrow. I **have to** go to the dentist.*

When you are not sure, use *have to*: it's always correct.

***must* and *should*: similar meanings**

Must and *should* suggest personal obligation – it's necessary because the speaker thinks it is.
You can use them to give advice. *Must* is much stronger than *should*.
*You **must** try and finish this report today.* (It's more than two weeks late!)
*You **should** try and finish this report today.* (You'll feel better if you do.)

***mustn't* and *don't have to*: different meanings**

Mustn't means you are not permitted to do something.
It is usually used only in writing and in formal speech.
We usually use *can't* instead of *mustn't*. (See below.)
Don't have to means it is not necessary for you to do something.
You ***mustn't*** park here. (It's a no-parking zone.)
You ***don't have to*** park here. (But you can if you want.)

***can* and *can't*: opposite meanings**

Can means something is permitted (or possible).
*You **can** park here. There's no restriction.*

Can't is similar to *mustn't*. It means you are not permitted to do something.
*You **can't** park here. It's a no-parking zone.*

UNIT 6: Exercises

Part 1

1 Complete the sentences with *in*, *on*, or *at*.

a I started my job ___in___ 2007.
b I usually get to work ________ about 8:15.
c I'm never late for work. I'm always ________ time.
d I work best ________ the morning.
e I don't like working ________ the weekend.
f Occasionally, I have to work ________ Saturdays.
g ________ the summer, I usually walk to work.
h I get paid ________ 28th of each month.
i We have a pay review ________ April.
j We have a big office party ________ the end of the year.

If necessary, change the verb (negative to positive, or positive to negative) or change the information to make all the sentences true for you.

2 Underline the correct alternative.

a I like to study **during** / **for** my summer vacation.
b I took a language course **during** / **for** August.
c I went to the USA **during** / **for** three weeks.
d I hadn't been abroad **during** / **for** a long time.
e I met an interesting couple **during** / **in** the flight.
f His father was a pilot **during** / **for** the war.
g He was a prisoner **during** / **for** four years.
h I saw him once more **during** / **in** my visit.

Part 2

1 Complete the table with the correct modal verb forms. Use *he* as the subject and *go* as the main verb.

	can	must	should	have to	need to
Affirmative	*He can go.*				
Negative	*He can't go.*				
Question	*Can he go?*				

2 Underline the most appropriate alternatives to complete the text.

Five ways to get your boss to like you

1 Flatter them
You **(1) don't have to / mustn't** tell your boss that he or she is the best boss you've ever had, or laugh hysterically every time they tell a joke. But you **(2) should / shouldn't** find subtle ways to make them feel good: for example, you **(3) should / have to** ask their advice when you have a difficult job to do.

2 Agree with them
You **(4) don't have to / mustn't** contradict your boss in front of other people, even if they're wrong.

3 Don't criticize
You **(5) don't have to / mustn't** criticize your boss behind their back. If you have something to say, say it to their face.

4 Be honest
When you're sick, you **(6) can't / don't have to** send a hospital report, but you **(7) should / can** call your boss directly. You **(8) mustn't / don't have to** send a text message or email – this will make it look as if you're lying.

5 Remember how they take their coffee
You **(9) should / can** remember how they take their coffee, so that next time they ask you to go to your local coffee shop, you **(10) shouldn't / don't have to** ask.

Which is the best piece of advice? Compare your ideas with a partner.

3 Work with a partner. Look at these things to do after the lesson and decide whether *must* or *have to* is the most appropriate way to complete each sentence.

a I ___*have to*___ go to the bank. I've got an appointment with the loan officer.
b I ________ go to the bank. I don't have any cash.
c I ________ remember to get my mother a birthday present.
d I ________ go straight back to work. I have an important meeting.
e I ________ pick up my children from school. It's the end of the semester.
f I ________ mail these letters. They've been in my purse since Monday!

Do you have any of these things to do after class?

UNIT 7: Passive

Passive = *be* (*am*, *was*, *have been*, etc.) + past participle (*used*, *built*, etc.)

TENSES		ASPECT			MODALS
		Simple	Progressive	Perfect	*will (would)*
Present	+	It's **used.**	It**'s being used.**	It **has been used.**	It **will be used.**
	-	It **isn't used.**	It **isn't being used.**	It **hasn't been used.**	It **won't be used.**
	?	**Is** it **used**?	**Is** it **being used**?	**Has** it **been used**?	**Will** it **be used**?
Past	+	It **was used.**	It **was being used.**	It **had been used.**	
	-	It **wasn't used.**	It **wasn't being used.**	It **hadn't been used.**	
	?	**Was** it **used**?	**Was** it **being used**?	**Had** it **been used**?	

The progressive forms *be being* and *been being* are very rare. Avoid using them.

In passive sentences, the object of the active verb becomes the subject of the passive verb. In other words, the "receiver" of the action becomes the subject and comes at the beginning of the sentence.

Active	Passive
subject verb object Somebody's stolen **my purse**!	subject verb **My purse** has been stolen!
subject verb object Detectives have arrested **two men**.	subject verb **Two men** have been arrested.
subject verb object President Roosevelt opened **the Golden Gate Bridge.**	subject verb by + agent **The Golden Gate Bridge** was opened by President Roosevelt.

In passive sentences, the "doer" of the action – known as the "agent" – is either not mentioned at all, or mentioned at the end of the sentence in a *by*-phrase.

There are several reasons why you might want to use passive verb structures.

1 The "doer" of the action is unknown.
Their house ***was built*** *in the 1980s.* (They don't know who built it.)

2 The "doer" of the action is not important in the context.
"When ***was*** *the Sydney Opera House* ***built****?" "In 1957."* (I want to know when it was ***built*** not who built it.)

3 The "doer" of the action is obvious.
Demonstrators ***were arrested*** *and* ***charged*** *with disturbing the peace.* (It is obvious that the police arrested and charged them.)

4 The "receiver" of the action is what we are talking about, and the "doer" is the new information.

Generally, you tend to put "known" information at the beginning of a sentence and "new" information at the end. Compare the following:

The Golden Gate Bridge is a popular tourist attraction in San Francisco. ***President Roosevelt opened it.***
The Golden Gate Bridge is a popular tourist attraction in San Francisco. ***It was opened by President Roosevelt.***

The second version is easier to process because it follows the order of "known" to "new."

The passive is much more common in written language than in spoken language.

Verbs with two objects have two possible passive structures:
I ***was given*** *this watch by my parents on my 18th birthday.* (The subject of the sentence is "me/I.")
This watch ***was given*** *to me by my parents on my 18th birthday.* (The subject of the sentence is "the watch.")

UNIT 7: Exercises

1 **Write the past participle forms for these verbs which are often used in the passive. What are the spelling rules for each group? Use your dictionary if necessary.**

a arrest, invent, jail, murder
arrested, … Rule: add ed
b accuse, create, produce, prosecute
c classify, identify, try, copy
d acquit, ban, kidnap, mug
e build, grow, make, steal

Rearrange the past participles into two groups according to their meaning. Use your dictionary if necessary.

Verbs used to describe crime	Verbs used to describe processes
arrested	*invented*

2 **Look at the following notices and announcements. Use your dictionary if necessary. Underline the passive structures and name the tenses.**

a The movie was written, directed, and produced by Steven Spielberg. *Simple past*
b Passengers are requested to remain in their seats until the plane has come to a complete standstill and the engines have been turned off.
c Lunch is now being served.
d Feeding the penguins is strictly prohibited.
e Applications must be submitted by December 31.
f The management cannot be held responsible for any loss of property.
g Pills to be taken three times daily.

Where would you expect to see these notices or hear these announcements? Discuss with a partner.

3 **Write affirmative and negative passive sentences. Use the verb in parentheses and an appropriate tense.**

a My mother (be born) ________________ in the 1950s.
My mother was born in the 1950s. /
My mother wasn't born in the 1950s.
b She (bring up) ________________ in a small village.
c She (educate) ________________ at a private school.
d She (teach) ________________ English from the age of eleven.
e She (award) ________________ a scholarship to study at college.
f She (marry) ________________ in the local church.
g She (employ) ________________ by the same company for the last twenty years.

Check (✓) the sentences which are true for you. Write three (true) passive sentences about your mother (or someone else in your family).

4 **Look at these general knowledge facts. Cross out *by* + the agent if it is not necessary.**

a Chess was invented in India by Indians.
b Snakes are not found in Ireland by anybody.
c 20% of the body's energy is used by the brain.
d The Statue of Liberty was built in France by French people.
e Fourteen muscles are used by people to smile.
f Forty-three muscles are used by people to frown.
g The first disposable safety razor was patented by King Camp Gillette.

How many of the facts did you know?

5 **Rewrite these sentences in the passive. Start each sentence with *I*.**

a People gave me money for my last birthday.
I was given money for my last birthday.
b My friend is showing me around her new apartment this evening.
c My employers don't pay me very much.
d People have sent me over twenty text messages so far today.
e Teachers taught me how to swim before I was seven.
f People tell me that I look like my father.

Are any of the sentences true for you?

UNIT 8: Modals of deduction. Past perfect

Part 1: Modals of deduction

There are many ways of expressing how certain or uncertain you are about something.

Degree of certainty	Modal auxiliaries	Other phrases
99% certain it IS ✓	It must be ...	I'm sure it's ...
	It may be ... It could be ... It might be ...	Perhaps it's ... Maybe it's ...
	It can't be ...	I'm sure it isn't ...
99% certain it ISN'T ✗		

*They **must** be home by now. They set off over an hour ago.*
*I **might** arrive late. I have to finish this report first.*
*Who's at the door? It **can't** be Jill – she's on vacation in Florida.*

The opposite of *must be* is *can't be*.
*The keys **can't be** in my coat because I wasn't wearing it. They **must be** in my purse.*

Part 2: Past perfect

Affirmative	Negative	Question	Short answer *Yes*	Short answer *No*
I/You/He, etc. **'d (had) worked.**	I/You/He, etc. **hadn't (had not) worked.**	**Had** I/you/he, etc. **worked**?	Yes, I/you/he, etc. **had**.	No, I/you/he, etc. **hadn't**.

You use the past perfect when you are talking about the past and you want to refer to an earlier past time. The past perfect clearly shows that one past event happened earlier than other past events.

*When we **arrived**, the concert **had already started**.*

*When we **arrived**, the concert **had already started**.*

Conjunctions such as *after*, *because*, *by the time*, and *when* are often used to combine a simple past clause with a past perfect one.

The movie started. I arrived. ➔ *The movie had started **when** I arrived.*
The train left. He reached the platform. ➔ ***By the time** he reached the platform, the train had left.*
He didn't check his tires. He had a flat tire. ➔ *He had a flat tire on the highway **because** he hadn't checked his tires.*
We had lunch. We went for a walk. We took the bus home. ➔ *We had lunch and then took the bus home **after** we had been for a walk.*

UNIT 8: Exercises

Part 1

1 Match the sentences so that they make sense.

a I'm going to set up my computer myself.
b You've been driving all day.
c Oh, no. I must be getting old.
d A new car? On my salary?!
e You must be Sarah's husband.
f Congratulations on your engagement.

1 She's told me so much about you.
2 You can't be serious! It's impossible.
3 I'm sure it can't be that difficult!
4 You must be delighted.
5 I'm afraid I can't remember your name!
6 You must be absolutely exhausted.

2 Rewrite these observations with the modal verb in parentheses so that the meaning is the same.

a I'm sure you're really cold! (must)
You must be really cold!
b I'm sure you're kidding. (must)
c I'm sure your keys aren't far away. (can't)
d Maybe you won't enjoy the movie. (might not)
e I'm sure you know who she is. (must)
f I'm sure it's not far from here. (can't)
g Maybe you'll meet the love of your life. (might)
h I'm sure she isn't that old. (can't)

Think about situations when you have made observations like these. Tell a partner.

Part 2

1 Test your irregular verbs. Use the verbs in the box to complete the three lists in the table with the infinitive, simple past, and past participle forms. There are eight verbs in each list.

~~bet~~ burst cost ~~dig~~ ~~drink~~ feed fight fly hurt let mean ring
rise shine shrink shut sing sink slide split spread stick swim win

1 All forms the same	2 Two forms the same	3 All forms different
bet – bet – bet	*dig – dug – dug*	*drink – drank – drunk*

Check your answers on page 167. Underline any verbs you weren't sure about.

2 Work with a partner. In each case write a second sentence, changing the verb in bold into the past perfect.

a I **had** breakfast when I got to work this morning.
I'd had breakfast when I got to work this morning.
b I **read** Harry Potter when I saw the movie.
c I **traveled** a lot when I started my job.
d I **did** the shopping when I got home yesterday evening.
e I **passed** my driving test when I went to college.
f The class **started** when I arrived.

In what way does the use of the past perfect change the meaning of the sentences? Are any of the sentences true for you?

3 Complete the sentences to make them true for you.

a By the time I was [age?], I had learned how to ... (swim? ski? drive? etc.)
b By the age of [age?], I had been to more than [number?] ... (countries? schools? concerts? etc.)
c By the time I was sixteen, I'd been learning [subject?] for [number?] years.
d By the age of [age?], I had moved [number?] times.
e By the age of [age?], I had realized that ...
f By the time I was [age?], I had decided that ...

Compare your sentences with your partner.

UNIT 9: Reported statements and questions

Reporting speech means using your own words to report what somebody has said (or thought).

Direct speech		Reported speech
Ana said, "I don't believe you."	→	Ana **said she didn't believe me**.
I said, "We can talk about it tomorrow."	→	I **told her we could talk about it the next day**.
She said, "Who do you think you are?"	→	She **asked me who I thought I was**.

When you report statements "using your own words", you need to decide which tenses, which pronouns, which time expressions, and which reporting verbs to use. When you report questions, you also need to change the word order.

Tenses

There is usually a logical "back-shift" of tense. This is because what the person said is now in the past. Present becomes past; present perfect or simple past become past perfect; *can* becomes *could*, etc.

Direct speech		Reported speech
"**I'm** really tired."	→	She said she **was** really tired.
"**I've had** a great day."	→	He said he**'d had** a great day.
"I **cut** my finger."	→	She said she**'d cut** her finger.
"**I'm going to take** a shower."	→	He said he **was going to take** a shower.
"I **was trying** to open a can of beans."	→	She said she **had been trying** to open a can of beans.
"I **can't find** the time to cook."	→	He said he **couldn't find** the time to cook.
"I **don't want** to go out."	→	She said she **didn't want** to go out.
"**I'll order** Chinese take-out."	→	He said he **would order** Chinese take-out.

Pronouns

Pronouns (*I*, *she*, *we*, etc.) and possessive adjectives (*my*, *your*, *his*, etc.) may change, depending on who is reporting and who/what they are reporting.

Direct speech: "**I** understand **your** ideas but **I** don't agree with **them**."
Report 1: *My mother told* ***me*** *that* ***she*** *understood* ***my*** *ideas but that* ***she*** *didn't agree with them.*
Report 2: *Ted's mother told* ***him*** *that* ***she*** *understood* ***his*** *ideas but that* ***she*** *didn't agree with them.*

Expressions of time or place

"Here-and-now" expressions in direct speech may change to "there-and-then" expressions in reported speech.
"Can you **come here tomorrow**?" → *He asked if I could* ***go there the next/following day***.

Reporting verbs

The most common reporting verbs are *say* (*that*) and *tell somebody* (*that*). Other verbs such as *admit*, *claim*, *explain*, *insist*, *reply*, or *suggest* can also be used. If you're not sure, use your dictionary to check on the correct verb pattern.
She said it was her fault. (NOT ~~She said me it was her fault.~~)
She told me she hadn't been thinking. (NOT ~~She told that she hadn't been thinking.~~)
She explained that she had been very tired. (NOT ~~She explained me that she had been very tired.~~)

Reported questions

In reported questions, the word order changes to subject + verb. You don't use *do*/*does*/*did*.
For *yes*/*no* questions you use *if* or *whether*.
"How **are you**?" → *He asked me how* ***I was***.
"Have you been here long?" → *He asked me* ***if/whether*** *I had been there long.*
"Where are you from?" → *He asked me where I* ***was from***.

Imperatives

You can report an imperative with *tell somebody to do something* or *ask somebody to do something*.
"Don't worry!" → *She told him not to worry.*
"Hurry up!" → *He asked them to hurry up.*

UNIT 9: Exercises

1 Match the beginnings and the ends of these famously "wrong" predictions and opinions.

- a In 1898, the Munich Technical Institute said that
- b In 1899, the Commissioner of US Patents said that
- c In 1907, Lord Haldane, British Minister of War, said
- d In 1927, Harry Warner of Warner Brothers asked
- e In 1943, Thomas Watson, IBM chairman, said
- f In 1962, the producers of *Doctor No* said that

1. Sean Connery couldn't play the sophisticated James Bond because he looked like a bricklayer.
2. who the heck wanted to hear actors talk.
3. Albert Einstein showed no promise.
4. there was a world market for maybe five computers.
5. everything that could be invented had been invented.
6. the airplane would never fly.

Rewrite the predictions and opinions as quotes.

a "Albert Einstein shows no promise."

2 Read the newspaper article about a great-grandmother's lucky escape. Complete the article by changing the direct speech into reported speech.

Lucky escape

A great-grandmother told the newspaper how she escaped death by centimeters after being hit by a meteorite traveling at 480 km/hr. Margaret Smithers said (**1** "It just missed my head and hit my arm.") it had just missed her head and (had) hit her arm.

Seventy-six-year-old Margaret was hanging out the laundry in her backyard when the brown metallic stone hit her. She said (**2** "I felt a nasty pain on my arm which started bleeding heavily.") ________________ . Her husband found the five-centimeter rock on the grass. She added that (**3** "I'm glad it didn't hit me on the head") ________________! Experts are analyzing the walnut-sized rock.

A spokesperson from the Astronomical Society said, (**4** "There's a good chance it is a meteorite.") ________________ . But he added that (**5** "The chances of being hit by one are incredibly small.") ________________ . He explained that (**6** "Most meteorites disintegrate as they enter the atmosphere.") ________________ . However, on average, one falls to Earth every week.

3 Complete the sentences with *asked*, *said*, or *told*.

- a She ____said____ she didn't believe me.
- b I ________________ her it was true.
- c She ________________ me why I hadn't told her.
- d I ________________ I'd wanted to.
- e She ________________ she'd been really upset.
- f I ________________ her I was sorry.
- g She ________________ me if I'd go with her.
- h I ________________ her I couldn't.

What do you think the conversation was about? Discuss with a partner.

4 Report the direct speech using the verb in parentheses.

- a "I hate spending money on new clothes." (said)
  He/She said that he hated spending money on new clothes.
- b "I'm not wearing this jacket again!" (told)
- c "Do you think I look fat in these pants?" (ask)
- d "I need to go on a diet." (said)
- e "I've checked the oil and put some air in the tires." (told)
- f "Don't forget that it's our anniversary tomorrow." (asked)
- g "I don't want to get married until I'm forty." (said)
- h "What time does your salsa class finish?" (asked)

Compare your ideas with a partner.

UNIT 10: Defining relative clauses. Real conditionals

Part 1: Defining relative clauses

A relative clause can define the thing or person introduced in the main clause. It comes immediately after the person or thing it is describing. You use *that* (or *who*) for people and *that* (or *which*) for things.

*The man **that/who cuts my hair** is named Jo.*
*A frog is an animal **that/which lives on land and in water**.*

The relative pronoun (*that, which, who*) can be the subject of the verb in the relative clause.

subject verb
*People **who come from** Rio de Janeiro are called Cariocas.*

subject verb
*A florist is a store **that sells** flowers.*

When the relative pronoun is the subject of the verb, it can never be omitted.

The relative pronoun (*that, which, who*) can be the object of the verb in the relative clause.

object verb
*The work **that** you **do** is very interesting.*

object verb
*The man **who I met** yesterday is a famous artist.*

When the relative pronoun is the object of the verb, it can be omitted.
The work ~~that~~ you do is very interesting.
The man ~~who~~ I met yesterday is a famous artist.

Part 2: Real conditionals

Real conditional sentences – sometimes called "first conditional" sentences – consist of an *if*-clause and a main clause. They are used to talk about present or future situations that are real or possible. These include promises, warnings, and threats.

If the weather improves, we'll go for a walk.
If you quit smoking, I'll be very happy.
If you touch that, you'll burn your finger.
If you don't go now, we'll call the police.

***if*-clause**
In most real conditional sentences, you use a present tense (simple, progressive, or perfect) in the *if*-clause, even when you are talking about the future.

	***if*-clause**	**Main clause**
Simple present	If you **arrive** early,	wait for me in the station café.
Present progressive	If you**'re spending** any time in Rio,	I can recommend a great hotel.
Present perfect	If you **haven't finished** by ten,	you'll miss the mail.
going to	If you**'re going to** talk to me like that,	I'm leaving!
Modal auxiliary	If you **can't** do it,	ask Tom for help.

Unless means the same as *if ... not*.
***Unless** you agree ... = **If** you **don't** agree ...*

***if*-clause**	**Main clause**
Unless you start studying now / **If** you **don't** start studying now,	you'll never pass your exams.

Main clause
You usually use the simple present, modal auxiliaries (especially *will/won't, can, must*, and *may*), or the imperative in the main clause.

***if*-clause**	**Main clause**
If he finds out the truth,	it's all over for you and me.
	we'll be in big trouble.
	you can forget about our vacation in Cuba.
	deny everything!

The *if*-clause and the main clause can often go in either order.
If I feel like going out, I'll give you a call. OR I'll give you a call if I feel like going out.
Use a comma after the *if*-clause when the *if*-clause comes before the main clause.

UNIT 10: Exercises

Part 1

1 Make one-sentence definitions using the relative pronouns *who/which/that*.

a A rolling pin is a kitchen utensil. You use it to flatten pastry.
A rolling pin is a kitchen utensil which/that you use to flatten pastry.
b A pestle is a tool. You use it to crush nuts and seeds.
c A woodlouse is a small insect. It eats dead wood.
d A farrier is a person. He/She makes and fits horseshoes.
e A fandango is a dance. It originated in Spain.
f A burglar is a person. He/She breaks into your house and steals things.

Check (✓) the sentences in which the relative pronoun can be omitted.

2 Insert a relative pronoun *who/which/that* where necessary.

a The school I went to was near my house.
b My mom is the only person really understands me.
c The issue worries me most is global warming.
d The biggest party I've had was for my 21st birthday.
e I've got a lot of friends live in Ecuador.
f I think it's better to have a job you enjoy than to have a well-paid job you hate.
g The people live next door to me are really friendly.

Which sentences are true for you? Discuss with a partner.

Part 2

1 Match the two halves of the sentences.

a They're not going skiing tomorrow — 2
b I'm not going to go for a walk
c You'll miss your flight
d You can still get your train
e I won't help you with your German
f I'll take care of their children
g He won't pass his exams
h She'll be top of her class

1 if you leave now.
2 unless they get fresh snow.
3 if they want me to.
4 unless you help me with my French.
5 if it's raining.
6 unless he studies hard.
7 if she really concentrates.
8 unless you take a taxi to the airport.

2 Look at the advice given by children to children and underline an appropriate alternative.

a **Unless** / **<u>If</u>** you get a bad grade at school, don't show it to your mom, **unless** / **if** she's on the phone.
b Don't make an enemy of the school bully **unless** / **if** he's smaller than you.
c **Unless** / **If** your mom is angry with your dad, don't let her brush your hair.
d **Unless** / **If** you like being hit, don't tell your mom her diet's not working.
e Don't hit your sister **unless** / **if** your parents are out.
f **Unless** / **If** your dad asks, "Do I look stupid?", don't answer him.
g **Unless** / **If** you want a kitten, start off by asking for a horse.

Which do you think is the best/funniest piece of advice? Discuss with your partner.

3 Write real conditional sentences using the verbs in brackets.

a If the weather (be) ____*is*____ good next weekend, I (go) ____*'ll go*____ for a long run.
b If it (rain) ________ tomorrow, I (not go) ________ out.
c My friends and I (go) ________ to the beach tomorrow if it (be) ________ sunny.
d If I (earn) ________ enough money this year, I (visit) ________ the USA.
e I (go) ________ snowboarding this winter, if there (be) ________ enough snow.
f I think I (see) ________ my family this weekend, unless I (have to) ________ work.

Which sentences are true for you?

UNIT 11: Wishes and regrets. Unreal conditionals

Part 1: Wishes and regrets

I wish / *If only* are two ways of talking about unreal situations. You can use them to express wishes or regrets about the present or the past. After *I wish* / *If only*, the tense backshifts to show that the situation described is/was unreal (see below).

Tense changes		
Fact		**Wish/Regret**
I**'m** a teacher.		If only / I wish I **wasn't/weren't** a teacher.
Simple present	→	Simple past
I**'m going** to the concert with Adam.		I wish / If only I **was going** with Carl.
Present progressive	→	Past progressive
I **haven't studied** any other languages.		I wish / If only I **had studied** another language.
Present perfect	→	Past perfect
I **left** school early.		If only / I wish I **hadn't left** school early.
Simple past	→	Past perfect

Other (non-tense) changes	
Fact	**Wish/Regret**
I don't have **enough/much** time.	If only / I wish I had **more** time.
I'm not very **good at** math.	If only / I wish I was/were **better at** math.

Part 2: Unreal conditionals

Unreal conditional sentences consist of an *if*-clause and a main clause. When forming unreal conditional sentences, the tense backshifts in the *if*-clause to show that the situation described is/was imaginary.

if-clause

To show that a present (or future) situation is imaginary, you use a past tense.
To show that a past situation is imaginary, you use the past perfect.

Fact		**Imaginary situation**
I**'m not** a teenager.	→	If I **was/were** a teenager, ...
I **didn't tell** him.	→	If I **had told him**, ...

If I/he/she/it were is more formal than *If I/he/she/it was*.
You always use *were* in the fixed expression *If I were you* ...

Main clause

For a present or future situation, you usually use *would/wouldn't* + infinitive in the main clause.
For a past situation, you usually use *would/wouldn't* + *have* + the past participle in the main clause.

***if*-clause**	**Main clause**
If I **could** sing,	I**'d be** in a band.
If I**'d had** a map,	I **wouldn't have gotten** lost.

Note: Unreal conditional sentences which refer to imaginary situations *in the present* (or future) are sometimes called "second conditional" sentences. Unreal conditional sentences which refer to imaginary situations *in the past* are sometimes called "third conditional" sentences

UNIT 11: Exercises

Part 1

1 **Make sentences, using *I wish* or *If only*.**

- a I can't play the piano.
  I wish I could play the piano.
- b I don't live near a beach.
- c I don't like my job.
- d I'm getting old.
- e I don't have enough free time.
- f I'm not good at English.
- g I have such a stressful life.
- h I don't earn a lot of money.

Which are true for you?

2 **Complete the second sentence so that it means the same as the first.**

- a I regret I wasn't born in another country.
  I wish ... I had been born in another country.
- b I regret that I didn't study English more at school.
  If only ...
- c I regret that I didn't go to a better school.
  I wish ...
- d I regret that I didn't travel much when I had the chance.
  If only ...
- e I regret that I got married so young.
  I wish ...
- f I regret that I didn't work hard in college.
  If only ...

Work with your partner. Discuss each regret and say if you share it.

Part 2

1 **Write complete questions.**

- a What / you / do / if / you / find / $100 / in the street?
  What would you do if you found $ 100 in the street?
- b If / you / be / able to / change your nationality, / what / you / be?
- c If / you / can / have dinner with a famous person, / who / you / choose?
- d If / you / have to / change one part of your body, / what / it / be?
- e What / you / do / if / you / see / someone stealing something in a store?
- f If / you / can / meet / one person from history, / who / you / like it to be?

Now answer each question so that it's true for you. Write full answers to each question.

- a If I found $ 100 in the street, I'd keep it.

2 **Make conditional sentences about these past situations, starting with *If* ...**

- a I wasn't paying attention. I walked into a lamppost.
  If I'd been paying attention, I wouldn't have walked into a lamppost.
- b I studied hard. I passed my exams.
- c I didn't study hard. I failed my exams.
- d I forgot to set my alarm clock. I overslept.
- e I missed the bus. I was late for work.
- f I bought a lottery ticket. I won some money.
- g I didn't have a map. I got lost.
- h The weather wasn't good. We didn't go camping.

Have any of these situations happened to you in the last year? Discuss with a partner.

3 **Complete these sentences so that they are true for you.**

- a If I had time, ...
- b I'd have been really happy if ...
- c If I were very rich, ...
- d If I had been born a member of the opposite sex, ...
- e If I were president of my country, ...
- f I'd have been furious if ...

Work with a partner. Compare your sentences. Are any the same?

UNIT 12: have/get something done

You can use *have something done* (*I'm going to* ***have my house painted****.*) when someone does something for you – often because you have paid them to do it. As a slightly more informal alternative to *have something done*, you can also use *get something done*.

Form: *have/get* + something (object) + past participle
I'll probably ***get my hair cut*** *next week.*
Have you ***had your ears pierced****?*
You really should ***get your eyes tested****.*

Compare the two sentences:

- *Mandy cut her hair last week.*
- *Mandy had her hair cut last week.*

In the first sentence, Mandy cut her own hair. In the second sentence, someone else cut her hair and was probably paid for it.

Sometimes *have something done* can mean you have a (usually) negative experience.
We had our house broken into yesterday.
This doesn't mean that you arranged for somebody to break into your house, but that something unfortunate happened to you.
I had my bike stolen last week.
He tried to cheat the Mafia and ended up having his legs broken.

UNIT 12: Exercises

1 Read the sentences and underline the most appropriate verb form in each case.

a We're **redecorating our house** / **having our house redecorated** right now. I'll be glad when the painters have finally finished and left.
b I'm going to **clean my car** / **have my car cleaned** later, so I bought a new pressure washer.
c Do you really think Angelina Jolie is ugly? I think you need to **test your eyes** / **have your eyes tested**.
d We're going to **fix the roof** / **have the roof fixed** soon. We have to wait until the builders can do it.
e I'm **cooking dinner** / **having dinner cooked** for some friends this evening. We get together once a week, and tonight it's my turn to be the host.
f My wife just **repaired her car** / **had her car repaired**. It's great that she's such a practical person – and it saves us a lot of money!

2 Complete the sentences with *have/get* + *something* + past participle, using the verb in parentheses.

a We (deliver) ________________ take-out ________________ to our home every week.
b I always (service) ________________ my car ________________ at the same garage.
c I (cut) ________________ my hair ________________ once a month.
d I usually (check) ________________ my teeth ________________ every six months. I've got a really good dentist.
e We (do) ________________ odd jobs ________________ in our house by professionals.
f I (take) ________________ my passport pictures ________________ in a professional studio. They look much better.

Work with a partner. Discuss which sentences are true for you.

3 Using the prompts, make questions with *have/get* + *something* + past participle.

a You / ever / appearance / change
Have you ever had your appearance changed?
b How often / you / eyes / test
c You / ever / anything / steal
d You / ever / ears / pierce
e You / ever / your car / vandalize
f How often / you / hair / cut

Work with a partner. Take turns asking and answering the questions.

Test yourself!

Underline the correct option in each sentence.

Units 1–3

1 Where (a) **is** (b) **does** (c) **was** he come from?

2 (a) **Has** (b) **Is** (c) **Does** she been here long?

3 (a) **I'm online always** (b) **Always I'm online** (c) **I'm always online**.

4 (a) **I'm on the phone all the time** (b) **All the time I'm on the phone** (c) **I'm all the time on the phone**.

5 We (a) **'ve** (b) **'s** (c) **'re** swum with dolphins.

6 She (a) **haven't** (b) **hasn't** (c) **isn't** been to the USA.

7 He (a) **'s** (b) **was** (c) **been** playing soccer when he twisted his ankle.

8 It's (a) **as** (b) **by** (c) **than** far the biggest fish I've ever seen.

9 She (a) **'s liking** (b) **like** (c) **likes** taking pictures.

10 I've (a) **knowing** (b) **been knowing** (c) **known** her for a long time.

Score: ____ /10

Units 4–6

11 If you don't know the word, (a) **look up it** (b) **look it up** (c) **it look up**!

12 I think (a) **I'm calling** (b) **I call** (c) **I'll call** Jan and see if she's free.

13 What happened? It's all gone dark! I can't see (a) **something** (b) **everything** (c) **anything**.

14 Is there (a) **many** (b) **much** (c) **a lot** cake left?

15 Were there (a) **many** (b) **much** (c) **a lot** people at the party?

16 I (a) **would** (b) **used to** (c) **could** be very thin when I was younger.

17 (a) **Would** (b) **Are** (c) **Did** you use to smoke?

18 I'm seeing Mr. Jones (a) **at** (b) **in** (c) **on** ten o'clock.

19 I'm always late for everything. I never get to work (a) **in** (b) **on** (c) **at** time.

20 She (a) **doesn't have** (b) **have** (c) **should** to see the doctor after all.

Score: ____ /10

Units 7–9

21 I can't stand (a) **wait** (b) **to wait** (c) **waiting** around.

22 He asked me (a) **help** (b) **to help** (c) **help** him.

23 She promised (a) **come** (b) **coming** (c) **to come** at 10:00 a.m.

24 Our office is (a) **cleaning** (b) **being cleaned** (c) **cleaned** right now.

25 The nominations (a) **have** (b) **has** (c) **having** been announced.

26 The lights aren't on: Sam must (a) **be** (b) **was** (c) **have been** out.

27 We (a) **are** (b) **have been** (c) **were** too late: the train had already left.

28 I knew I (a) **haven't** (b) **hasn't** (c) **hadn't** been there before.

29 She said that she (a) **'ll** (b) **'d** (c) **'ve** bought some new clothes.

30 We asked him (a) **whether** (b) **when** (c) **how** he had ever had problems.

Score: ____ /10

Units 10–12

31 A truant is a pupil (a) **who** (b) **he** (c) **which** stays away from school without permission.

32 If you (a) **wanted** (b) **will want** (c) **want** to join us, bring some food.

33 Jon won't come (a) **unless** (b) **if** (c) **if not** you ask him.

34 They wouldn't be so popular if they (a) **weren't** (b) **wouldn't be** (c) **aren't** so talented.

35 Do you know how she (a) **does feel** (b) **feels** (c) **feel**?

36 If I (a) **can** (b) **could** (c) **would** sing, I'd be in a band.

37 I wish I (a) **took** (b) **have taken** (c) **had taken** swimming lessons when I was at school.

38 If I (a) **'ve** (b) **'d** (c) **'d have** had a map, I wouldn't have gotten lost.

39 She's wearing (a) **an expensive white silk** (b) **a white expensive silk** (c) **a silk white expensive** blouse.

40 I'm having my eyes (a) **test** (b) **tests** (c) **tested** tomorrow.

Score: ____ /10

main verb · adjective · conjunction · modal auxiliary verb · adverb · article · pronoun · main verb

Learn these useful words and you can understand more about the language you are studying.

determiner · noun · pronoun · main verb · preposition · noun · auxiliary verb

Agents are people or things that perform an action in a passive sentence.
*He was brought up by **his aunt and uncle**.*

Antonyms are words that mean the opposite of other words.
rich ↔ poor   dead ↔ alive   tall ↔ short

Back-shift is when a verb moves "one tense back" in a conditional clause or reported statement.
*If you **were** a woman, you'd understand.   "I can't come." → He said he **couldn't** come.*

Clauses are groups of words containing a subject and a verb.

main clause	subordinate clause	main clause	time (subordinate) clause
I waited	*but she didn't come.*	*I'll call*	*when I get there.*

Note: Subordinate clauses are introduced by conjunctions.

Collocation refers to words that frequently occur together.
common sense   get along well   Merry Christmas

Complements refer to adjective or noun phrases which give more information about the subject of a clause.
*She was **very happy**.   It's **my fault**.   I feel like **a complete idiot**.*
Note: Complements usually follow verbs like *be, seem, feel.*

Conjunctions show a connection between one clause and another.
***Just as** we were leaving the hotel, I spotted a friend.*

Consonants are all the letters of the English alphabet except for the five vowels *a, e, i, o,* and *u.*
b, c, d, f, g, h, j, k, l, m, n, p, q, r, s, t, v, w, x, y, z

Expressions are groups of words that belong together where the words and word order never or rarely change.
black and white   That reminds me.   How do you do?

Idioms are groups of words with a meaning which cannot be understood by taking the meaning of each individual word.
*My father **footed the bill**.   Let's **play it by ear**, OK?*

Intransitive verbs do not take an object.
*He **arrived**.   **Is** Marta still **sleeping**?   Stop **shouting**!*
Note: Many verbs can be either intransitive or transitive. It depends on the meaning or context.
*He **opened** the door.* (Transitive)   *The door **opened**.* (Intransitive)

Linkers show a connection between one sentence and another.
*Many drivers drive too fast. **As a result**, there are more and more accidents.*

Numbers can be cardinal (*1, 2, 3, ...*) or ordinal (1st, 2nd, 3rd, ...).

Objects usually come after the verb and show who or what is affected by the verb.
*She closed **the door**. My dog hates **me**. I made **a cup of coffee**.*
Note: Some verbs take both a direct object (DO) and an indirect object (IO).
*She gave **him*** (IO) ***a kiss*** (DO). *He sent **her*** (IO) ***some flowers*** (DO).
*I teach **students*** (IO) ***English*** (DO).

Participles are the forms of verbs used in compound tenses and as adjectives.
*What are you **doing**? I've **finished**. It's **freezing**! He's **injured**.*

Particles are the adverbs or prepositions that form part of a phrasal verb.
*turn it **on** take **off** get **along with** her*

Partitives are words or expressions that show that only part of something is being referred to, rather than all of it.
***a piece of** cake **a pack of** gum **a bunch of** flowers*

The **phonetic alphabet** is a set of special symbols which shows speech sounds in writing.
mother = /ˈmʌðər/ coffee = /ˈkɑfɪ/

Phrasal verbs are combinations of a verb and one or two particles.
switch on come up with

Pronouns are words used in place of nouns or noun phrases. There are many classes of pronoun.
Subject pronouns: *I, you, she*, etc.
Object pronouns: *me, you, her*, etc.
Possessive pronouns: *mine, yours, hers*, etc.
Demonstrative pronouns: *this, that, these, those*

Proper nouns are words that refer to a particular person, place, or institution.
Janet, Mexico City, the United Nations

Proverbs or sayings are short, well-known statements that give practical advice about life.
When the cat's away, the mice will play.

Register describes a level and style of a piece of language which is appropriate for the circumstances in which it is used.
I am very grateful for your help. (More formal) *Thanks.* (More informal)

Relative clauses are clauses that modify a noun or a noun phrase. They give additional information about the noun and are joined to a previous clause by words such as *who, that,* or *which.*
*That's the man **who helped me**. This the pen **(that) I lost**.*
*Everyone is well, **which is really great**.*

Synonyms are words or expressions which mean the same as another word or expression.
tolerate sb = put up with sb I'm off now. = I'm going now.

Transitive verbs take an object.
*You're wasting **your money**. He cut **his finger**.*
*I can't pronounce "**comfortable**."*

Vowels are the letters *a, e, i, o,* and *u*.

Unit 1

1.03

a 5% equals one twentieth
b 12.5% equals one eighth
c 25% equals one quarter
d 30% equals three tenths
e 33.3% equals a third
f 50% equals a half
g 75% equals three quarters
h 80% equals four-fifths

1.05

Adam
(A = Adam; I = Interviewer)
I: Hi, excuse me. We're doing some research into how people use technology to talk to their friends. Do you mind if we ask you a couple of questions?
A: Well, I'm in a bit of a hurry.
I: It'll only take a few minutes.
A: Well, OK then.
I: Ok, how do you usually contact your friends - by phone, email, text, ...?
A: I am at the office all the time so I usually use my business email.
I: Do you usually use it to write to friends?
A: No, that's only for business! I hardly ever check my personal email. There's a lot of spam today. I voice message my friends. It's so much quicker, and I'm very bad at texting.

Carole
(C = Carole; I = Interviewer)
I: Hi, excuse me. Can I ask you a question for some research we're doing?
C: Certainly.
I: How do you usually contact your friends?
C: Oh, I pick up the phone ....
I: And do you ever use email?
C: Yes, of course. I regularly check my email. Oh, and I use Skype now and then. One of my grandchildren lives in Australia and she calls me on Skype every weekend.
I: When was the last time you wrote a letter?
C: Oh, I love receiving letters. But I must admit, I never write letters nowadays. It's a shame really, don't you think?

Sharon
(S = Sharon; I = Interviewer)
I: Hi, excuse me. We're doing some research into how people use technology to talk to their friends. Do you mind if we ask you a couple of questions?
S: OK.
I: How do you usually contact your friends - by phone, email, text, ...?
S: I use my smartphone. I'm always online so I chat with several friends.
I: Do you speak on the phone?
S: Not very often - it's too expensive. I text message them. I talk to my school group, and my family group, so I chat with them at the same time.
I: Which social media do you use? Facebook, Twitter, Instagram...
S: Hmm, I love to chat, but I like to make instant videos too. So I often use Whatsapp, Snapchat and Facebook.

1.06

I suppose I've got five or six close friends, and most of them are really similar to me. But my friend, Jackie, is the exception. In many ways, we're opposites. We met about ten years ago in Guatemala. I was taking an intensive Spanish language course, and she was in my class. We were also living in the same student accommodation. I arrived a few weeks after her, and she was really friendly. I guess we became friends because we were in the same situation and we were both from the USA. I'm amazed we got along so well, because we have nothing in common. For a start, we come from very different backgrounds. She grew up on a farm in the country with lots of brothers and sisters and dogs and horses. I grew up with my mother in a small apartment in the city with a pet hamster! We don't share the same taste in music, clothes, books, art, or anything really. Our personalities are very different - she's very artistic, and I'm not. I'm very neat and organized, and she's not. We even look different - she's tall and dark, and I'm small and fair. But we do have one very important thing in common. We're both crazy about baseball, and we like the same team - the Red Sox. We meet about three or four times a year and we usually go out for lunch and talk about baseball or the good times in Guatemala.

1.07

a
(C = Cathy; H = Harry)
C: Hey! How's it going?
H: Not bad.
C: What have you been up to lately?
H: Not a lot, really. What about you?
C: Oh, this and that.
H: Hey, I have to run. I'll give you a call.

b
(C = Cathy; J = Jim)
C: Hello, stranger!
J: Cathy! How's life?
C: Great! What are you up to these days?
J: Oh, keeping busy, you know.
C: You should come over for dinner some time.
J: That would be great. Better get back to the office. See you.

c
(C = Cathy; E = Ed)
C: Hi. How are things going?
E: Fine. What about you?
C: Oh, pretty good. Are you doing anything special this weekend?
E: No, just taking it easy.
C: Me, too.
E: Sorry, I can't stop. Take care.

1.08

Greetings
How's it going?
How's life?
How are things going?

Saying things are OK
Not bad.
Great!
Fine.

Asking for news
What have you been up to lately?
What are you up to these days?

Saying you're in a hurry
Hey, I have to run.
Better get back to the office.
Sorry, I can't stop.

Goodbyes
I'll give you a call.
See you.
Take care.

1.09

1-4 (*in different emotions*) Please go into the sitting room and sit down. I'll be back in minute.

Unit 2

1.11

a It's very hot in here.
b He's very angry.
c She's very pretty.
d My car's very dirty.
e They're very tired.
f This class is really interesting.

1.12

(I = Interviewer; A = Andy; B = Beth; C = Cindy)

Andy

I: Have you ever had an injury?

A: Yes, I have. I was playing basketball for the local team. I was jumping up to catch the ball, when a player from the other team knocked me over, and I fell heavily on my left leg.

I: Oh, no. Were you badly hurt?

A: Yes, I twisted my ankle and couldn't play basketball for more than three months.

Beth

I: Have you ever been in a dangerous situation?

B: Yes, I have. I was walking my dog one day with my sister, and we were crossing this field. There was a horse in it, and it suddenly started running towards us, looking really crazy.

I: What did you do?

B: Well, I know you aren't supposed to run away from animals, because they can sense your fear. But we ran away as fast as we could.

Cindy

I: Have you ever been really scared?

C: Yes, I have. Last summer I was driving on the highway in California. We were getting close to Los Angeles so I started to slow down, ready to turn off the road. Suddenly, this black convertible appeared out of nowhere, pulled in front of me, and stopped! I almost drove into the back of it, but I just managed to turn off the road in time. I've never been so scared in my life.

1.13

(J = Jake; F = Friend)

J: Have I ever told you about the time a dog almost attacked me?

F: No. What happened?

J: Well, it was a few years ago. I was still in high school, actually, so I guess I was sixteen or seventeen. It was the weekend and it was summer - the sun was shining, and I was with some friends in the backyard. We were playing soccer. Well, we weren't exactly playing soccer, because there were only three of us, but we were playing with a ball. In fact, we were using my older brother's ball. Anyway, we were having fun and enjoying the game, when suddenly one of my friends kicked the ball really hard, and it went up in the air, over the fence, and into my neighbor's backyard. I couldn't believe it. My brother really loved that ball and he never let me use it.

F: Oh, no. What did you do?

J: Well, I went and knocked on the neighbor's door, but there was no answer. So I had to climb over the fence. It was really high, and my friends had to push me over. Anyway, as soon as I dropped down on the other side, I realized I wasn't alone.

F: The dog?

J: Yes, an enormous dog was running towards me, barking like crazy. I've never been so scared in my life!

F: What did you do?

J: I was absolutely terrified. I couldn't move. But then I noticed a chair near the fence, so I jumped up on it and managed to climb back over the fence.

F: What about the ball?

J: I didn't get the ball, but fortunately, the neighbors came back before my brother did. So in the end, he never knew about it. Which is good because my brother is almost as scary as the neighbor's dog!

1.14

(I = Interviewer; T = Toby; K = Kate)

I: Toby, where did you learn?

T: At the beach this summer. It's the most exciting thing I've ever done.

I: Is it hard?

T: Yes, you have to be strong and healthy and also the kind of person who likes showing off!

I: What equipment do you need?

T: A wetsuit, a board, a kite, and a harness.

I: Is it similar to windsurfing?

T: I think it's a little more difficult than windsurfing. But it's similar, because you do it in the ocean and you need the right amount of wind.

I: What's so good about it?

T: Everything! But hangtime is by far the best thing about it. That's when you jump, and try to stay suspended in the air for as long as possible. It's awesome.

I: Kate, where do you do it?

K: Wherever there are good cliffs. One of the best places I've ever been is Yosemite, in California. But I usually go to Minnesota. The cliffs are not as high as in Yosemite, but they're much closer to where I live.

I: Do many women do it?

K: No, there aren't as many women as there are men, but there are female-only courses to get women into the sport.

I: Is it very dangerous?

K: Yes, it is, so you have to take the right equipment: waterproof clothes, climbing shoes, and ropes.

I: Is it an expensive sport?

K: Not really. In fact, it's slightly less expensive than many other sports, because the mountains are free.

I: Why do you do it?

K: When you get to the top, it's the best feeling in the world.

1.15

a

A: How did you get that black eye?

B: I was playing baseball, and the ball hit me in the face.

A: You'd better put an ice pack on it. It looks terrible.

b

C: Why are you limping?

D: I've twisted my ankle.

C: Oh, no. It looks really painful. You really should lie down and keep your leg up.

c

E: Did you have a good swim?

F: It was OK at first, but then I got a cramp and I had to stop.

E: Oh, that's horrible. You're probably dehydrated. You need to drink more water.

d

G: My feet are killing me. I have terrible blisters.

H: You need to put some plasters on them. And then you should wear sandals for a while.

G: But it's winter!

e

I: How was the sailing?

J: Great, but I think I got sunburned. My nose is really red.

I: You need to put some cream on it immediately.

f

K: Are you OK?

L: No, I think I broke my thumb.

K: Oh, no. You probably need an X-ray. You'd better go to the hospital.

1.16

1. You'd better put an ice pack on it.
2. You need to drink more water.
3. You'd better go to the hospital.
4. You need to put some cream on it immediately.
5. You really should lie down and keep your leg up.
6. You need to put some plasters on them.

Unit 3

1.17

Kim

After that party I got in touch with Dan and suggested a bike ride. We had a good time although he cycled very fast and I could hardly keep up with him! We didn't go for some juice afterwards as I was too tired! He contacted me again a week later to ask me to the cinema but I was visiting my family that weekend so I couldn't make it. We've been trying to arrange another date, but it's been difficult. I've relocated to San Francisco because of my job, so we're a long way from each other. Also, he's been on his own for a long time. I'm not sure he's ready to share his life.

Dan

I was really pleased when Kim got in touch after the party. She had said that she enjoyed cycling but when we went out on our bikes she didn't seem very happy. In fact, she seemed to be a bit annoyed with me at the end - I don't know why. We tried to arrange another date, but I don't think she wanted to. And of course, she's in another city now. Kim works very hard, and doesn't have much time left.

1.21

(M = Mia; R = Rita)

M: So what do you think of Liz's new boyfriend?
R: John? He seems nice. I don't really know. He wasn't very talkative.
M: Well, he's a little shy. And Liz tends to dominate the conversation, doesn't she?
R: Yes, I guess so. But when John did say something, it wasn't particularly interesting.
M: Oh, no. You can be so mean.
R: I'm not mean – just honest.
M: But he's not bad-looking, is he?
R: He's OK. Isn't he a little young for her?
M: Young? Liz isn't exactly old.
R: That's true. But she looks older than she is.
M: Yes, I know what you mean. But she's so nice – she deserves someone really special.
R: Actually, she can be really difficult.
M: Really?
R: Yes, she can be a little bossy.
M: Oh, no. Why can't everybody be perfect, like us?
R: And so modest. Ha-ha!

1.22

1. He wasn't very talkative.
2. Liz tends to dominate the conversation.
3. It wasn't particularly interesting.
4. You can be so mean.
5. He's not bad-looking.
6. Liz isn't exactly old.
7. She can be really difficult.
8. She can be a little bossy.

REVIEW A

1.24

(A = Alice; G = Gretchen)

A: Hi Gretch! How are you?
G: Fine thanks, what's up?
A: I just had a text from Luke. He's moving out!
G: Oh no - why?
A: He's met a woman in Spain. He's completely in love and he's moving there.
G: How exciting! What's her name?
A: Valeria. She works at the university in Seville.
G: I'll miss him ... when is he leaving?
A: In a month's time, at the end of August.
G: So soon!
A: I know, I think we should give him a farewell party, don't you?
G: That's a really good idea... let's talk to the others tonight.
A: We could make it a surprise for Luke, couldn't we?
G: Yeah, but how could we make sure he's at home that night? He's always at the gym in the evenings!
G: Good point. I'll think of something... leave it to me!

Unit 4

1.25

(T = Tom; H = Hua)

T: We're in Beijing, and it's mid-January. Hua, we've already celebrated the New Year in the USA, but you don't celebrate New Year's Day on January 1, do you?
H: No, we don't. Our New Year usually takes place in early February but not always. It depends on the Chinese calendar.
T: I see. So how are you going to celebrate this year?
H: Well, everybody spends the month before the New Year preparing for it. First of all, I'm going to help my mother do the housework. We're going to sweep away all the bad luck and make room for good luck to come in.
T: Does everybody do that?
H: Yes, and some people paint their doors and windows, usually red.
T: Is red a lucky color?
H: Yes, traditionally, red is the color that scares away bad luck. For the New Year, we put red paper decorations on the walls.
T: And do you have plans for New Year's Eve?
H: Yes, we're having a big family dinner.
T: Is there a traditional New Year's Eve dinner?
H: Yes, we always eat jiaozi, which are dumplings cooked in boiling water.
T: Oh, I'm sure it's really good. Are you going to a New Year's Eve party after dinner?
H: No, we always spend New Year's Eve with our family. After dinner, everybody watches TV or plays cards or other board games, and at midnight, lots of fireworks and firecrackers go off. It's really exciting.
T: How long do the celebrations go on?
H: For about three days.
T: Do you make New Year's resolutions?
H: Not exactly - we make wishes on New Year's Day.
T: What are you going to wish for?
H: I can't tell you, because it might not come true.
T: Well, I hope all your wishes come true. Happy New Year. How do you say that in Chinese?
H: Guo Nian Hao.
T: Guo Nian Hao!

1.28

(Z = Zoe; D = David; S = Sandy)

Z: Hello.
D: Is Sandy there, please?
Z: Yes, just a minute – I'll get her for you. ... It's David.
S: Oh, hello, David.
D: Look, I'm really sorry I didn't call earlier, but I'm still at the office and ...
S: Oh, that's all right. I forgot you were going to call anyway.
D: Listen, I'm afraid I can't come to the party. I'm having dinner with some important clients tonight.
S: It doesn't matter. – I'm going to the party with someone else.
D: Oh, OK, well I'll call you.
S: When? I mean, all right. Goodbye.
D: Bye.
Z: So?
S: Well, he apologized – and he's having dinner with an important client. Anyway, I have to go. See you later.

1.29

(S = Sandy; J = James; A = Alex)

S: Hi, James. Hi, Alex. Where's Suzy?
A: Oh, she changed her mind at the last minute. David called her and asked her to go to dinner at that new Japanese restaurant.
S: What? Now I'm definitely going to tell him it's over.
J: Who's David?

1.32

I went to a great party last summer. My friend, Maggie, was leaving town and moving abroad to live. So she had a farewell party, but she came up with a really good theme - it was a costume party, and everybody had to dress up as something beginning with the letter M. She chose the letter M because it's the first letter of her name. I thought it was a great idea, and people came dressed as all kinds of things - Mickey Mouse, Madonna, Medusa. I went as Marilyn Monroe. It was fun, but I didn't particularly enjoy wearing lipstick or high heels. I don't know how women do it all the time. The party was at Maggie's house, but it was summer, so we were in the backyard a lot of the time. It looked really beautiful. They had lights in the trees and lots of mirrors, so that the lights were reflected, and it made the yard look much bigger. There must have been at least seventy people there. I think she invited everyone she knew. I didn't know everybody, but it didn't matter. Wearing costumes was a perfect ice-breaker and everybody mixed really well. The food was great, too. Maggie was moving to Thailand, so the food was Thai. She got the local Thai restaurant to do it, and it was delicious. We even had Thai iced tea to go with it. Maggie's brother is a DJ, so the music was fantastic, and I danced a lot - without my shoes on.

1.34

a

Do you want to go to the movies tonight?
Would you like to come to the movies tonight?
I was wondering if you'd like to go to the movies tonight.

b

Yes, good idea.
Yes, that sounds great.

c

I'd love to, but I'm working tonight.
No, I'm afraid I can't.

d

Are you doing anything tonight?

e

Oh, what a shame.
Oh, too bad.

1.35

M: Hi there! How are you today?
F: Fine thanks, and you?
M: Oh, I'm fine, thanks. What can I do for you?
F: I'd like 4 rib eye steaks, please.
M: Sure, here you are, 4 good juicy rib eyes.
F: Great, thanks. How much is that please?
M: That'll be 9 dollars and 89 cents please.
F: Oh, I'm sorry, I only have a 20 dollar note.
M: No problem ma'am, here's your change, 10 dollars and 11 cents.
F: Thank you - bye!
M: Thank you. Have a nice day now!

Unit 5

1.36

a True. Cheese is made from the milk of cows, sheep, goats and sometimes buffalos.
b False. France produces an average of 1.8 million tonnes of cheese per year. The United States produces 5.4.
c False. There are hundreds of different types of cheese.
d False. Parmesan is a hard cheese from Italy.
e False. NASA made an announcement on April 1st, 2006 that they had discovered the moon's surface contained cheese. It was an April Fool's joke.
f True. Cheese is a good source of protein and calcium.
g False. Cheese often contains saturated fat and salt. This means eating too much could lead to high cholesterol and high blood pressure leading to heart disease.

1.38

(I = Interviewer; M = Mark)

I: Mark, you've tasted some of the more unusual dishes from around the world. Can you tell us about them and what they taste like?
M: Yes, well, I've just come back from China where I ate baked cobra for the first time.
I: Cobra? I imagine it tastes fishy.
M: No, not at all. In fact it tastes meaty, like chicken. It was a little tough and chewy, but delicious.
I: Really? I find that hard to imagine.
M: And before that I was in Thailand. I ate lots of fried grasshoppers there. They're really crisp and tasty, but a little greasy.
I: Hm. I'm not sure I'd like to eat insects.
M: Well, that's because you're not used to them. In many parts of the world, insects are a good source of protein and minerals. Last time I was in Indonesia, I had a feast of insects. In fact, for one meal, the main course was roasted cockroaches.
I: What did that taste like?
M: Well, they're crunchy on the outside, and on the inside there's a rich liquid which tastes pretty sweet and fruity.
I: What other insects have you eaten?
M: While I was in Africa, I ate caterpillars. They boil them and dry them in the sun, so they taste a little dry and bland. But they're really good for you.
I: Oh.
M: One of my favorite insects to eat is ants. Did you know that in Colombia, some movie theaters serve roasted, chocolate covered ants instead of popcorn?
I: Really? What are they like?
M: Sweet and crisp - like popcorn.
M: Oh, ha-ha.
I: What about you? Have you ever eaten anything unusual?
M: Well, I'm not as adventurous as you, and I haven't traveled much. But the strangest thing I've ever eaten was in the USA recently. It was a chocolate cookie Pizza.
I: What? You mean, like a pizza with chocolate cookies on it?
M: That's right. Very sweet.
I: Sounds disgusting! Was it very greasy?
M: No, it was delicious!

1.39

There were five of us at home when I was growing up: my father, my mother, my brother, my sister, and me. My mother did most of the cooking, but we all helped her. Well, sort of helped her. We each had a special job: I used to chop vegetables, my brother helped with the dishes, and my sister set the table. I used to love everything my mother cooked, except for one thing - meat. I didn't like it, and that made life difficult for my mother, because everyone else liked it. So she used to cook meat for everyone else, and a vegetarian meal for me. Teatime was always really important in my house - I think it's because my mother is half British. We'd have tea and cakes at about four o'clock in the afternoon. My mother would invite the neighbors over, and we'd have a tea party! I used to love those times. My father would come home from work at about seven o'clock in the evening, and then we used to have our dinner in the kitchen. Then we would help to clear the table, and we'd be in bed by 8:30. The weekends were a little different. Every Saturday, we used to go to a restaurant for dinner, and on Sundays we'd have pasta as a treat. My father is of Italian origin, so pasta was his favorite dish. My favorite dish when I was a child was rice and beans. It's a popular dish in Brazil, but nobody makes it like my mom.

1.40

(W = Waiter; M = Man; WO = Woman)

W: Good afternoon. Do you have a reservation?
M: Yes. The name's Brown.
W: Oh, yes. Is this table OK for you?
M: No. We want to sit near the window.
W: Yes, of course. Follow me.
M: Are you ready to order yet?
WO: No. Go away and come back a bit later.
M: Of course. Would you like to order some drinks?
WO: Yes. Two lemonades.
WO: Hey! Come here. We want to order now.
W: Very good. What can I get you?
WO: Give me the lamb.
W: OK. And sir?
M: I want the grilled salmon.
W: Would you like to see the dessert menu?
WO: No.
M: Bring me two cups of coffee and the check.
W: Certainly. How was your meal?
WO: Good.

1.41

(W = Waiter; M = Man; WO = Woman)

W: Good afternoon. Do you have a reservation?
M: Yes, a table for two in the name of Brown.
W: Oh, yes. Is this table OK for you?
M: Do you have anything near the window?
W: Yes, of course, follow me.
W: Are you ready to order yet?
WO: Not quite. Could you give us a few more minutes?
W: Of course. Would you like to order some drinks?
WO: Yes, two lemonades, please.
WO: Excuse me. We're ready to order now.
M: Very good. What can I get you?

WO: I'll have the lamb, please.
W: OK. And sir?
M: I'll have the grilled salmon.
W: Would you like to see the dessert menu?
WO: No, I'm all right, thank you.
M: Can we have two cups of coffee and the check, please?
W: Certainly. How was your meal?
WO: It was great, thank you.

Unit 6

1.46

I love working from home. I don't have to drive to work, I don't have to sit in traffic, and parking is not my problem anymore. I don't have to get dressed in the morning – I can wear my sweatpants all day. In fact, I don't have to get up in the morning at all! If I want, I can work all night. It's up to me. There's nobody to tell me, 'You must be punctual. You mustn't make personal phone calls. You can't do your shopping online ...' There are only a couple of downsides. I have to call somebody if I want to talk, and I can't blame anything on anybody else – I'm the only person here!"

1.47

a
I work in Seattle for a big law firm. It's an American firm, and the head office is in Washington, DC, so I have to go there about once a month for meetings. Here in Seattle, we're supposed to start work at nine, but I often start later and work until nine or ten o'clock at night. Unfortunately, we don't get extra money for working overtime. We have to dress formally, so I always wear a suit and tie to work. Lawyers aren't allowed to wear bright colors or jeans. Recently, the head office brought in a new rule: we're not allowed to have relationships with people in the same company. I think it's ridiculous to ban office romance. Where else are you going to meet somebody?

b
This is the newsroom, where I work as a journalist. I'm actually responsible for foreign news. As you can see, we work in open-plan offices, so it can get pretty noisy. We're allowed to work at home one day a week, so when I want to do some quiet work, I don't come into the office. We work flexible hours because news is coming in all the time. We're supposed to have a break every two hours, but when you're working to meet a deadline, you can't afford to take time for a break. Sometimes I work right through my lunch hour - it's crazy. In fact, you have to be crazy to work here. As far as dress is concerned, we can wear anything we like.

c
You have to be at least twenty-one to be a train driver, but you don't have to have any particular qualifications to get on a training course. I earn a good salary, but my job involves a lot of responsibility, and I work unsociable hours. I often work at night or on weekends, and I'm supposed to work four or five shifts a week. You can't work a shift of more than twelve hours and you have to have twelve hours off between shifts. My job affects my social life, because I can't have a few drinks and go to bed late in the evening if I'm driving the next day. We have to wear a uniform and we're supposed to wear our hats all the time, but it gets a little bit hot.

1.48

(I = Interviewer; M = Mr. McClusky)

a
W: We're making good time.
M: Yes, hopefully we'll be there in time for dinner.
W: Oh, yes, I think so. In fact, we may even have time to spare.
M: Well, that's OK. If we have some time before dinner, we can go to the gym.
M: The gym? I'd rather kill time in the mall!

b
The Global Earth Party will put the environment at the top of the agenda. We've asked the same question time and time again: when will the government do something about global warming? We're running out of time – we need to act now. Vote for the Global Earth Party today!

c
W: Come on, guys. Stop running. OK, one at a time. Ruben, stop pushing. Let's go back to class.
BOY: But we didn't have time to finish our game.
W: Yes, I know, time flies when you're having fun. But we have work to do.

1.50

(S = Sandy; A = Amy)
A: Hi Sandy, how's it going?
S: Hey Amy. OK I think. I got some cute gadgets for camping. A little pan to heat up my food in and a small stove which folds up into a tiny metal box. Oh, and a kit for purifying water.
A: Right, so where are you going exactly?
S: I'm doing the PCT, the Pacific Crest Trail which goes for 1,000 miles along the west coast of the States, but I haven't planned my route in detail yet.
A: But when are you leaving?
S: A week from tomorrow.
A: So, you have your flight booked and all your gear sorted?
S: Well, I haven't got my tickets yet. I guess I should do that. I did some shopping as I said: I got the camping stove and pan - and some sunscreen.
A: What about your hiking boots? Shouldn't you try wearing them before you go?
S: Oh yeah, I forgot about that. I'll get some nice soft, light boots.
A: What about a tent and sleeping bag?
S: I'm borrowing my brother's. I just hope he has cleaned them since he went travelling last year.
A: And ... you've checked that your passport is okay?
S: I think so, I have it right here... Oh no, it expired a month ago!

REVIEW B

1.52

W: What are you doing for Christmas this year? Are you staying here in Chicago?
M: Oh, I don't know, actually.
W: Do you want to come and spend it in Vermont with my family?
M: Maybe. What are you planning?
W: Well, I'm going to take the day off and drive on Christmas Eve, because Mom's having a little party. She always does. Everyone will be there - my brother, Ken, and his wife, Michelle, with their kids. And my sister, Diane. My Grandma - she's 92 now! And my mom's sister, Betty, with all my cousins.
M: Oh!
W: Then, we'll have dinner together. Dad always used to make it, but since they split up, Mom does it. We always have fish, usually salmon or something, with a light fruit dessert. Then, before bed, we're allowed to open one present each, from under the Christmas tree.
M: We always used to do that too, when we were kids! What do you usually do on Christmas Day?
W: We get up early and have a smoked salmon for breakfast before we spend the morning opening presents. After that, we have lunch. I think Ken is going to cook it again this year. He's a great cook. We usually have turkey, cranberry sauce, and mashed potatoes, followed by three or four desserts - you know, the traditional stuff.
M: What about the afternoon?
W: Dad's coming over in the afternoon, with his new wife. I'm a little worried about it, actually. I don't know what Mom's going to say. She isn't too happy about it. But she had to invite him, and Christmas just wouldn't be the same without Dad.
M: Oh.
W: Anyway, in the afternoon we'll all stay at home and play games, or watch a movie on TV and eat chocolate.
M: And are you coming home the next day?
W: No, I'm staying in Vermont. We always have a big lunch on that day, with friends. We eat cold meat and salad for lunch, with fresh fruit. Then we go for a walk, if it's not too cold. I'll come back the next day.
M: That sounds wonderful, Carol, but I think I'll stay at home on my own.

Unit 7

2.02

(H = Host; J = Jack)
H: People are increasingly obsessed with reading stories and looking at pictures of celebrities. Today there are more

paparazzi on the streets than ever, all of them trying to get the definitive celebrity picture. We're here with Jack, a paparazzo with fifteen years of experience, about his job. Jack, thank you for joining us.

J: You're welcome.

H: Jack, why are people so interested in reading about the private lives of celebrities?

J: Because they're young, beautiful, rich, and photogenic, and they lead glamorous lifestyles.

H: But the pictures that appear in the tabloid press are not always glamorous. They're often unflattering pictures of celebrities just trying to lead their lives. For example, I remember seeing a picture of Matt Damon getting a parking ticket. What's so interesting about that?

J: Well, people also want to think that these celebrities are just normal people, so they enjoy seeing pictures of them doing ordinary things like shopping. I also think it's fine to take unflattering pictures of them because it gives us hope when we realize that they're just like us really!

H: I understand that, but where do you draw the line?

J: Well, we're not completely insensitive. We try not to involve children. For example, Kate Moss asked us not to take pictures of her daughter, and we haven't. Do you remember seeing pictures of her daughter in the press?

H: No, but I did read an interview with Kate Moss, where she said that she can't walk anywhere because the paparazzi follow her everywhere. That must be awful. In the same interview she said that a female photographer was chasing her in New York and fell over a water hydrant. She cut her lip and was bleeding, so Kate stopped to ask her if she was OK. The woman just continued taking pictures! That's a little desperate, isn't it?

J: The woman was just doing her job. Listen, so many of these celebrities refuse to cooperate with the paparazzi. We try reasoning with them. We explain that we don't want to upset them, but they shout and swear at us. So we follow them everywhere. It's a game. Have you ever seen a bad picture of Nicole Kidman in the press?

H: Er, no.

J: That's because she plays the game. She always agrees to smile for the camera, and we get our shot. Then we leave her alone. If you ask me, I think these celebrities are hypocritical. On the one hand they need to have their pictures in the press, and on the other hand they tell us that we're invading their privacy. If they don't like the attention, I suggest that they change jobs.

2.04

/t/ checked, escaped, forced, stopped
/d/ described, involved, named, used
/Id/ expected, needed, reported, treated

2.05

a Talks between the UN and delegates from major African nations have been suspended after the African team stormed out, complaining about budget issues. After three weeks of non-stop discussions, the chief negotiator has called for a one-week cooling-off period before talks start again.

b President Liga has announced his resignation after a difficult 12 months in office. He will remain until the end of the year and then step down, allowing Vice President Lopez to take his place.

c Hundreds of holidaymakers slept on beaches last night as forest fires continued to sweep through the Mediterranean. Foreign consulates are working hard to help many travelers who want to return home.

d Skywatchers in the US are preparing for the spectacular sight of a total solar eclipse. The moon is set to pass in front of the sun, casting a shadow that will sweep over the nation from Oregon in the west to South Carolina in the east. It is the first total solar eclipse to be seen exclusively in the US since independence in 1776. The next is not due until 2024.

e High school student Elana Banker has been barred from returning to school after the summer vacation. The reason: the tattoos that she acquired during the vacation, which are banned according to the school rules. The Principal, Brad Martin, says Elana will not be allowed to return until she has had the tattoos removed.

f A jogger caught on camera pushing a woman into the path of an oncoming bus in London England, has been arrested thanks to a huge response from the public. The police put out a request for help after failing to find the man for two months. One of the man's co-workers came forward when they saw the TV appeal.

2.07

Positive responses
Good job!
Lucky you!
Oh, congratulations!
Oh, that sounds interesting.
How exciting!
Negative responses
Oh, I'm sorry to hear that.
Oh, no, that's terrible.
How annoying!

2.08

a We got engaged last week.
b My internet's down again.
c I'm going snowboarding for the first time this weekend.
d I just won $1,000 in the lottery.
e I'm reading Barack Obama's autobiography.
f My wallet was stolen.
g My mom's going to give me her car.
h I think my boyfriend might lose his job.
i I passed all my English exams.

Unit 8

2.09

(W = Woman; M = Man)

W: Have you heard from Conrad lately? Is he still going around the world?

M: Yes, lucky guy. He's in South America now - I had a message from him yesterday.

W: How's he doing?

M: He's having a great time. Come and take a look at the pictures on his blog.

W: Oh, great.

M: Here we go.

W: Oh, wow! Look at those waterfalls. Where is that?

M: Well, he hasn't put the name of the place, but I guess it could be Vietnam.

W: Or it could be India.

M: No, it can't be India, because he hasn't been there. I'm pretty sure it's Vietnam. I know he went trekking in the hills there.

W: Oh, I'd love to go to Vietnam.

M: Mm, me, too. Now this one must be Singapore. Look at that skyline - it's so built-up.

W: Or it could be Hong Kong.

M: No, he didn't go to Hong Kong, but I know he stopped off in Singapore.

W: Ah. Wow, look at these statues. They look really old. Is it a Buddhist temple?

M: Yes, I think so. That's probably Thailand. He was there for the New Year.

W: Lucky guy. Now this is different. I didn't know Conrad could ride a horse.

M: He can't. I don't think that's him.

W: So where is this then?

M: I'm not sure, but it's probably southern Argentina.

W: Oh look, here's a good one. What is he doing?!

2.11

Continents
Asia, Antarctica, Europe
Mountain Ranges
the Himalayas, the Andes, the Pyrenees
Oceans
the Pacific, the Atlantic, the Indian
Rivers
the Nile, the Amazon, the Danube

2.12

[P = Peter; M = Marc]

P: Hi Marc, how's it going?

M: All good thanks. Have you recovered from your jet lag?

P: Just about - I slept till noon today.

M: So, when can I take you to dinner? I'm free this Friday if you are?

P: Ah, sorry no. My parents have invited me for dinner on Friday. How about Saturday?
M: Err ... I had planned to ... see someone on Saturday...
P: Oh yes? Did you meet someone while I was away?!
M: Err ... well, this is what I wanted to talk to you about over dinner ... it's Carla.
P: ... Marc ... you are joking aren't you? Please tell me you are joking ...

2.13

I once went on a trip through the Sinai desert in Egypt, from the Red Sea to a historical place called St. Catherine's Monastery. I was actually on a windsurfing vacation with some friends in a small resort called Dahab. It's a perfect place for windsurfing and other water sports. But one day, the weather was terrible for windsurfing; basically, there was no wind at all. My friends decided to go diving, but I don't like being under the water, and I hate lying on the beach. So I signed up for a trip to St. Catherine's Monastery. We left the hotel at about 10:00 a.m., and the weather was just beginning to get hot. There were ten of us in a minivan including eight tourists, one guide, and one driver. Fortunately, the minivan had air-conditioning. The guide spoke five languages, so during the trip, he told us the history of the monastery in English, Spanish, French, and German. The trip took about two hours, and as we drove through one of the driest deserts in the world, I just stared out of the window at the wonderful scenery. The sandy color of the mountains looked fantastic against the blue sky. We stopped once on the way at a place where the view is spectacular and everybody got out and took pictures. There were Bedouins selling souvenirs, and I bought a beautiful necklace. By the time we arrived at the monastery, it was really hot and there were a lot of other tourists there, but I was glad I'd come. It's a very special place, and I'd love to do the trip again, but next time I'd rent a car and do it on my own time.

2.16

Tim called his girlfriend, Fiona, at Los Angeles International airport last Monday. He was at the gate and about to board his plane to the UK. He was visiting for the second time and they talked about their plans for the weekend. That was the very last time Fiona heard from him. He didn't arrive at Fiona's apartment in West London and he has not been seen since.

Fiona called the police who did some investigating together with the Californian authorities. Northeast Airlines employees remember seeing Tim at the gate, and their records show that Tim checked in and took the flight. But there is no record of him entering the UK. Several passengers interviewed by police were certain that seat 32B - which was Tim's seat - was empty for the whole flight. His phone was switched off and he didn't return to his Santa Monica home. So, it's a complete mystery! What has happened to Tim?

Unit 9

2.17

No one wants to appear superficial when using social media. Nowadays it seems most people want to make a statement when they post on the internet. Many people turn to different online environments where they can tell their friends their opinions on a great variety of issues, such as politics, food, travel, shopping, entertainment, news, etcetera. See below for current trends in internet use.
On politics: 63% of people *said* that they liked to express how they voted on social media whereas 30% didn't like to risk causing offence to friends so *preferred* to keep their political opinions private. A minority, 7%, thought it was boring to read about other people's political views online.
On food: 27% *stated* that they posted successful recipes online to share with friends, while 13% *admitted* that they had read food blog posts and had watched demo videos but rarely cooked anything themselves. The majority of respondents reported that they had surfed the net for good recipes before having friends round for a meal.
On travel: The majority of people thought that the best way to research destinations and make bookings was via the net (55%) and a lot of people (43%) enjoyed sharing their experiences via blogs. Only 2% *preferred* to keep quiet about their travel in case their favorite places were over-run with tourists.
On shopping: The vast majority of respondents (65%) *said* that they had bought their clothes online.
24% *explained* that they had looked at their favorite brands on the net, then went to the mall to try them on before they made a purchase. Only 11% *claimed* that they had bought mostly from stores.
On entertainment: 68% *said* that they had downloaded or streamed most of their videos and movies from the net.
25% *preferred* to use the net mainly to catch up on TV programs. A minority of 7% *declared* that they rarely used the internet for entertainment.
On news: 59% *insisted* that they had the news from social media rather than from the newscasts or newspapers. 38% *said* that they looked at Twitter first when a news item broke and only 3% said that they had *refused* to use social media for news.

2.18

1
A: Which is your favorite track on the album?
B: The last one - it's amazing. I can't wait to see them performing live.

2
A: What did you think of it?
B: I thought the acting was fantastic and the cinematography's superb. Apart from that, it was so boring.

3
A: Have you finished it yet?
B: Almost.
A: What's it like?
B: Really good. I think it's going to be a bestseller.

4
A: I enjoyed that. What did you think of it?
B: I thought it was awful - a sentimental tearjerker - and the ending was predictable.
A: Well, it made you cry anyway.
B: No, it didn't - I've got a cold.

5
A: Are you enjoying it?
B: Yes. It was a little difficult to get into, but now that I'm past the first few chapters, I can't put it down.

6
A: What did you think of the special effects?
B: What special effects?
A: It was all done with computers.
B: Oh, no. I thought it was real. You've spoiled it now.

7
A: Did you have a good time?
B: Not really. I can't stand all that techno stuff. I like it when you can actually hear the lyrics.
A: Old hippy.
B: What did you say?
A: Nothing.

2.20

One of my favorite movies is *Forrest Gump*. I know it's an old movie but I've never seen anything better. Actually, I've seen it three times. The last time I saw it was the other night on TV, and it made me laugh and cry all over again. I love Tom Hanks and I think he's great in this movie. Robin Wright played the part of his girlfriend, and Sally Field was his mom. I can't remember who else was in it, or who directed it. But I do know that it won six Oscars including best picture, best director, and Tom Hanks got best leading actor.
Apparently it's based on a novel, but I have no idea who wrote it. There are so many things I love about this movie. I guess it's a drama, but it's historical and it's funny and it's really sad, too. The character of Forrest Gump is amazing. He's not very smart, and at the beginning of the movie he can't walk properly, but he manages to succeed in life without meaning to, and without realizing it. I particularly like the parts where he meets famous people like President Kennedy or Elvis Presley. It's so good the way they mix old black and white footage from the 60s. It's hilarious when Forrest meets Elvis. Forrest has a strange way of walking, and when Elvis imitates him, it looks like the dance that he was famous for.
The soundtrack is great too. There are all these classic rock songs including some

by Elvis. But the ending is a tearjerker - I cry my eyes out every time. I won't spoil it for you in case you haven't seen it, but you should see it because it's the best movie of all time.

2.25

M: Hey, Rosa! I need the car tonight. I'm going to that gig downtown and I said I would give Mike and Jeff a ride. That's OK, right?
W: Not going to happen, Rob. I need the car in case Mom needs picking up from the station - she's arriving this evening, remember?

2.26

M: Hey, Rosa! I need the car tonight. I'm going to that gig downtown and I said I would give Mike and Jeff a ride. That's OK, right?
W: Not going to happen, Rob. I need the car in case Mom needs picking up from the station - she's arriving this evening, remember?
M: Oh, come on. I've promised. How about doing a favor for your favorite brother?
W: Sorry, I told Mom that I'd pick her up if she needed it. You'll have to get a taxi.
M: I don't have the money. Look - if I can have the car tonight, you can have it for the rest of the weekend.
W: You're just not listening, Rob. It's my car and it's a no.
M: But what do I tell Mike and Jeff...?
W: Sorry, not my problem. Look at the time - you'd better get going. The bus leaves in 5 minutes...

REVIEW C

2.28

Bryn: Hi there, you're listening to WBC on 94.6 FM and I'm your host, Bryn Partridge. This morning we are talking about Prince Harry's recent outburst at the media. What do you think about this? Do you agree that the media are too intrusive or do you think it's important we know what the British royal family is up to? Give me a call, I am ready and waiting to hear your views. We have our first caller ... Megan from West Virginia. Hi Megan, what do you think about all this?
Megan: Hi, Bryn. I just wanted to say I completely agree with Prince Harry.
Bryn: You do?
Megan: Yes, I think it is outrageous that the British royal family have no privacy at all. They are human beings just like us and none of us would like to be watched all the time!
Bryn: Thank you, Megan. I think we have Charlie on the line?
Charlie: Hi, Bryn. I think it's a bit of a fuss about nothing. What do they expect? Everyone wants to know about them - why shouldn't they put up with a bit of intrusion?
Bryn: Ah, so you think it's part of their job do you, Charlie?
Charlie: I do. They have to be popular. They represent their people. If they have to smile and pose for the camera whenever they go out, what's the problem?
Bryn: Thank you, Charlie. I think we're going to hear from Steven now. Hello Steven, are you there?
Steven: Yes, I am, Bryn. I'm British and I totally disagree with your last caller. If we want our royal family to represent us around the world we have to respect them and give them some space. If they are constantly stressed how are they going to do their job properly? Ordinary people have no idea how hard it must be to live your life under a microscope and have every move watched and judged...
Bryn: Well, thank you, Steven, you have put your view across very clearly. It's time to go to the news now, but we'll be back with more of your calls in a couple of minutes...

Unit 10

2.29

1
A: It's something that lived a very long time ago. It looks very scary.
B: A thing that lived a long time ago.
C: Um ... It's a big monster.
2
A: It's a person who takes care of animals when they are sick.
B: A person that helps animals.
C: It's the doctor that takes care of our pets.
3
A: It's something that's very cold and it's ... it's a ... it's a stone.
B: It's kind of a big piece of ice that cracks off a bigger piece.
C: It's a big ice cube.
4
A: A place where animals have been put up to show people.
B: Somewhere where they show you things that are very old.
C: It's somewhere people show things like dinosaurs and olden days things.
5
A: It's a person who takes toys away.
B: It's someone that comes in the middle of the night ... and he has ... something on his face with round holes and he has a T-shirt that's black and white and he robs things.
C: It's someone who steals things when you're asleep.

2.31

Dale: Welcome to Dale's Dilemmas. I'm Dale Rogers, and the subject of today's dilemma is pushy parents. Are today's parents too ambitious for their children? Should they let children be children and stop organizing their lives? Should we congratulate them for developing their children's potential, or should we say "back off and leave the kids alone"? In the studio, we have George and Rachel from Chicago. They disagree about how to bring up their daughter, and we're going to hear what they have to say. ... George and Rachel, welcome to the show.
M: Thanks.
W: Thanks.
Dale: Rachel, if we could start with you. Can you tell us a little about your daughter?
W: Yes, my daughter Hayley is five years old, and I think she has what it takes to be a movie star. So I'm doing everything I can to get her into the movies.
Dale: And what exactly does that involve?
W: Hayley goes to acting classes twice a week. She has a singing teacher who comes to the house once a week, and we watch a lot of movies together at home. Then on weekends we go to auditions. Sometimes we have to travel to New York or Los Angeles, but I'm willing to do whatever it takes.
Dale: That's a lot of traveling. What do you think about it, George?
M: I think my wife is obsessed. I don't think she should make Hayley do this. It isn't Hayley's choice. Rachel wanted to be a child star, and that's why she's making Hayley go though this.
W: I'm not making her do anything against her will. Hayley loves it and she wants to be a star.
Dale: But at five years old, does she understand what it means?
W: No, of course not. I want to let Hayley grow up like a normal child. There's too much pressure in the movie world. She's a kid. Let her play, let her have friends.
Dale: It's true that being a child star can be a very isolating experience.
W: I know that, but if you don't try, you don't succeed. When Hayley is famous and she's making movies, you're going to look back and thank me.
Dale: Thank you, Rachel and George. In just a moment, we'll be meeting Mark and Charlene, who want their two-year-old son to be the next Tiger Woods. But first, it's over to the studio audience. Who has a question for Rachel and George?

2.32

Dale: Who has a question for Rachel and George? Yes, the woman in the red dress, please ...

W2: Do you know how Hayley feels?
W: She enjoys her life and she wants to be a movie star.
M: I think she's too young to know how she feels. She says she's happy because she wants to please her mom.
Dale: Thank you. Another question now, please. Yes, the woman with the blue shirt.
W3: Can you tell me what you're going to do when Hayley starts school?
M: I'd like her to stop doing auditions and focus on being a normal school kid.
W: Well, I think it would be wrong to stop now after all the time and money we've invested. After all, you don't invest in a business and then give up after six months if you're not making a profit.
M: But Hayley is not a business - she's a child. Our daughter.
Dale: OK, ... let's have one from the man in the green jacket.
M2: Do you think you're depriving Hayley of a normal childhood?
M: Yeah. I worry about that.
W: Well, I don't. She's special and I want to help her to fulfill her potential.
Dale: Yes, the young man with the gray sweater.
M3: Could you tell me whether you have any other children and how they are affected?
M: We have a seven-year- old son, and he misses his mom.
W: He's very proud of his little sister.
Dale: The woman in the red dress again.
W2: Do you have any idea how stressful it is to be a movie star?
M: Very stressful. I don't think my wife has thought about the negatives at all.
W: We can cope. I just hope that I can come back here in ten years and we can do a follow-up story when Hayley's a star.
Dale: Well, I'm afraid that's all we have time for now. Thank you to our guests...

2.34

My mother plays the piano really well, so she wanted me to learn the piano, too. I had lessons for a while, but I wasn't very good, and eventually my piano teacher begged my parents to stop sending me. So that was the end of my music career! But what I really wanted to do was martial arts, and my parents let me join a club when I was about nine. I used to love those kung fu movies and Bruce Lee was my hero. I had posters of him all over my room, and that was how I got the idea. I was a little disappointed at first, because our classes weren't like the movies, but then I got obsessed with it and I was doing martial arts two or three times a week. We did it at a gym on the other side of town, so my parents drove me there because it was pretty far away from my house. But when I was about fourteen, I decided that I didn't want my friends to see my parents dropping me off, so I took the bus instead. I'm still doing martial arts now after ten years, and I've started getting more and more interested in kick-boxing. I'd definitely encourage my own children to do martial arts. It's not just about fighting - of course, you learn self defense - but you also learn other skills such as mental discipline and self-confidence.

2.37

a
I took my three year-old, Johnny, with me to the grocery store yesterday. It was a disastrous outing and it ended with him crying loudly because I wouldn't buy him a bag of candy. I tried to be strong and calm but he just would not listen even when I told him he was a very naughty boy and I was very unhappy. I gave him the candy to make him quiet, but by that time he was so furious he threw them onto the floor. Finally, I had to drag him out of the store crying and shouting. It was so embarrassing. When we got home I made him sit on his own on the bottom step for 5 minutes as a punishment, though I'm not sure he understood why. Maybe I should have given him the candy at the very beginning!

b
Ellie, who normally has a sunny personality, was not in a good mood at all the other day. Maybe she had needed a snack before we left for the supermarket, but anyway, by the time we got there she was in a very bad mood. She started complaining and pulling things out of the cart that I had put in. I kept calm and told her that was making me feel angry. But I could see things were getting worse, so I gave her a comic from the shelf and an apple from the cart, and sat her in the cart to look at the comic. As soon as she started looking at it and took the first bite of the apple, I praised her for behaving well. I asked her about the apple - what it tasted like, what color it was, to distract her. She read the comic and ate her apple all the way round the store. The checkout girl even commented on how good she was, which was lovely. In the car going home I told Ellie she made me feel very proud when she sat so quietly in the cart.

Unit 11

2.41

M1: Why don't you tell me something that I would never have guessed?
M2: Err, I like to snowboard.
M1: Huh?
M2: That's right, it doesn't even exist! And voice-over acting, you don't know what that is, do you?
M1: Nope but if I did know, I don't think I would want to do it. So, if you didn't become a super star - what did you do?
M2: Hey, listen I didn't do things exactly like you wanted, but I have done some things. Look, I wrote some novels.
M1: Great, I'm very pleased, oops ... did you get any less clumsy?!

2.42

a
I picked up the money and put it in my pocket and went into my office. I thought about it for a long while and then I walked out of the office and went to the local police precinct to hand the money in. I doubt whether the person who dropped the money - about 5,000 dollars in total - would have noticed it had gone, much less have gone to the cops to report it missing, but if I hadn't given it in, I couldn't have lived with myself. The good news is that the cops told me that if it isn't claimed in six months, I can keep the cash!

b
I decided to keep quiet. I figured that it was none of my business. My friend's boyfriend may just have been carried away by the circumstances. I do want to be honest with my best friend but I don't want to be the reason they split up.

c
Ed went back to the restaurant the next day and paid the difference. The restaurant owner was so grateful; he gave us some vouchers for a free main course when we next go to the restaurant.

2.44

Conversation A
1 Hello.
2 Is Maddy there?
3 Is this Phil?
4 Hold on, I'll go and get her.
5 It's me.
6 What are you up to later?
7 See you tomorrow.

Conversation B
1 Good morning.
2 I'd like to speak to Mr. Moore, please.
3 Who's calling, please?
4 Just a moment, please. I'll try to put you through.
5 Philip Jones here.
6 Are you available later on today?
7 I'll look forward to seeing you tomorrow.

2.45

Brainstorming
How is it that some people always seem to be able to generate new ideas and think creatively, and others seem to struggle to do so?
Well, the good news is that you can learn to think creatively using brainstorming techniques.
Nobel prize winner Linus Pauling said: 'The best way to have a good idea is to have lots of ideas'.
A brainstorming session is a great way to generate a whole bunch of ideas - and it's fun.

The rules are simple:
- everyone in the group has a say
- all ideas are accepted
- no criticism of others' ideas is allowed

Unit 12

2.46

1 Al

I'm really proud of my fabulous Mexican snakeskin cowboy boots. Most of my friends hate them and wouldn't be seen dead in boots like these, but I like that fact that they're different. I wear them for work with a suit and tie, and I think the contrast looks great. I like to stand out from the crowd.

2 Fran

I usually wear jeans and a sweatshirt during the day, but for going out, my favorite thing is my red low-waisted miniskirt. I wear it with a wide black leather belt and short boots, and it looks fantastic with my old black leather jacket.

3 Jay

I have about twenty-five pairs of jeans, but my favorites are my old black skinny jeans. I play the guitar in a band and I always wear my black skinny jeans and a black turtle neck sweater when we're playing. It's like a uniform.

4 Brooke

I'm really into vintage clothes and I just bought a beautiful long purple silk evening dress. I haven't worn it yet - I'm waiting for the right occasion. It would look great on the red carpet at the Oscars.

2.47

a /i/ medium green jeans
b /u/ two blue suits
c /ɜr/ third worse fur
d /ɔ/ tall bald author
e /eɪ/ plain beige suede
f /er/ wear their hair

2.48

I was invited to a friend's birthday party recently, and there were a few people there who I'd never met before. I'm not very good at introducing myself to strangers, so I just stayed with the people I knew, and that was great because I hadn't seen them for a while. But then this woman came over and introduced herself, and asked who I was. I thought she seemed really friendly and very confident. She was tiny, with long curly black hair, and I remember she was wearing a beautiful turquoise necklace. I admired the necklace, and she told me that it was from Mexico. We talked about Mexico, and it turned out that we'd both been on vacation to the same Mexican resort, but not at the same time. Small world. I haven't seen her since then, but she works with my friend, so I think I'll probably run into her again some time. I hope so.

2.49

A: Did you see Ten Years Younger last night?
B: No, I missed it. I had to work. Why, was it good?
A: It was amazing. They had a man and a woman on, and honestly, the transformation was incredible.
B: What did they look like?
A: Well, the man looked about sixty, even though he was forty-nine.
B: Oh, no!
A: He had this long gray hair, and he was dressed a little like an old rock star.
B: Urgh!
A: Anyway, he had his hair cut and colored, and he had his teeth whitened.
B: Oh yes, that makes such a difference.
A: And I think he had his eyelids lifted.
B: Oh well, of course, if you can afford to have plastic surgery, you're bound to look better.
A: Yes, but I think that's all he had done. Oh, and he had his clothes chosen by a stylist.
B: What about the woman? Did she have lots of plastic surgery?
A: No, she didn't actually. But she looked as if she'd had a major face-lift. It was amazing. Before the makeover, everybody thought she was about forty-nine, but she was thirty-seven.
B: Oh. What did she have done?
A: She had her hair cut and colored, of course. And she had her make-up done by an expert and her clothes chosen by a stylist.
B: Oh, I'd love that. How old did they think she was after the makeover?
A: Thirty-two.
B: Oh, she must have been thrilled. Hey, do you think I need to have my hair cut?

2.52

Making positive comments

a Oh, she looks so beautiful.
b What a beautiful day!
c This dessert is delicious.

Giving and receiving compliments

d What a beautiful dress!
Oh, this? I've had it for ages.
e Blue really looks good on you. Do you think so? Thank you.
f That's a very nice hat.
I'm glad you like it.

Thanking and accepting thanks

g Thank you so much for a wonderful day.
You're welcome.
h Thank you for inviting us.
Don't mention it.

REVIEW D

2.54

I: Colin, tell me about your childhood. You never knew your real parents, did you?
C: That's right. I was brought up in children's homes. I moved several times when I was very young and then went to live with my foster parents, Ida and Bud, when I was ten.
I: Was it a difficult childhood?
C: Well, some people might see it that way, but I have very good memories. In that part of New York at that time, everyone was poor – we never had any money – but we didn't complain. There was a real neighborhood spirit. Everyone helped each other.
I: Can you tell me what your memories of that time are?
C: We used to make our own entertainment - there was no TV, no video games. We played in the streets and down by the railroad tracks. All the kids together.
I: And you left school pretty young, didn't you?
C: Yes. I left school at fourteen and went to work in a factory. But I didn't like it. I only stayed there two years. I always wanted to work for myself, so I became a cab driver. I worked as a driver for ten years until after I got married.
I: But you didn't stay a cab driver?
C: No. I was ambitious! I wanted a good life for my kids. So when we had our third baby, I started my own business from nothing. Soon had fifty taxi cabs and drivers! I sold the business a few years ago, and made enough money to buy a second home in Florida.
I: How did you meet your wife?
C: We met at a dance. She was wearing a beautiful yellow silk dress. I thought she was the prettiest thing I'd ever seen. We got married six months later.
I: Any regrets? Would you change anything about your life?
C: Not a thing! I feel like the luckiest man in the world!

Vowels

/ɪ/	ship	/ʃɪp/	(build, business, gym, spinach, women)
/i/	need	/nid/	(bean, he, key, niece, people, sardine)
/ʊ/	put	/pʊt/	(could, foot, woman)
/u/	pool	/pul/	(flew, fruit, lose, rule, shoe, through, two)
/e/	egg	/eg/	(breakfast, friend, many, said)
/ə/	about	/əˈbaʊt/	(arrive, husband, lemon, nervous, police)
/ɔ/	saw	/sɔ/	(abroad, caught, talk, thought, water)
/æ/	back	/bæk/	(bag, fast, laugh)
/ʌ/	bus	/bʌs/	(blood, does, enough, onion)
/ɑ/	father	/ˈfɑðər/	(car, heart, pasta)

Diphthongs

/ɜr/	verb	/vɜrb/	(learn, curly, skirt, word)
/eɪ/	face	/feɪs/	(break, eight, fail, say, they)
/ɔɪ/	boy	/bɔɪ/	(noise)
/oʊ/	nose	/noʊz/	(although, coat, know, shoulder)
/aɪ/	white	/waɪt/	(buy, die, eye, height, high, my)
/aʊ/	mouth	/maʊθ/	(town)
/ɪr/	hear	/hɪr/	(near)

Consonants

/p/	pen	/pen/	(happy)
/b/	bag	/bæg/	(rabbit)
/t/	tea	/ti/	(ate, fatter, worked)
/d/	dog	/dɔg/	(address, played)
/ʧ/	chip	/ʧɪp/	(natural, watch)
/ʤ/	jazz	/ʤæz/	(age, bridge, generous)
/k/	cake	/keɪk/	(chemistry, kitchen, knock, toothache)
/g/	girl	/gɜrl/	(foggy)
/f/	fat	/fæt/	(different, laugh, photographer)
/v/	very	/ˈveri/	(of)
/θ/	thin	/θɪn/	(think)
/ð/	these	/ðiz/	(they)
/s/	snake	/sneɪk/	(city, message, race)
/z/	zoo	/zu/	(has)
/ʃ/	sugar	/ˈʃʊgər/	(description, machine)
/ʒ/	measure	/ˈmeʒər/	(garage, usual)
/m/	map	/mæp/	(summer)
/n/	name	/neɪm/	(sunny, knife)
/ŋ/	ring	/rɪŋ/	(thanks, tongue)
/h/	house	/haʊs/	(who)
/l/	leg	/leg/	(hill, possible)
/r/	road	/roʊd/	(carry, write)
/w/	wine	/waɪn/	(one, why)
/j/	yes	/jes/	(used, usual)

Stress

Word stress is shown by underlining the stressed syllable: *water, amazing, Japanese*.

Letters of the alphabet

/eɪ/	/i/	/e/	/aɪ/	/oʊ/	/u/	/ɑ/
Aa	Bb	Ff	Ii	Oo	Qq	Rr
Hh	Cc	Ll	Yy		Uu	
Jj	Dd	Mm			Ww	
Kk	Ee	Nn				
	Gg	Ss				
	Pp	Xx				
	Tt					
	Vv					
	Zz					

Infinitive	Simple past	Past participle
be	was/were	been
beat	beat	beaten
become	became	become
begin	began	begun
bend	bent	bent
bet	bet	bet
bite	bit	bitten
blow	blew	blown
break	broke	broken
bring	brought /brɔt/	brought /brɔt/
build /bɪld/	built /bɪlt/	built /bɪlt/
burn	burned	burned/burnt
burst	burst	burst
buy /baɪ/	bought /bɔt/	bought /bɔt/
can	could /kʊd/	(been able)
catch	caught /kɔt/	caught /kɔt/
choose	chose	chosen
come	came	come
cost	cost	cost
cut	cut	cut
deal /dil/	dealt /delt/	dealt /delt/
dig	dug	dug
do	did	done
draw	drew	drawn
dream	dreamed/dreamt	dreamed/dreamt
drink	drank	drunk
drive	drove	driven
eat	ate	eaten
fall	fell	fallen
feed	fed	fed
feel	felt	felt
fight	fought /fɔt/	fought /fɔt/
find	found	found
fly	flew	flown
forget	forgot	forgotten
forgive	forgave	forgiven
freeze	froze	frozen
get	got	gotten
give	gave	given
go	went	gone/been
grow	grew	grown
hang	hung	hung
have	had	had
hear	heard /hɜrd/	heard /hɜrd/
hide	hid	hidden
hit	hit	hit
hold	held	held
hurt /hɜrt/	hurt /hɜrt/	hurt /hɜrt/
keep	kept	kept
kneel	knelt/kneeled	knelt/kneeled
know	knew /nju/	known
lay	laid	laid
lead	led	led
leave	left	left
lend	lent	lent

Infinitive	Simple past	Past participle
let	let	let
lie	lay	lain
light	lit/lighted	lit/lighted
lose	lost	lost
make	made	made
mean	meant /ment/	meant /ment/
meet	met	met
pay	paid	paid
put	put	put
read	read /red/	read /red/
ride	rode	ridden
ring	rang	rung
rise	rose	risen
run	ran	run
say	said /sed/	said /sed/
see	saw /sɔ/	seen
sell	sold	sold
send	sent	sent
set	set	set
shake	shook	shaken
shine	shone	shone
shoot	shot	shot
show	showed	shown
shrink	shrank	shrunk
shut	shut	shut
sing	sang	sung
sink	sank	sunk
sit	sat	sat
sleep	slept	slept
slide	slid	slid
speak	spoke	spoken
spend	spent	spent
split	split	split
spread	spread	spread
stand	stood	stood
steal	stole	stolen
stick	stuck	stuck
swear	swore	sworn
swell	swelled	swollen/swelled
swim	swam	swum
take	took /tʊk/	taken
teach	taught /tɔt/	taught /tɔt/
tear	tore	torn
tell	told	told
think	thought /θɔt/	thought /θɔt/
throw	threw	thrown
understand	understood	understood
wake	woke	woken
wear	wore /wɔr/	worn
win	won /wʌn/	won /wʌn/
write	wrote	written

Macmillan Education

Companies and representatives throughout the world

American Inside Out Evolution. Student's Book Intermediate

Adapted by Peter Maggs and Catherine Smith / The Content Station team: Simon Campbell, George Wells and Catherine Gray
Macmillan is a registered trademark.
First edition published 2017

ISBN: 978-607-473-640-3

Based on New American Inside Out Student's Book Intermediate

Editorial Manager: Patricia Muradas
Editorial Operations Coordinator: Veronica Teodorov Ferreira
Editor: Cintia Zaitune
Concept design: Martha Tadaieski
Page make-up: The Content Station
Illustrations: Karen Ahlschläger pp33, 42 (b), 50 (b), 79, 95, 109, 116; Gustavo Gialuca pp14, 22, 30, 42 (t), 50 (t), 58, 70, 78, 86, 98, 103, 106, 114.
Graphic Production: Kelly Gobbo
Photographic research: The Content Station
Cover concept and design: Jean Aranha
Cover photo: Vitaliy Pozdeev | Dreamstime

The authors and publishers would like to thank the following for permission to reproduce the photographic material:
Album / Touchstone Pictures p111 (r); **Dreamstime** / Monkey Business Images p9, Dreamstime / Antonio Guillem p10(t), Dreamstime / Rvlsoft (icons), Dreamstime / Nanditha Rao p11(t), Dreamstime / Axel Bueckert p11(c), Dreamstime / Felix Mizioznikov p11(b), Dreamstime / MinervaStudio p12, p13(t), Dreamstime / Jason Stitt p13(b), Dreamstime / Dzeinmail p14 (emojis), Dreamstime / Wollertz p16, Dreamstime / Ammentorp p17, Dreamstime / Mikael Damkier p18(t), Dreamstime / Rido p18(bl), Dreamstime / Alenin p18(bc), Dreamstime / Kiosea39 p18(br), Dreamstime / Alexey Maximenko p19, Dreamstime / Artyom Bondarovich p20(tl), Dreamstime / Wavebreakmedia Ltd p20 (tr), Dreamstime / Chris Van Lennep p20(1), Dreamstime / Stefan Dahl Langstrup p20(2), Dreamstime / Georgy Dzyra p20(3), Dreamstime / Fabio Lamanna p20(6), Dreamstime / MNStudio p20(7), Dreamstime / Alexey Poprotskiy p20(8), Dreamstime / Nenad Kostic p20(9), Dreamstime / Creativei p21, Dreamstime / Wavebreakmedia Ltd p24 (tl-1), Dreamstime / Travnikovstudio p24 (tl-2), Dreamstime / Jeanne Provost (bl1, bl2), Dreamstime / Nyul (tr-1), Dreamstime / Inara Prusakova (tr-2), Dreamstime / Mimagephotography p24 (br-1), Dreamstime / Anke Van Wyk (br2), Dreamstime / Nyul p26(l), Dreamstime / Helder Almeida p26 (r), Dreamstime / jfkimage p27(t), Dreamstime / Dragonimages p27(b), Dreamstime / Flair Images p28(a), Dreamstime / Gpointstudio p28 (b), Dreamstime / Christine Langer-püschel p28(c), Dreamstime / Piotr Marcinski p28(d), Dreamstime / Gualtiero Boffi p28(e), Dreamstime / Vlue p28(f), Dreamstime / Pe3ak p29(a), Dreamstime / Ocusfocus p29(b), Dreamstime / Shao-chun Wang p29(c), Dreamstime / Lunamarina p29(d), Dreamstime / Alena Kratovich p29(e), Dreamstime / Roberto Caucino p32, Dreamstime / Tijanap p34, Dreamstime / Stepanida Popzoglo p35, Dreamstime / hijodeponggol pp36&37, Dreamstime / Eagleflying p38(t), Dreamstime / Ronnie Wu p38(b), Dreamstime / Photographerlondon p39(t), Dreamstime / Vadymvdrobot (p39(b), Dreamstime / David Pereiras Villagra p40(t), Dreamstime / AleksandarNakic p40(b), Dreamstime / Ian Allenden p41(t), Dreamstime / Geotrac p41 (c), Dreamstime / nicomenijes p41(b), Dreamstime / Pipa100 p44, Dreamstime / Voyagerix p45(l), Dreamstime / Strannikfox p45(r), Dreamstime / Martin Hatch p46, Dreamstime / Adogslifephoto p47 (snake), Dreamstime / Teekaygee p47 (grasshopper), Dreamstime / Dave Bredeson p47 (cockroach), Dreamstime / Cameramannz p47 (caterpillar), Dreamstime / Ryan Pike p47 (ant), Dreamstime / Heinz Teh Chee Siong p47 (cookies), Dreamstime / Diego Vito Cervo p48 (t), Dreamstime / Daria Garnik (b), Dreamstime / Kadettmann p49, Dreamstime / Fizkes p52, Dreamstime / Cebas1 p54, Dreamstime / Viacheslav Iacobchuk p55, Dreamstime / Arne9001 p56 (tl), Dreamstime / Monkey Business Images p56 (tc), Dreamstime / Belish p56 (tr), Dreamstime / Iegor Liashenko p57(t), Dreamstime / Tea p57(b), Dreamstime / Kathywooding90 p61, Dreamstime / M. Rohana p62(t), Dreamstime / Jill Lang p62(b), Dreamstime / Liquidanbar p63(t), Dreamstime / Arinahabich08 p63(b), Dreamstime / Photographerlondon pp64&65, Dreamstime / Ratz Attila p66(1), Dreamstime / Calvin Leake p66(2), Dreamstime / Tommaso79 p66(4), Dreamstime / Bigjiang p66(5), Dreamstime / Carrienelson1 p67, Dreamstime / Igor Kovalchuk p68(a), Dreamstime / Damed01 p68(b), Dreamstime / Toxawww p68(c), Dreamstime / Americanspirit p68(d), Dreamstime / Photographerlondon p68(e), Dreamstime / Stefan Dahl Langstrup p68(f), Dreamstime / Ilona Saibarakova p70 (News logo), Dreamstime / Petre Bucur p70 (woman), Dreamstime / Hongqi Zhang (aka Michael Zhang) p70 (man), Dreamstime / muratart p70 (TV), Dreamstime / Eric Overton p70 (house), Dreamstime / Prochasson Frederic P72, Dreamstime / Alekosa p73(a), Dreamstime / Juan Moyano p73(b), Dreamstime / Tomas Marek p73(c), Dreamstime / Paop p73(d), Dreamstime / Travnikovstudio p74(t), Dreamstime / Kobby Dagan p74(a), Dreamstime / Sven Hanscge p74(b), Dreamstime / Bvh2228 (c), Dreamstime / Manuelaudio p74(d), Dreamstime / Esviesa p75(t), Dreamstime / Serban Bogdan p75(b), Dreamstime / Wrangel p77, Dreamstime / Tom Wang p80, Dreamstime / Iuliia Lisitsyna p82(l), Dreamstime / Mikkolem p82(c), Antonio Guillem p82(r), Dreamstime / Sbukley p83(t), Dreamstime / Featureflash p83(b), Dreamstime / Nadino p84(a), Dreamstime / Opolja p84(b), Dreamstime / Dan Grytsku p84(c), Dreamstime / Volodymyr Melnyk p84(d), Dreamstime / Ruslan Huzau p84(e), Dreamstime / Nadino p84(f), Dreamstime / Roberto Caucino p85(t), Dreamstime / Yunuli123 p85(a), Dreamstime / Vbaleha p85(b), Dreamstime / Lekcej p85(c), Dreamstime / Mimagephotography p85(d), Dreamstime / Vadymvdroboto p91(t), Dreamstime / Jackbluee p91(b), Dreamstime / Oksun70 p92, Dreamstime / Weedezign p94, Dreamstime / Photoeuphoria p96, Dreamstime / Imagesolution p97, Dreamstime / Germanskydiver p100(l), Dreamstime / Julian Bound p102, Dreamstime / Photographerlondon p108(t), Dreamstime / Iryna Kalchenko p108 (br), Dreamstime / Sharplaninac p108(bl), Dreamstime / Sabphoto p109(a), Dreamstime / Anna Kraynova p109(b), Dreamstime / Makidotvn p109(c), Dreamstime / George Mayer p109(d), Dreamstime / Ampyang p110, Dreamstime / Viorel Dudau p117, Dreamstime / Andrey Popov p118 (l), Dreamstime / Yobro10 p118(c), Dreamstime / Photographerlondon p118 (r), Dreamstime / Frizzantine p119(t), Dreamstime / Rido p119 (bl), Dreamstime / Pemotret p119(br), Dreamstime / Featureflash p120, Dreamstime / Subarashii21 pp123&127, Dreamstime / Chrisstanley p133, Dreamstime / Iakov Filimonov p135, Dreamstime / Monkey Business Images p137, Dreamstime / Pavel Siamionau p139, Dreamstime / Katarzyna Bialasiewicz p141, Dreamstime / Robert Kneschke p143, Dreamstime / Antonio Guillem p145, Dreamstime / Ocskay Mark p147, Dreamstime / Doodkoalex p149, Dreamstime / Awlend p151, Dreamstime / Monkey Business Images p152; **Getty Images** / Kyodo News p100(r), Getty Images / Twentieth Century Fox Pictures / Sunset Boulevard p111(l), Getty Images / Frederick M Brown / Stringer p111(c); **iStock** / abu p20(4), iStock / erikreis (p20(5), iStock / yanik88 p20(10), iStock / Likoper p33, iStock / Kerkez p35, iStock / innovatedcaptures p112(all), iStock / alptraum / innovatedcaptures p122; Peter Emshwiller p104, Social media icons - iStock / tnrsmr.

CANIEM No. 2275

Macmillan Publishers S.A. de C.V.
Insurgentes Sur 1886
Col. Florida, CP 01030
Álvaro Obregón
Ciudad de México
Tel: +52 (55) 5482 2200
elt@grupomacmillan.com

www.grupomacmillan.com www.macmillan.com.mx www.macmillanenglish.com

Printed in Brazil

This book was printed in January, 2025 by: Eskenazi Indústria Gráfica Ltda, Avenida Miguel Frias Vasconcelos, 1023 - Jaguaré - São Paulo - SP.

Notes

Notes